Africa and the Bible

Africa and the Bible

CORRECTIVE LENSES

Critical Essays by Gene Rice

Edited by Alice Ogden Bellis
Foreword by Cain Hope Felder
Preface by Jonathan Rice

CASCADE *Books* • Eugene, Oregon

AFRICA AND THE BIBLE
Corrective Lenses—Critical Essays

Cascade Books
An Imprint of Wipf and Stock Publishers
199 W. 8th Ave., Suite 3
Eugene, OR 97401

www.wipfandstock.com

PAPERBACK ISBN: 978-1-5326-5864-8
HARDCOVER ISBN: 978-1-5326-5866-2
EBOOK ISBN: 978-1-5326-5867-9

Cataloging-in-Publication data:

Names: Rice, Gene, 1925–2016, author. | Bellis, Alice Ogden, 1950–, editor. | Felder, Cain Hope, foreword. | Rice, Jonathan, 1962–, preface.

Title: Africa and the Bible : corrective lenses—critical essays / Gene Rice ; edited by Alice Ogden Bellis ; foreword by Cain Hope Felder ; preface by Jonathan Rice.

Description: Eugene, OR: Cascade Books, 2019. | Includes bibliographical references and indexes.

Identifiers: ISBN: 978-1-5326-5864-8 (PAPERBACK). | ISBN: 978-1-5326-5866-2 (HARDCOVER). | ISBN: 978-1-5326-5867-9 (EBOOK).

Subjects: LCSH: Bible—Africa—History. | Bible. Old Testament—Criticism, interpretation, etc.

Classification: BS511.2 R51 2019 (print). | BS511.2 (epub).

Manufactured in the U.S.A. NOVEMBER 7, 2019

Royalties are being donated to the Dr. Gene and Betty Rice Scholarship Fund at Howard University School of Divinity

Dedicated

to

all students of

The Howard University School of Divinity

Past,

Present,

and

Future

Be still and know that I am God.

PSALM 46:10

Contents

Foreword

It is indeed an honor to have this unique opportunity to fulfill a secret promise, known to only a few of Dr. Gene Rice's closest colleagues and personal friends. For perhaps many more years than we might want to admit, Gene would come to a few of us on the faculty, asking us to collaborate with him in publishing with him several critical studies on the Black presence in the Bible. Over the years, Dr. Rice himself had published several such scholarly articles for European academies and for Howard University's own *Journal of Religious Thought*. Given the limited linguistic, historical, and classical framework that buttressed foundations for Hebrew Bible studies in Jewish, Catholic, and Protestant seminaries and graduate schools, scholarly voices like that of Gene Rice were somewhat akin to modern-day John the Baptists—crying in a virtual hermeneutical wilderness.

Of course, today the heretofore wilderness of persons wrestling with narrow and exclusive understanding of ancient biblical texts is gaining new, more inclusive tools to convert tears into laughter and joy where there has been pain! Professor Gene Rice for half a century in so many a classroom and lecture hall made ancient Israel come alive and regain her strength in times of great adversity as the pages of the Hebrew Bible would jump off the page anew! With his "still" soft voice Gene Rice was able to re-enliven the psalms of old. Yet in such unassuming modest ways he seemed never to forget his service in Iwo Jima of World War II. The horrors of war evidently fueled his passion for peace and the rich diversity of people and ancient cultural heritages—not least Africa in the pages of the Bible itself. Rice found ways as a Quaker, an Episcopalian, and a worshipper in the Howard University School of Divinity chapel, to help seminarians prepare for ministry and find their voices to serve others!

Please receive the contents and careful insights of this book and know that you are with a holy man, who walked the corridors of our Divinity

School with Howard Thurman, Benjamin Mays, and Lawrence Neal Jones! Clearly, our hope is that through the remarkable spirit of Professor Gene Rice, we as fellow pilgrims have in this book a publication that reaches and still teaches us from the grave, to demonstrate the true power of the resurrection. *Africa and the Bible* is a collection of critical studies and short essays that re-focuses attention on a subject that has for too long been disparaged and rejected in the western academy. Isn't it nice to have such advocacy in the struggle to teach that God inspired: two of our most beloved faculty members—Alice and Gene—to join us in our research and teaching at Howard University School of Divinity.

Cain Hope Felder
Montgomery, Alabama
August 2018

Preface

ONE OF MY FATHER'S first scholarly articles, "The Curse That Never Was (Genesis 9:18–27)," carefully dismantled and repudiated the so-called biblical justification for slavery and racism. Genesis 9:18–29 had long been interpreted by many American Christian leaders as providing theological legitimacy for the slave system and the persistence of white supremacy long after the nominal abolition of slavery. It's fair to say that what my father called the "Big Lie" about the irremediable otherness of African people was the central preoccupation of his long academic career, motivating him to research and write about the neglected subject of the positive presence of Africans in the Bible. And it was to the Big Lie that my father returned after his retirement from Howard University and especially in the last months of his life.

In the years after his retirement from Howard University in 2009 my father was deeply troubled and indeed preoccupied by the direction race relations in the United States were moving. Thrilled by the election of Barack Obama, a milestone that seemed to indicate that America had undergone a profound transformation in terms of its attitudes about race, my father was appalled as it became increasingly obvious that a substantial number of white people were opposed to the Obama presidency, not so much because of disagreements over policy but because they denied the very legitimacy of Barack Obama's presidency. Those white Americans who challenged Obama's American citizenship were, in effect, calling the nation's first African-American president an illegitimate usurper. Just at the time when superficial observers began to celebrate the milestone of a post-racial America, white racism was resurgent and its undeniable reality was daily being captured by cellphone cameras all across the country.

Inspired by the prophetic tradition of the Old Testament, my father toward the end of his life wanted to put together, not a scholarly article, but an impassioned appeal to the nation as a whole: a genuine reconciliation between the races must be achieved for the nation to move forward. My father believed that people could open their hearts to the timeless and transcendent values of love and justice that lie at the foundation of Christianity as well as all the other major faith traditions. Inspired in part by the success of South Africa's Truth and Reconciliation Commission, he believed the essential prerequisite for a meaningful and lasting reconciliation would be for white Americans to explicitly acknowledge and turn away from the path of bigotry and hatred. Slavery and racism are sins of such magnitude and persistence that they require, in effect, their own Yom Kippur or Day of Atonement. He was clearly outraged that Christianity, which claims to champion transcendent standards of right, had been complicit in rationalizing one of the greatest evils ever perpetrated on a people. My father came back to the Big Lie about the Curse of Ham because he had a keen sense of how deeply rooted and persistent the notion of African inferiority or "otherness" is in American life.

As a white man born in Kentucky in 1925, my father would seem to be an unlikely proponent of meaningful racial equality (like reparations). Kentucky, a sharply divided state, joined the Civil War on the side of the Union. Yet Confederate monuments are so plentiful today that most Kentuckians now think their state fought for the Confederacy. Our family was pro-Union (I recently discovered ancestors with such politically unsubtle names as "General Grant Rice" and "General Sherman Rice") and some of our ancestors were involved in the Republican Party (way back when the Republicans were truly "the party of Lincoln" while the Democratic Party was unabashedly the party of Jim Crow). But being pro-Union does not in itself carry over to a belief in racial equality: Kentucky did not ratify the thirteenth amendment until 1976. And the old Republican Party's opposition to Jim Crow was ineffective and half-hearted at best.

Nonetheless, my father's conviction that a genuine reconciliation between the races must be achieved for the nation to move forward was clearly deeply rooted. The strongest source is the most obvious: a belief in a Christianity that is faithful to its highest ideals. A second important source seems unlikely at first glance: his military service. Most people who knew my father during his teaching career were surprised to find out he had been an underage volunteer for the US Marine Corps during World War II and had been wounded in battle at Iwo Jima. Most who knew my father's background believed the soft-spoken and pacifist Quaker professor they knew must have been a very different young man. Undoubtedly, Private Rice grew considerably before becoming Professor Rice but there's more similarity than difference between the teenager who lied about his age to join the Marines and the young professor who led a small group of Howard students in the March on Selma. Like many Americans, he understood the Second World War as a fight for *freedom*. It is not uncommon for soldiers returning from war to think more critically about the nature of the societies they risked their lives to defend. The United States had just gone to war to fight for the freedoms of people oppressed by explicitly racist regimes—the atrocities committed by Imperial Japan, no less than Nazi Germany, were driven largely by a sense of racial hierarchy. When my father returned home after the war, he found himself outside the complacent majority of white America in recognizing the disconnect between America's goals abroad and its long legacy of white supremacy at home. Having been wounded in battle and seeing so much death and destruction, he saw life as a gift from God and he returned home with the restless determination to do something worthwhile with his own.

One of the things about my father's experience in World War II that made a lasting impression on him was the realization that a truly united America could achieve great things. He frequently expressed disappointment that that unity of purpose that had harnessed the nation's resources to fight the Second World War could not be sustained for the broader social purposes of peace and justice. Coming from a poor family in Appalachia, my father was well aware of the formidable obstacles of class that had to be overcome to achieve his own professional goals. That experience made him painfully aware of the far greater obstacles of race in American life and the most important fault line in American society was the legacy of slavery and the persistence of racism. Nonetheless, my father believed that America could live up to its ideals and that institutions like Howard University could help lead the way. He began his teaching career at Howard University in 1958 with an idealism and enthusiasm that remained undiminished over his fifty-one year teaching career. He would be delighted to know that all proceeds from the sale of this book go to the support of the Howard University School of Divinity Scholarship Fund.

Jonathan Rice
Charlottesville, Virginia
August 2018

Acknowledgements

The editor wishes to acknowledge the unflagging, enthusiastic support and thoughtful guidance in the journey of this volume from inspiration to publication of the Rev. Delores McCoy Delegall, Dr. Gene Rice's widow, in shaping this volume. Her wisdom, belief in the project, and steady assurance have kept us on the track to completion.

Introduction

In 1971 I entered what was then called Howard University School of Religion to begin work on my Master of Divinity degree. It was then that I first met Dr. Gene Rice, Professor of Old Testament Language and Literature. He had already served in that role for almost twenty years when I entered Howard. Dr. Rice's field was the one that I would ultimately make my own. I did not take many courses from him, however, because I had already taken the introductory Hebrew Bible courses in undergraduate school as a religion major and at the time Howard did not offer introductory Hebrew, which I took through a consortium school and then continued most of my language study at Catholic University nearby where I ultimately completed my MA and PhD degrees in Semitic languages. Even though I did not take many courses from Dr. Rice, I was impressed by his scholarship. Though his ethnicity was not African, his passion for the African presence in and influence on the Hebrew Bible was deep and unwavering.

He also impressed me as a deeply caring individual. In the one course that I did take from him, which was an intermediate-level language course, he had planned a final exam, but he was delayed from administering it due to a neighborhood emergency. There was a fire in someone's home, and due to his involvement in helping the family, I never took that exam. Although he had strong standards, he also had his priorities straight.

After I completed my PhD, I was amazed to find myself as Dr. Rice's junior colleague. It had never occurred to me when I was a student at Howard that I would ever find myself on the faculty there. Although I had learned a great deal as a pastor, the role into which I moved after completing the coursework for my PhD, I was ready for the move to academia when I finished my dissertation, and Gene Rice was a most gracious and cordial mentor.

Dr. Rice was a quiet man. One of my favorite stories about him is one told by the students. He had a very soft voice, so sometimes the students would have trouble hearing him in class. They would occasionally ask him to speak up and he would agree to do so, but then would keep on speaking in much the same way. They learned that they would have to be very quiet and listen intently to hear him. Because they admired him so much, they did not ever seem to mind doing this. They told this story with good humor. It always seemed odd that someone who had been a Marine and fought at Iwo Jima could be so gentle and quiet, but Dr. Rice had a quiet strength that was not to be mistaken for weakness and the students understood this.

The other story that he told me himself is about how he came to be at Howard. When he was a student at Columbia, the placement office received a request from what was then called the School of Religion at Howard, but they did not tell him about it because they assumed that a young white man from Kentucky, which is where Gene Rice grew up, would not have any interest in an academic position in a historically black school. Somehow, though, he found out about the position, and he was interested, very interested, and as they say, the rest is history. Perhaps, like me, growing up in the segregated South had done something to him that could only be dealt with by spending his career at a place like Howard. His son Jonathan Rice's preface also explains some of the other factors that probably led to his eagerness to come to Howard.

Even before Dr. Rice died, I wanted to see his articles on the Black presence in and influence on the Bible published in a volume of their own, as I felt then—as I have continued to feel—that their combined impact should be much stronger than the sum of their parts scattered across various issues of our journal. I have been pleased to work with Dr. Rice's widow Rev. Delores (Didi) McCoy DeLegall and his son, Jonathan Rice, both of whom also are excited about bringing his scholarship to a larger audience, to both the faith and wider academic communities than they have reached through the Divinity School's journal, the *Journal of Religious Thought*. *Africa and the Bible: Corrective Lenses* is a collection of articles by Gene Rice, who served for over fifty years as Professor of Old Testament at Howard University School of Divinity. His legacy is—in part—his students, as was evident at his memorial service at the chapel at Howard University School of Divinity, where on short notice in the summer, former students packed the house and an impromptu choir sang heavenly music, including a hymn of Dr. Rice's own composition. But it is certainly also these articles, which are gems of scholarship, crafted with care and compassion for the ages. Dr. Rice wrote many other fine articles, published in the *Journal of Religious Thought* and in many other academic journals. They are all worth reading, but these have a special place in academic history and in my heart.

In the first article, "Joseph and Jim Crow,"[1] Gene Rice retells the story of Joseph and his brothers, emphasizing its twin themes of brotherhood and betrayal, and ultimately its profound message of reconciliation, which is not vengeful but demands real repentance before genuine reunion can occur. The themes in the story are read as having implications for race relations in mid-twentieth century America when the article was written (and indeed, sadly, they are equally relevant fifty years later).

The second article, "The Curse That Never Was (Genesis 9:18–27),"[2] is about the so-called curse of Ham. Many have claimed that Gen 9:18-27 justifies slavery and segregation, in spite of Canaan being the one who is cursed rather than Ham who represents Africa. In this passage Gene Rice shows that two versions of the naming of Noah's three sons—Shem, Ham, and Japheth—coexist. One involves naming Japheth as the youngest; the other names the youngest as Ham, suggesting that two versions have been edited together. An attempt to harmonize the two versions using Canaan just confuses matters more. The biblical text does not directly address the question of why Noah curses Canaan for the wrong of his father Ham. However, the passage has nothing to do with cursing people of African descent as is shown by the generally positive attitude the Bible has toward Ethiopians (Kushites), what the biblical authors call people from Africa. At the time of Dr. Rice's death he was working on a revision of this article, which he was planning to rename "The Big Lie," as Jonathan Rice describes in his preface. Dr. Rice was very passionate about the horrendous effects the misinterpretation of this verse has had on the African-American community.

In the third article, "Two Black Contemporaries of Jeremiah,"[3] Jeremiah's two named black contemporaries, Ebed-Melek and Jehudi ben Nathaniah ben Shelemiah ben Kushi, are considered. Their character, status, and ethnic origin are all scrutinized. Ultimately their Ethiopian origins are tied to the period a century earlier when Judah was in alliance with the

1. Rice, "Joseph and Jim Crow," 3–14, and chapter 1 in this book, 1–12.

2. Rice, "The Curse That Never Was," 5–27, and chapter 2 in this book, 13–34.

3. Rice, "Two Black Contemporaries of Jeremiah," 95–109, and chapter 3 in this book, 35–49.

Twenty-fifth Ethiopian dynasty of Egypt and the Assyrian empire posed a serious threat to its existence.

The fourth article, "Was Amos a Racist?,"[4] begins with a survey of the commentaries available at the time of the writing of the article and finds that about half of them believed that this verse was racist, but with little justification. Dr. Rice finds instead that the Ethiopians were regarded positively by the biblical authors, and thus there is no basis for a negative view in the original historical context. The Israelites were probably compared to the Ethiopians because the Ethiopians were the most distant nation known to the Israelites. The underlying theological motivation was that God cared about all nations, no matter how far away they were from Israel. It had nothing to do with race.

In the fifth article, "The African Roots of the Prophet Zephaniah,"[5] Dr. Rice discusses the fact that the prophet Zephaniah is unique among the biblical prophets in that his genealogy includes four generations, including his father Kushi (the Ethiopian) and his great grandfather Hezekiah. Gene Rice scrutinizes Zephaniah's family history and his message to make the case that the most natural way of reading this prophet is as both a person of Ethiopian origin and a descendant of King Hezekiah. Part of the rationale for understanding Zephaniah as Kushite is historical. At the turn of the seventh century BCE, Judah was in alliance with the Twenty-fifth Ethiopian dynasty of Egypt, an alliance that brought lasting ties between Judah and the Kushites. Part is based on the references to Ethiopia in Zephaniah's prophecy. There are many grounds for understanding the reference to Hezekiah as meaning King Hezekiah: 1) if King Hezekiah had not been intended, the author would have had to make that plain, 2) the prophet's authority lay not with his royal background; 3) nevertheless, only someone with a royal background could have prophesied such judgment and survived.

The sixth article, "Africans and the Origin of the Worship of YHWH,"[6] begins with Gene Rice's initial proposal that the Midianites/Kenites were the first worshippers of YHWH, a thesis supported by other scholars. He presents intriguing archaeological evidence including names on Egyptian togographic lists: the land of Shasu-yhw. The Shasu were a nomadic people

4. Rice, "Was Amos a Racist?," 35–44, and chapter 4 in this book, 50–58.

5. Rice, "The African Roots of the Prophet Zephaniah," 21–31, and chapter 5 in this book, 59–71.

6. Rice, "Africans and the Origin of the Worship of Yahweh," 27–44, and chapter 6 in this book, 72–90.

similar to the Hapiru. W. F. Albright identified the *yhw* component of the name as the equivalent of YHWH. The second piece of evidence is some heavy red and yellow flax and wool fabric embedded with beads with regularly placed postholes found in a former Temple of Hathor. This was found in Timna about eighteen miles north of the Gulf of Aqaba. Along with it was a copper snake. Much Midianite pottery was also located at the site. These finds were dated to 1150 BCE. Based on the location within ancient Midian it is believed that they are from an ancient Yahwistic tent shrine. What evidence suggests that the Midianites/Kenites were from Kush? Rice points out that the Kushites lived all over Palestine. Most important is the fact that Moses' wife Zipporah (assuming she is the person referenced) is called Kushite in Num 12:1.

The seventh article, "The Alleged Curse on Ham,"[7] is the only article that is not from Howard's *Journal of Religious Thought*. Instead, it is one of the articles at the beginning of the American Bible Society's African American Jubilee Bible (KJV). The subject is the same as the second article, "The Curse That Never Was," but whereas the second article is heavily footnoted and dense, this article was written for a more general audience.

The eighth and final chapter is an extended book review of *The Rescue of Jerusalem: The Alliance between Hebrews and Africans in 701 BC* by Henry T. Aubin.[8] In this review, Rice gives a thoughtful and positive review to a book, the thesis of which is that the Twenty-fifth Ethiopian dynasty of Egypt played a significant part in saving Jerusalem from destruction by the Assyrian empire in 701 BCE, a perspective that has not frequently been championed in academic circles for many years, and that the reason that this viewpoint has not received a great deal of attention during the last century and more is at least in some cases subtle and in others not so subtle forms of racism. (This book is the subject of a book-length review of essays currently in progress by biblical scholars, Egyptologists, and Nubiologists, and a Classicist, Assyriologist, and Ancient Near Eastern historian to be published by the *Journal of Hebrew Scriptures*, of which I am the editor).

Alice Ogden Bellis
Professor of Hebrew Bible
Howard University

7. Rice, "The Alleged Curse on Ham," 127–43, and chapter 7 in this book, 91–104.

8. Rice, Review of *The Rescue of Jerusalem*, 181–92, and chapter 8 in this book, 105–20.

Abbreviations

ABD	*Anchor Bible Dictionary*, edited by David Noel Freedman, 6 vols., New York: Doubleday, 1992
ANET	*Ancient Near Eastern Texts Relating to the Old Testament*, edited by James B. Pritchard, 3rd ed., Princeton: Princeton University Press, 1969
ATJ	*Africa Theological Journal*
AuOr	*Aula Orientalis*
BN	*Biblische Notizen*
BASOR	*Bulletin of the American Schools of Oriental Research*
BZAW	Beihefte zur Zeitschrift für die alttestamentliche Wissenschaft
CEV	*Common English Version*
ErIsr	*Eretz Israel*
EvT	*Evangelische Theologie*
ExpTim	*Expository Times*
HUCA	*Hebrew Union College Annual*
JBL	*Journal of Biblical Literature*
JEA	*Journal of Egyptian Archaeology*
JPOS	*Journal of the Palestine Oriental Society*
JTS	*Journal of Theological Studies*
KAT	Kommentar zum Alten Testament
OTL	Old Testament Library

OtSt	*Oudtestamentische Studiën*
PEQ	*Palestine Exploration Quarterly*
ScrHier	*Scripta Hierosolymitana*
VT	*Vetus Testamentum*
ZAW	*Zeitscrift für die alttestamentlische Wissenschaft*

1

Joseph and Jim Crow[1]

Of all the personalities in the Bible, Joseph is surely one of the noblest and most admirable. Envied and hated by his brothers, sold into slavery, betrayed by Potiphar's wife and forgotten by Pharaoh's butler, Joseph does not despair in adversity, nor become bitter, nor lose faith in God. Suddenly precipitated into a position of great authority and made a member of the Egyptian court, Joseph does not become vain, nor vengeful, nor ashamed of the foreign origin of his family and their humble circumstances. Apart from Jesus, Joseph stands alone in the Bible as one whose character is virtually above reproach.

The excellence of Joseph's character is matched by the excellence of the Joseph story as literature. Unlike the Abraham and Jacob narratives, which are garlands of short, terse, individual stories often of no more than ten verses, the Joseph story is a single, organic composition with a beginning, a middle, and an end. It is developed in sufficient length and detail (Gen 37–50), in fact, that it may properly be called a short story. The contents of the story fall naturally into four "acts": I. The conflict between Joseph and his brothers (ch. 37); II. Joseph's rise to power in Egypt (chs. 39–41); III. The reunion and reconciliation of Joseph and his brothers (chs. 42–45); IV. Jacob's reunion with his son, his death in peace, and the death of Joseph after a full and rich life (chs. 46–50). The conflict between the brothers, the motif of robe and of dream, the reversal of the brothers' intention, and the recognition scene between Joseph and his brothers are treated with a

1. *Editor's note*: The language in this article has been updated to be gender inclusive and contemporary in terms of how various ethnic groups are labeled. Rice would undoubtedly have written it the way it has been edited if he were writing the article now.

mastery that places the Joseph story among the best examples of prose literature in the Bible—and in world literature.

Yet for all the admirable qualities of Joseph's character and for all the excellence of the Joseph story as literature, the story is not concerned primarily to praise Joseph nor to demonstrate the ability to tell a story well. Two powerful themes run through the Joseph story that transcend the interest in Joseph's personality and character, and it is for the sake of embodying these themes that the story has been so admirably shaped. It is in these two themes that the Joseph story becomes transparent to the Word of God and it is to the understanding of these themes and their relevance for today that this study is directed.

I. Conflict

The first of these great themes is that of brotherhood. This theme is struck at the very outset of the story. The action begins with the development of a conflict between Joseph and his brothers. The conflict grows out of Jacob's great love for Joseph, the child of his old age and the offspring of his favorite wife, Rachel, and a sense of destiny on the part of Joseph that, to the minds of his brothers, smacks of "delusions of grandeur." The smoldering resentment of the brothers comes to a head when Jacob gives Joseph a princely robe and Joseph tells his brothers of dreams that suggest they will become subservient to him. Maddened with jealousy, the brothers plan to kill Joseph. Their chance comes when Joseph is sent by his father to see how his brothers are getting along with the flocks. But the intervention of Reuben and Judah and the fortuitous appearance of a caravan conspire to avert actual murder and instead Joseph is taken to Egypt and sold to a certain Potiphar. The brothers dip Joseph's robe in goat's blood and take it to their father who draws the inevitable conclusion that Joseph is the victim of a wild beast and is plunged into inconsolable grief.

At this point we do not know how the subject of brotherhood is to be treated. We are simply made to witness—without any interpretative help from the story itself—the violent disruption of a family. One comes to the end of chapter 37 with the picture of Jacob scalded with grief, of Joseph's brothers hardened with hatred, and of the young Joseph suddenly wrenched from father and home, degraded to the status of a slave, and placed at the mercy of a strange and alien world, and one silently wonders how such a breach can ever be made whole again.

II. Betrayal

With chapter 39 the setting abruptly shifts to Egypt and as we become absorbed in the vicissitudes of Joseph, the sorrowing Jacob and the hardened brothers gradually fade from the horizon of our thoughts and our attention focuses exclusively on Joseph. Sold to Potiphar, Joseph quickly proves himself an able and dependable man and soon becomes the trusted overseer of his master's affairs.

Joseph's very winsomeness and attractiveness, however, lead to his downfall. Potiphar's wife has an eye for a handsome man and she is not fussy about the sanctity of her marriage. Contemporary authors could learn much from the manner in which the relationship between Joseph and Potiphar's wife is treated. There is no dallying with or sentimentalizing of the rousing emotions of Potiphar's wife and no compromising of the moral issue. To be sure, the episode is narrated with candid realism, but it is a healthy realism that exposes the affair for what it really is. There is no suggestion that Potiphar's wife is neglected by her husband, or that Joseph secretly loves her. As her actions after the showdown with Joseph reveal, her feeling for him is something less than love. Ironically it is Joseph's *robe*, clutched as Joseph frees himself from her, that is used in evidence against him. The fact that Potiphar has Joseph imprisoned rather than put to death, as was normally the penalty in such a case, suggests how deep was his regard for Joseph even in his outrage—and perhaps also that he knew more about his wife than he pretended.

Even in prison, however, the ability of Joseph is recognized by the keeper of the jail and Joseph is placed in a supervisory capacity over the other prisoners. In the course of time Pharaoh's butler and baker are placed in this prison and come under Joseph's care. He in turn makes a profound impression on them by correctly interpreting, to the good fortune of the butler and to the misfortune of the baker, two especially perplexing and troubling *dreams* they dreamed—and one is reminded that Joseph also was a dreamer in his youth. But upon being released, the butler, who had promised Joseph to speak to Pharaoh for the purpose of securing his release, promptly forgot Joseph and Joseph is again betrayed. This is the nadir of the Joseph story. The hope of ever seeing his family and his homeland again seems utterly impossible. At this point his childhood dreams of eminence must have seemed a mockery. Psalm 105:19 refers to this period of Joseph's life as one in which God tested him. That Joseph bore the test well and was strengthened as a result of it is indicated by the manner in which he conducts himself throughout the rest of his career.

III. The Turning Point

The turning point of the Joseph story comes some two years after Pharaoh's butler was released from prison and it is occasioned by a famine. The famine is anticipated by Pharaoh himself in two portentous dreams (dreams always come in pairs in the Joseph story), which his wise men and magicians are unable to interpret. Then Pharaoh's butler belatedly remembered Joseph and spoke of him to Pharaoh. Hastily called before Pharaoh, Joseph interprets Pharaoh's dreams as referring to a coming famine of seven years duration and moreover recommends some prudent measures to cope with it. Pharaoh was so impressed that he both believed Joseph and appointed him to a position of authority second only to himself that he might take the action he had recommended. As a part of his equipment for his office, Joseph is provided with a robe of fine linen—and one is reminded of the robe soaked in blood and the one clutched in passion-turned-to-hatred. The famine came as Joseph said it would and, as it had been the occasion of Joseph's elevation from prison to prime minister, so it was also the occasion of Joseph's meeting his brothers again. For the famine prevailed also in the land of Canaan and led Joseph's brothers to seek grain in Egypt.

IV. Reconciliation and Reunion

Chapter 42 tells of the first encounter of Joseph with his brothers. It is an encounter that takes place without reconciliation and reunion. Joseph, who has grown to full manhood since he last saw his brothers, is not recognized by his brothers but he recognizes them. Yet Joseph chooses not to reveal himself to his brothers. As a matter of fact, Joseph treats his brothers harshly. He charges them with being spies, throws them in jail for three days and when he releases them, keeps one as a hostage who can be reclaimed only if they return and bring their youngest brother, Benjamin. Why does Joseph behave this way? Is he merely playing with his brothers and tormenting them so as to take vengeance on them? No; Joseph feels that there are certain conditions that must be met before genuine reconciliation and reunion can take place, and he acts the way he does in order to bring these conditions about. And a careful examination of the story at this point discloses that Joseph goes about this brilliantly and profoundly.

Quickly composing himself after his initial surprise, Joseph asks his brothers, in a harsh voice, where they are from, and upon hearing that they are from Canaan, charges them with being spies. The implication of his charge is that there is something suspicious about *ten* adult men coming to Egypt to purchase grain. Sensing the thrust of Joseph's charge, the brothers affirm that they have come only to buy grain and that they are all the sons of one man—brothers—and not a band of spies. Thus very skillfully Joseph focuses the attention of the brothers upon their common sonship in the family of Jacob.

Having gained this opening, Joseph seeks to focus the thoughts of his brothers still more sharply by scoffing at their claim and by reiterating his charge that they are spies. This leads the brothers to define more precisely their family relationship. They explain that originally there were twelve, that one of their number is at home with their father, and *one is no longer among them*—and another strategic opening is gained. (One wonders how long it has been since the thought of Joseph has crossed the minds of the brothers.) Joseph now brings the thoughts of his brothers to the focus he had intended all along by propounding a test allegedly of their veracity. If they are telling the truth, let them return home and bring this other brother back with them. Then Joseph will know that they are indeed brothers and eleven in number. But one of them must be left behind as a hostage. This also will test whether they are brothers or not, for if they are really brothers they will demonstrate this by returning for him.

Prior to stating these terms, Joseph had kept his brothers in jail for three days. This experience, with all its uncertainty together with having to leave a hostage behind, leads to a breakthrough in the spirits of the brothers at the point so carefully prepared for by Joseph. Upon hearing Joseph's terms, the brothers say to one another, "In truth we are guilty concerning our brother, in that we saw the distress of his soul, when he besought us and we would not listen; therefore is this distress come upon us" (42:21). At long last the ghost of Joseph returns to haunt his brothers and the first step toward reconciliation and reunion has been taken. Before there can be genuine reconciliation and reunion the brothers must become aware of the suffering inflicted upon their brother by their crime.

But Joseph does not seek only to make his brothers aware of what had happened in the past. He seeks also to place before them a decision in the present. By requiring them to leave their brother, Simeon,[2] in prison in Egypt, they are once again confronted with a choice to be made about brotherhood. They must now decide whether or not they will violate their brotherhood with Simeon by abandoning him in Egypt. The decision was not easy—as decisions like this never are—for Benjamin, the child of Jacob's sorrow and of the mother of Joseph, had somewhat taken the place of Joseph in the old man's life, and the brothers knew that their father would be most reluctant to consent to Benjamin's being taken to Egypt. Jacob's fear for Benjamin's safety had prevented him from accompanying his brothers to Egypt in the first place. To make the choice still more difficult and real, Joseph gives the brothers an excuse to rationalize not returning to Egypt. He secretly returns the money they had paid for the grain they had purchased. If they return to Egypt, they must do so knowing that they will be charged with stealing government grain.

Joseph's brothers are very human and very much like us. In the security of their home the ghost of Joseph is forgotten, and silently, imperceptibly, the brothers yield to temptation. They do not tell their father of the condition that they must take Benjamin with them if they are to redeem Simeon; they keep postponing their return for him, and Simeon is in effect abandoned. Thus ends the first encounter of Joseph and his brothers. Some progress is made, but the conditions for reconciliation and reunion have not been realized.

But the grain that was purchased in Egypt slowly dwindles away and again the family of Jacob is stalked by hunger. There is no alternative but again to seek grain and the only place where grain is to be found is Egypt. Now Joseph's brothers must tell their father that before they can have access to "the man" (Joseph) in Egypt again they must take Benjamin with them. Somehow overriding his feelings, Jacob consents for Benjamin to go. With steps that are made against their will, the brothers return to Egypt. Their anxiety is such that while still in the doorway of Joseph's "office" they effusively protest their innocence about the money and the charge that they are

2. Simeon is the next to the oldest of Jacob's sons. Normally the oldest son, Reuben, as the most responsible of the brothers, would have been kept as the hostage. That he was not is due to a statement he made to his brothers after they recognize in the fate that has befallen them the nemesis of their sin against Joseph. Unaware that Joseph understood him, Reuben said to his brothers, "Did I not tell you not to sin against the lad? But you would not listen" (42:22). In this way Joseph learns of Reuben's efforts on his behalf and his gratitude to Reuben, by passing over him as the hostage, is a subtlety that the other brothers and even Jacob fail to perceive. Judah also is a leader of his brothers and the defender of Joseph.

spies to Joseph's "executive secretary." To their amazement Joseph's secretary cordially receives them, dismisses the matter of the money, returns Simeon to them, and invites them to have dinner with Joseph! That evening Joseph welcomes the brothers graciously and cordially, asks about their father, and is genuinely interested to meet their younger brother. The brothers feel nervous and ill at ease, but gradually Joseph's cordiality conquers their fear and they give themselves up to the conviviality of the evening. Only two incidents out of the ordinary happen. The seating arrangement was such that they were arranged in order of age, and for some reason Benjamin was given more food than the rest. For a moment their old fear clutched their throats, but nothing was made of this and they soon dismissed it as coincidence. And so the evening passed without mention of the money or the spy charge. Nevertheless they would breathe easier when they were safely on their way home again.

It is understandable, therefore, that they arose somewhat earlier than usual the next morning. They tried to appear not too eager as they prepared to depart. Somehow all went smoothly and without incident. Not a word was said about the money or the spy charge and no effort was made to retain Simeon or Benjamin. At last they were on their way and with each step the spring in their stride increased a bit. With a sigh of relief they passed through the city gate and settled into the long trek that lay before them. Suddenly the thundering of hoofbeats shattered their home-bent thoughts; all at once a contingent of royal troops surrounded them, and the stern charge, "Why have you stolen Joseph's silver cup?" is leveled against them. Protesting their innocence vehemently, they dismount and open their baggage to be searched. The search proceeds from oldest to youngest. In spite of their sureness of their innocence, each time a bag is opened they hold their breath and each time the inspection fails to disclose the cup a load falls away from them. Ten times this happens and now only one sack is left, Benjamin's. With all eyes focused upon it and with hands that have become all thumbs it is opened and what each brother had suspected deep in his heart is confirmed. In utter despair they trudge back to the city. And again the ghost of Joseph arises to haunt them. They know that in some mysterious way God has been at work in these events and, as Judah says to Joseph upon their return, "has found out the guilt of your servants" (44:16).

In the light of the legal customs of the day Joseph is unexpectedly lenient. It would have been proper to hold all the brothers responsible and to demand the death penalty. Instead Joseph holds only Benjamin responsible and demands only that Benjamin become his slave. The rest of the brothers are free to return home! But by giving the brothers a way out, Joseph is again testing them. This time, however, the brothers stand the test. In a moving speech, Judah describes the love of Jacob for Benjamin, how his grief would be unbearable were they to return without their youngest brother, and offers himself in Benjamin's place. At the time of the first trip, Joseph had tested his brothers so that they perceived something of his own agony of soul as a result of what they had done. Here they become aware of the agony of their father over the loss and abuse of a son—and here I think Jacob can also represent God. With this awareness and with Judah's willingness to give himself in place of Benjamin the climax of the story is reached. Genuine reconciliation and reunion having become possible, Joseph reveals himself to his brothers and the story moves on to a happy and satisfying close.

In bringing about this reconciliation Joseph avoids two extremes. On the one hand, he avoids a cheap and meaningless reconciliation and reunion on the occasion of the initial encounter with his brothers or at the banquet table. On the other hand, he avoids taking revenge or playing God. At the time of Joseph's initial encounter with his brothers there is a hint that he may have been motivated by revenge. This is suggested by the fact that he first puts all of them in jail and is willing for only one to return to Canaan and fetch Benjamin (42:16). After three days, however, Joseph releases all the brothers but one and permits them to return home. Whether he conquers his desire for vengeance at this time or whether he is motivated by concern that the brothers carry food to his languishing father is not clear. But from the manner in which Joseph conducts himself during the second visit of the brothers it is evident that whatever thoughts he may have had about vengeance have been completely overcome and this is stated explicitly at the end of the story.

After Jacob dies, the brothers fear that Joseph may have spared them only for the sake of their father and will now have his revenge. Joseph dispels their anxiety by saying in 50:19: "Fear not, for am I in the place of God?" With remarkable restraint and skill, Joseph brings his brothers to an awareness of their violation of brotherhood and fatherhood and keeps this ever before them until the conditions are right for genuine reconciliation and reunion. Thus the violent breach made in Jacob's family was healed and the brotherhood between the sons of Jacob is renewed on a level even deeper than it was in the beginning.

V. Providence

Running parallel to and interwoven with the theme of brotherhood, a second and even grander theme is to be found in the Joseph story. It is not as obvious as that of brotherhood; and while it is present all along it does not become explicit and articulate until the great recognition scene between Joseph and his brothers. Immediately following Joseph's disclosure of himself he says to his brothers, "And now do not be distressed, or angry with yourselves, because you sold me here; for God sent me before you to preserve life" (45:5). Again, after the death of Jacob, when the brothers are fearful that Joseph will take vengeance on them, Joseph allays their fears with the words: "As for you, you meant evil against me; but God meant it for good, to bring it about that many people should be kept alive, as they are today" (50:20). This second theme, then, is that of the providence of God.

As one thinks back over the Joseph story in the light of these luminous statements of Joseph to his brothers he begins to marvel at the way God's providence becomes visible. At the time the brothers were so blinded by jealousy that they were determined to kill Joseph, a caravan came along that was in the market for a slave. This caravan, moreover, was on its way, not to Arabia, or Mesopotamia, or Phoenicia, but to Egypt. In Egypt, Joseph was sold, not to anyone, but to Potiphar, a man who had the capacity to appreciate his potential and the generosity to permit him to develop it. Framed by Potiphar's wife by circumstantial evidence that legally condemned him to death (and without hope of mercy because of his foreign birth and status as a slave), Joseph's sentence is magnanimously commuted to one of extended imprisonment. Even in prison the circuit of God's providence remains intact, for there Joseph came to know Pharaoh's butler and impressed him with his ability to interpret dreams. When the butler forgot Joseph's request to speak to Pharaoh on his behalf, Pharaoh dreamed some puzzling and disturbing dreams that none of his magicians and wise men could interpret. And, as was stated earlier, the famine both precipitated Joseph into a position of authority where he was able to help his brothers and brought them to him. The brothers had been determined to destroy Joseph and thereby to frustrate his childhood dreams (37:20). The result of their efforts was that Joseph was placed on a path that led him to the place where he was able to save them as well as many others. Nowhere in the Joseph story does God manifest himself tangibly or speak directly to Joseph or his brothers or intervene outwardly in the course of events. Yet silently, wonderfully, awesomely, God was present and at work every step of the way.

VI. The Sign of Our Covenant

The Joseph story, then, is more than a rousing story well told. It is transparent to a profound understanding of the meaning of brotherhood and of the ways of God with humanity. The ancient theme of broken brotherhood with which the Joseph story deals is by no means, however, peculiar to the family of Jacob. This is one of humankind's perennial problems and especially is it so for modern people. As one surveys the world scene today, it is the rule rather than the exception to find brother ranged against brother. There is North Korean against South Korean, Vietnamese against Viet Cong, Nationalist Chinese against Communist Chinese, Indian against Pakistani, Israeli against Arab, Turk against Greek, Algerian against Frenchman, Tutsi against Hutu, white South African against colored South African—and white American against Americans of color.

It is especially important that the differences between the white and Black American be understood as one of broken brotherhood. The stirring events that gave birth to America and the soaring words by which our birth was announced destined us to a great adventure in brotherhood. A nation christened with the words, "We hold these truths to be self-evident, that all men are created equal, that they are endowed by their Creator with certain unalienable Rights" and who greets the immigrant and visitor with a Statue of Liberty on which is inscribed: "Give me your tired, your poor, your huddled masses yearning to be free" must be opposed to any form of injustice among its citizens and must seek to maintain a society in which humans are truly brothers. As a matter of fact, America has committed herself to such an adventure in brotherhood in a solemn and binding covenant, the Constitution.

But noble words can become platitudes and conduct can make a mockery of professed ideals—and the human heart knows many ways to rationalize and explain away the contradiction. Such a covenant needs a sign and a safeguard to prevent this from happening. African Americans, precisely because of the difference of the color of their skin, constitutes such a visible reminder and test of the ideals enshrined in the covenant of our political and spiritual destiny. As God made the rainbow the sign of his covenant with Noah, so he has made African Americans the sign of his covenant with America. The protest of Blacks against the violation of brotherhood by the practices of segregation and discrimination, then, is a solemn responsibility he owes both to himself and the nation. How the nation treats this protest is not a matter of secondary importance nor is it one it can choose to ignore. The presence and the protest of African Americans place the nation inexorably before a decision. Because violated sisterhood stands in such violent conflict with our purpose for being as a nation, the decision is a matter of national life or death. America cannot be America unless there is a reconciliation and reunion of the white and Black American as brothers. It is because this is the nature of our problem that the Joseph story is so relevant today.

To approach this problem as one of broken sisterhood to which the solution must be a reconciliation and reunion as sisters will not be easy. It will mean that just as Joseph's brothers had to become aware of the agony of soul they had caused Joseph and their father, so must the white American become aware of the agony of soul that Blacks have suffered at her hands and of the pain this suffering has caused God. And not only must the white American become aware of the violation of brotherhood in the past; she must, as did Joseph's brothers, stand the test of brotherhood in the present. In his present relationship to African Americans as neighbor, employer, or employee, as fellow citizen, white Americans must pass the test of brotherhood—and especially so when they have a legitimate way to avoid it. It will mean that there can be no cheap and meaningless reconciliation and reunion. Once the white American has arrived at the point where there is openness to personal friendship with the Black American, she may feel that she has demonstrated that she is a "true Christian" and that the Black American ought to be grateful to her and to receive her with open arms. But this is only to arrive at the approximate point of Joseph's brothers at the end of their first trip. The problem is not this easily solved. As the brothers of Joseph had to make two trips to Egypt, so must the white American go a second mile in his relationship with his African American brother. He will know that he has completed this second mile when he can stand with Judah at the moment of his great speech to Joseph in Gen 44:18–34, when he can risk ridicule, ostracism, violence, or financial loss for the sake of his Black brother.

If this approach is hard for the white American, it is equally difficult for her Black brother. The more freedom and dignity the African American experiences, the greater is her awareness of the indignity and outrage of the past. The greater her wrath for white people, the more effective is her struggle against them. The clearer she sees the sin of her white sister, the less likely she is to be aware that she also is subject to sin. It will be as hard for the African American to forgive and accept white people as it is for the white American to acknowledge his sin and to seek to atone for it. If there is to be genuine reconciliation and reunion as brothers it will mean that the Black American must be patient with the first and often offensive overtures of the white American and he must, as did Joseph, refrain from acting out of revenge or seeking to play God. The remarkable thing is that in an age of violence, when minority groups throughout the world have resorted to terror and indiscriminate slaughter to gain their objectives, the African American Negroes alone, especially as they have been guided by Martin Luther King Jr., have conducted themselves strikingly in the spirit of Joseph. This is one of the greatest sources of hope for a reconciliation and reunion as brothers and sisters and one of the brightest chapters in modern history.

If America fails to be true to her destiny, only two paths are open to her: Either she will become hardened into a fanatical reactionaryism or through a failure of nerve lapse into weakness and indecision. The former case would inevitably lead to a global holocaust. In the latter case, the Communist bloc of nations, deprived of the alternative and challenge provided by America, would surely become completely demonic. But if we in America achieve a reconciliation and reunion as brothers and witness to the ideal of brotherhood, not only will the sin of the past and the present be redeemed, but the cause of brotherhood everywhere will be strengthened and possibly a way will be opened to a reconciliation and reunion of the Communist and non-Communist nations as brothers. In a world brooded over by the threat of atomic and hydrogen annihilation, is there any other way?

The recognition scene in the Joseph story is one of the great passages of the Bible. It is aglow with surprise, wonder, and joyful weeping. A great recognition day awaits us in America, a day when the white American and the African American discover that they are genuinely brothers. When this happens, perhaps the Black American will be able to say to her white sister, as Joseph said to his brothers: "As for you, you meant evil against me; but God meant it for good, to bring it about that many people should be kept alive, as they are today" (50:20).

2

The Curse That Never Was

(Genesis 9:18–27)[1]

Of all the passages of the Bible none is more infamous than Gen 9:18–27. Many a person has used this text to justify to himself and others his prejudice against people of African descent. Indeed, it has been widely used to claim divine sanction for slavery and segregation. Often the location of the passage is unknown and one is not familiar with the details, but with the certainty of unexamined truth it is asserted that the Bible speaks of a curse on Black people. And this notion has exercised so powerful an influence precisely because its adherents by and large have been "good church people." While the heyday of this understanding of Gen 9:18–27 was during the nineteenth and early twentieth centuries, it persists to this day. Whether wittingly or unwittingly, a recent article by F. W. Bassett of Limestone College, Gaffney, South Carolina, lends aid and comfort and helps to perpetuate it.[2] It is time that the misunderstanding and abuse of this passage come to an end.

I

Rarely have such clear and unambiguous claims been made of so obscure and difficult a passage. Its complexity is apparent from the outset. It begins

1. I would like to express appreciation to Kingsley Dalpadado, Samuel L. Gandy, Jack H. Goodwin, and Frank M. Snowden, Jr., without whose generous help this article in its present form would not have been possible.

2. Bassett, "Noah's Nakedness and the Curse on Canaan," 232–37.

by naming the sons of Noah who went forth from the ark, namely, Shem, Ham, and Japheth, but goes on to add in a statement that takes one completely by surprise: "Ham was the father of Canaan." And this information is repeated in verse 22. By its position immediately following the account of the flood, it is implied that the episode of 9:18–27 took place shortly thereafter. Moreover, the account gives the impression that Noah's sons have not yet set up separate households but are still unmarried and living with their father in the family tent. This impression is strengthened by the fact that one of the sons is designated as "the youngest" (v. 24). Also the offense against Noah is the kind one might expect from a teenager but hardly from a mature, married man. Yet the two references to Ham as the father of Canaan presuppose that Noah's sons have left their father's tent, set up separate households, and that a number of years have passed in the course of which Canaan, who is Ham's fourth son (Gen 10:6), was born and has become either a teenager or a young adult.

While the reference to Ham as the father of Canaan is awkward in every respect, one can infer from the context that it was introduced because later on Canaan is cursed for the misdeed of Ham. But instead of clarifying matters, this only creates another problem. Why should Canaan be cursed for the wrong of his father? The biblical text provides no answer to this question.

The attentive reader of Gen 9:18–27 is confronted, in the third place, by two different conceptions of the extent of Noah's family. Genesis 9:19a states that from Shem, Ham, and Japheth "the whole world was peopled." But according to 9:25–27 the sons of Noah all live in the land of Palestine.

In the fourth place, there is the perplexing fact that the sons of Noah are listed in the order Shem, Ham, and Japheth in 9:18 and on the basis of Gen 5:32 this is most naturally understood as the order of their birth. In 9:24, however, the offender against Noah is expressly identified as Noah's "youngest" son. From the order Shem, Ham, and Japheth, the youngest son is Japheth. But Japheth is not cursed.

This brings us to the fifth and most enigmatic of all the difficulties of Gen 9:18–27. In 9:24–25 Noah identifies the offender against him both as his youngest son and as Canaan: "When Noah awoke from his wine and knew what his youngest son had done to him, he said, 'Cursed be Canaan; a slave of slaves shall he be to his brothers.'" Then in vv. 26–27 Noah names the two brothers to whom Canaan is to be slave: "Noah also said: 'Blessed be the LORD, the God of Shem; and let Canaan be his slave. God enlarge

Japheth, and let him dwell in the tents of Shem; and let Canaan be his slave.'" Thus whereas the sons of Noah are Shem, Ham, and Japheth in 9:18, they are Shem, Japheth, and Canaan in 9:24–27.

II

How does one deal with a passage so in tension with itself? It is helpful to be aware that this is not the only such passage in Genesis. In fact, this kind of inner tension is the rule rather than the exception throughout the first six books of the Old Testament. We have not one but two versions of the creation, the genealogy of the first men, the flood, the family of nations, God's covenant with Abraham, Abraham's betrayal of Sarah, the covenant ceremony at Mt. Sinai, etc. And these parallel versions frequently differ sharply from each other. The universe in Gen 1:1—2:4a, for example, is brought into being by eight creative acts over a period of six days whereas in Gen 2:4b–25 there are only four creative acts and there is no reference to the time involved. The names in the two parallel genealogies of mankind before the flood (Gen 4:17–26 and ch. 5) are spelled differently at times and do not consistently follow the same order. According to one version of the flood Noah takes seven pairs of clean and one pair of unclean animals into the ark (Gen 7:2, 3) and the flood lasts sixty-one days (7:4; 8:6–12) while in the other version Noah takes two of every kind of animal into the ark (6:19, 20; 7:9, 15) and the flood lasts for one year and ten days (7:11; 8:13, 14).

We may find these parallel but different versions of things confusing and troubling, but that they exist is a givenness of the biblical witness, the recognition and clarification of which has been one of the most fundamental and widely accepted achievements of the study of the Old Testament during the past century. Nor is this phenomenon confined to the Old Testament. We have not one but four versions of the ministry and teaching of Jesus and the difference between the version of Mark and John is just as sharp as anything we have in Genesis. For that matter, Protestants and Catholics do not understand Jesus's last meal with his disciples in the same way nor do all Protestants understand it alike! While a profound unity underlies the biblical witness, it speaks not with a single voice and the recognition of this is the necessary condition for the proper understanding of Gen 9:18–27.

All the tensions of Gen 9:18–27 are resolved when it is recognized that this passage contains two parallel but different traditions of Noah's family. In one tradition Noah's family consists of Shem, Ham, and Japheth, and these three are the ancestors of all the peoples known to ancient Israel. This tradition is universal, catholic in scope. It is found in Gen 9:18–19a (and elsewhere in 5:32; 6:10, 7:13; 10:1; 1 Chr 1:4). In the other tradition, Noah's family consists of Shem, Japheth, and Canaan, and they all live in Palestine. This tradition is limited, parochial in scope. It is found in 9:20–27 (and seems to be presupposed in 10:21, where Shem is referred to as the elder brother of Japheth).

The understanding of Gen 9:18–27 is so confused because the text in its present form represents an effort to minimize the discrepancy between these two traditions by equating Ham in the one with Canaan in the other. This was done by the notation in 9:18b, "Ham was the father of Canaan," and by adding in 9:22a, "Ham the father of" before Canaan. When these two harmonizing notes are recognized as such the two different traditions of Noah's family stand out sharply: verses 18–19a reflect one tradition, verses 20–27 embody the other. Instead of trying to harmonize them, each should be considered in its own right. When this is done it becomes clear that Noah's discovery of wine and his cursing and blessing of his sons is an independent, coherent narrative in which the offender against his father as well as the one cursed is Canaan. This becomes graphically clear if the harmonizing notes are placed in brackets or removed as in the following citation of the text:

> [20]Noah was the first tiller of the soil. He planted a vineyard; [21]and he drank of the wine, and became drunk, and uncovered himself in his tent. [22]And . . . Canaan saw the nakedness of his father, and told his two brothers outside. [23]Then Shem and Japheth took a garment, laid it upon both their shoulders, and walked backward and covered the nakedness of their father; their faces were turned away, and they did not see their father's nakedness. [24]When Noah awoke from his wine and knew what his youngest son had done to him, [25]he said,
>
> "Cursed be Canaan;
> a slave of slaves shall he be to his brothers."
> [26]He also said,
> "Blessed be the LORD, the God of Shem;
> and let Canaan be his slave.
> [27]God enlarge Japheth,
> and let him dwell in the tents of Shem;
> and let Canaan be his slave."[3]

3. This translation follows the RSV except at two points. In v. 21 the RSV has "lay uncovered" instead of "uncovered himself." The rendition adopted above is defended in

This is not a new interpretation. It was first proposed by J. Wellhausen in 1876.[4] Among those who have subsequently adopted and defended it are: K. Budde (who devotes ninety pages to Gen 9:18–27!),[5] A. Kuenen,[6] A. Westphal,[7] W. R. Harper,[8] B. Stade,[9] H. Holzinger,[10] B. W. Bacon,[11] C. H. Cornill,[12] W. E. Addis,[13] E. Kautzsch,[14] D. S. Margoliouth,[15] J. E. Carpenter and C. Hartford-Battersby (with reserve),[16] H. Gunkel,[17] S. R. Driver (with reserve),[18] W. H. Bennett,[19] E. Meyer,[20] A. R. Gordon,[21] C. F. Kent,[22]

n. 96 of this study. "Blessed be the Lord" in v. 26 is given as an alternative translation in a footnote by the RSV and of the two alternatives it is closest to the Hebrew text.

4. Wellhausen, "Die Composition des Hexateuchs," 403–4. This was the first of three long articles (the third article was published in vol. 22, 1877). They were reprinted in the 4th ed. of Bleek, *Einleitung in das Alte Testament*, 181–267, and published (unchanged) by Wellhausen in book form in 1885 under the same title as above.

5. Budde, *Die Biblische Urgeschichte*, 290–370; 506–16.

6. Kuenen, *An Historico-Critical Inquiry into the Origin and Composition of the Hexateuck*, 234.

7. Westphal, *Les sources du Pentateuque*, 1:243.

8. Harper, "The Pentateuchal Question. I. Gen 1:1—12:5," 61–62.

9. Stade, *Geschichte des Volkes Israel*, 1:109.

10. Holzinger, *Genesis erklärt*, 91; and Holzinger, *Einleitung in den Hexateuch*, 141.

11. Bacon, "Notes on the Analysis of Genesis I.–XXXI"; and Bacon, *The Genesis of Genesis*, 114, 115, 231.

12. Cornill, *Introduction to the Canonical Books of the Old Testament*, 86, 87.

13. Addis, *The Documents of the Hexateuch*, 14–15.

14. Kautzsch, *Die Heilige Schrift des Alten Testaments*, 154.

15. Margoliouth, "Ham," 288–89.

16. Carpenter and Hartford-Battersby, *The Hexateuch*, II, 14–15.

17. Gunkel, *Die Genesis übersetzt und erklärt*, 78–81, 84, 87; and Gunkel, *Die Urgeschichte und die Patriarchen*, 88.

18. Driver, *The Book of Genesis*, 109, 111–12.

19. Bennett, *Genesis*, 155.

20. Meyer, *Die Israeliten und ihre Nachbarstämme*, 219–22.

21. Gordon, *The Early Traditions of Genesis*, 3–4, 240, 260, 263.

22. Kent, *Narratives of the Beginning of Hebrew History*, 60, see 69; and Kent, *The Heroes and Crises of Early Hebrew History*, 47–48, 51.

J. Skinner,[23] F. Böhl,[24] R. Smend,[25] C. Steuernagel,[26] O. Procksch,[27] H. E. Ryle,[28] W. Eichrodt,[29] J. R. Dummelow,[30] W. M. Patton,[31] E. S. Brightman,[32] A. S. Peake,[33] O. Eissfeldt,[34] S. Mowinckel,[35] R. H. Pfeiffer,[36] W. Zimmerli,[37] E. G. Kraeling,[38] C. A. Simpson,[39] G. von Rad,[40] A. Lods,[41] E. B. Redlich,[42] J. Chaine (with reserve),[43] A. Clamer,[44] C. T. Fritsch,[45] J. Heemrood,[46] A. Halder,[47] R. L. Hicks,[48] J. H. Marks,[49] A. H. McNeile and T. W. Thacker,[50]

23. Skinner, *A Critical and Exegetical Commentary on Genesis*, 182, 184, 186, 195, 202, 219.

24. Böhl, *Kanaanäer und Hebräer*, 6, 68.

25. Smend, *Die Erzählung des Hexateuch*, 17–18, 21, 27, 28.

26. Steuernagel, *Lehrbuch der Einleitung in das Alte Testament*, 140.

27. Procksch, *Die Genesis*, 71ff.

28. Ryle, *The Book of Genesis*, 127, 128, 129.

29. Eichrodt, *Die Quellen der Genesis von neuem untersucht*, 118–19; see 145.

30. Dummelow, "Genesis," 16.

31. Patton, *Israel's Account of the Beginnings*, 107–8.

32. Brightman, *The Sources of the Hexateuch*, 38.

33. Peake, "Genesis," 145.

34. Eissfeldt, *Hexateuch-Synopse*, 7, 8; see 89, 14*–15*, 256* and "Genesis," 372.

35. Mowinckel, *The Two Sources of the Predeuteronomic Primeval History (JE) in Gen 1–11*, 15–16.

36. Pfeiffer, *Introduction to the Old Testament*, 274–75.

37. Zimmerli, *1. Mose 1–11*, 355–56.

38. Kraeling, "The Earliest Hebrew Flood Story," 291.

39. Simpson, *The Early Traditions of Israel*, 63–64, 451–452, 498; and Simpson, "The Book of Genesis," 555–56, 560.

40. Von Rad, *Genesis*, 131–32.

41. Lods, *Historic de la Littérature Hébraïque et Juive*, 174, 175.

42. Redlich, *The Early Traditions of Genesis*, 113–14.

43. Chaine, *Le Livre de la Genèsis*, 144, 145.

44. Clamer, *La Genèsis*, 201–3.

45. Fritsch, *The Book of Genesis*, 46–47.

46. Heemrood, "Kanaän Vervloekt," 129–30.

47. Halder, "Canaan," 494.

48. Hicks, "Ham," 515.

49. Marks, "Noah," 555.

50. McNeile and Thacker, "Ham," 361.

R. Graves and R. Patai,[51] G. Fohrer,[52] E. H. Maly,[53] and T. E. Fretheim.[54] A variation of this interpretation is represented by A. Dillman,[55] J. Hermann,[56] and L. Rost,[57] who maintain that originally the passage had to do only with Canaan (Dillmann) or with Canaan and Shem (Herrmann, Rost) and that the reference to the other brother(s) has been added later.[58]

The above roster of scholars is sufficient to indicate that after its introduction in the 1870s the interpretation presented above quickly won the assent of the majority of authorities and has maintained that position to the present. And it would be difficult to draw up a more distinguished company of scholars. Nevertheless this interpretation has not lacked for opposition nor have there been wanting vigorous defenders of an alternative point of view.

III

Among those who assume the unity of Gen 9:18–27 and therefore regard Ham as the offender are: A. Köhler,[59] C. A. Briggs,[60] Franz Delitzsch,[61] W. H. Green,[62] H. L. Strack,[63] J. Halévy,[64] C. J. Ball,[65] T. K. Cheyne,[66] M. Dods,[67]

51. Graves and Patai, *Hebrew Myths*, 121–22.

52. Fohrer, *Introduction to the Old Testament*, 162.

53. Maly, "Genesis," 16–17.

54. Fretheim, *Creation, Fall, and Flood*, 127 n.2.

55. Dillman, *Genesis*, vol. 1, 302, see 306, 307.

56. Hermann, "Zu Gen 9:18–27," 127–31.

57. Rost, "Noah der Weinbauer," 169–78.

58. Kennett in his, "The Early Narratives of the Jahvistic Document of the Pentateuch," 17–19, argues that the sons were Shem, Japheth, and Canaan but that Ham rather than Noah was their father.

59. Köhler, *Lehrbuch der Biblischen Geschichte: Alten Testament*, I, 54 n.4, 66.

60. Briggs, *Messianic Prophecy*, 79–81.

61. Delitzsch, *A New Commentary on Genesis*, I, 290ff.

62. Green, "The Pentateuchal Question," 127–30.

63. Strack, *Die Bücher Genesis, Exodus, Leviticus und Numeri*, 28.

64. Halévy, *Recherches Biblique*, I, 174ff.

65. Ball, *The Book of Genesis*, 56.

66. Cheyne, *Traditions and Beliefs of Ancient Israel*, 150–54. Cheyne attempts to master the problems of Gen 9:18–27 by understanding Ham to be a North Arabian people. To achieve this understanding, however, he freely and arbitrarily emends the text.

67. Dods, *The Book of Genesis*, 78.

A. Ehrlich,[68] W. Möller,[69] L. Murillo[70] E. König,[71] P. Heinisch,[72] B. Jacob,[73] H. C. Leupold,[74] U. Cassuto,[75] H. Junker,[76] H. Frey,[77] A. Richardson,[78] W. M. Logan,[79] R. H. Elliott,[80] J. de Fraine,[81] and F. W. Bassett.[82] To these may be added a small group of scholars who take the position that there is only one tradition of the sons of Noah, namely, Shem, Ham, and Japheth, but that part or all of the cursing of Canaan and the blessing of Shem and Japheth is later than the story about Noah's discovery of wine. Among these are: B. D. Eerdmans,[83] J. Hoftijzer,[84] H. W. Wolff,[85] and D. Neiman.[86]

Perhaps the most serious obstacle to those who defend the unity of 9:18–27 is the fact that Ham is regularly named as Noah's second son whereas the offender is specifically designated as Noah's youngest son (v. 24). One of the oldest and simplest expedients to avoid this difficulty is to accept the order Shem, Ham, and Japheth as the proper one chronologically but to construe the adjective, young, not as a superlative but as a

68. Ehrlich, *Randglossen zur Hebräischen Bible*, I, 41–42.

69. Möller, *Wider den Bann der Quellenscheidung*, 106 n.2.

70. Murillo, *El Génesis*, 408ff.

71. König, *Die Genesis*, 385–86.

72. Heinisch, *Das Buch Genesis*, 184–86.

73. Jacob, *Das erste Buch der Tora: Genesis*, 258ff.

74. Leupold, *Exposition of Genesis*, 343ff.

75. Cassuto, *A Commentary on the Book of Genesis*, II, 141ff.

76. Frey, *Genesis*, 35–36.

77. Junker, *Das Buch der Anfänge*, 132–35.

78. Richardson, *Genesis I–XI*, 113–15.

79. Logan, *In the Beginning God*, 69–73.

80. Eliott, *The Message of Genesis*, 70–71.

81. De Fraine, *Genesis*, 95ff.

82. Bassett, "Noah's Nakedness and the Curse on Canaan," 232–37. The unity of the passage is assumed but not defended by Hughes, *A Critical Study of the Meaning of 'RWR in Genesis 9:18–27*.

83. Eerdmans, *Alttestamentliche Studiën I: Die Komposition der Genesis*, 77–78, 84.

84. Hoftijzer, "Some Remarks on the Table of Noah's Drunkenness," 22–27.

85. Wolff, "Das Kerygma des Jahwisten," 87.

86. Neiman, "The Date and Circumstances of the Cursing of Canaan," 113–34. By a questionable interpretation of Genesis 10, Dussaud infers that Canaan, Shem, Ham, and Japheth are brothers and issue of the same father. It was the author of Gen 9:18–27, he maintains, who put Canaan in a secondary role in relation to his brothers ("Cham et Canaan," 221–30).

comparative. That is, in relation to Shem, Ham is Noah's "younger" son.[87] Not two but three sons are compared, however, and when this is the case the proper construction is the superlative.

There is an old and well represented tradition, on the other hand, that the order Shem, Ham, and Japheth is not chronological and that Ham actually was Noah's youngest son.[88] This understanding is arrived at by construing Gen 10:21 to read, "Shem, the brother of Japheth, the eldest" and by taking "youngest son" in 9:24 to refer to Ham. But almost all authorities are agreed that the proper construction of Gen 10:21 is "Shem . . . , the elder brother of Japheth." And if the "youngest son" in 9:24 is Ham the cursing of Canaan is completely unmotivated and without meaning.

Still others would solve this problem by contending that "youngest" in 9:24 should not be understood chronologically but morally in the sense of "the least, the contemptible."[89] But there are a number of words in the Hebrew language better suited to express moral condemnation and it is difficult to see why so ambiguous a term would have been chosen in this context.

Accepting that "youngest son" is to be understood chronologically and that the reference is to Canaan, some have sought a way out of the dilemma by calling attention to the fact that son is sometimes used in the

87. Both the Septuagint and the Vulgate construe the adjective "young" as a comparative. This construction was defended among older scholars by Schumann, Ewald, Keil, and Schrader (cited by Dillmann, *Genesis*, 306 n.7). Leupold (*Exposition of Genesis*, 348) and Hughes (*A Critical Study of the Meaning of 'RWR in Gen 9:18-27*, 117) are virtually alone among more recent scholars in adopting this position.

88. This view is already found in Bereshith Rabbah 26:2; Numbers Rabbah 4:8; Babylonian Talmud, Sanhedrian 69b; Josephus, *Antiquities* i.4.1, see i.6.3; *Jubilees* 7:10; Justin Martyr, *Dialogue* 139; Köhler, *Lehrbuch der Biblische Geschichte*, 54 n.4, see 66; Möller, *Wider den Bann der Quellenscheidung*, 106 n.2; Murillo, *El Génesis*, 410; König, *Die Genesis*, 386; Heinisch, *Das Buch Genesis*, 184, 185; Cassuto, *A Commentary on the Book of Genesis*, 165; Hoftijzer, "Some Remarks on the Table of Noah's Drunkenness," 23–24; de Fraine, *Genesis*, 97, 98.

Delitzsch argues for Shem being the oldest (see 10:21) and Ham the youngest (*A New Commentary on Genesis*, 290, 293–94). Jacob, largely on the basis of his understanding of Gen 11:10, maintains that the proper chronological order is Ham, Shem, Japheth (Ibid., 306–7).

89. Bereshith Rabbah 36:7; Targum of Pseudo-Jonathan on Gen 9:24; the early Syrian Fathers; Rashi; Jacob, *Das erste Buch der Tora: Genesis*, 264–265; see 291, 308. Cassuto thinks that "possibly" the Hebrew word has both a chronological and moral sense in this context (*A Commentary on the Book of Genesis*, 165). Procksch asserts that the word is used in the absolute rather than the comparative sense to emphasize that the offense against Noah was not the deed of a mature person (*Die Genesis*, 71, 73).

sense of grandson.[90] Such usage is attested but never in conjunction with son used in the literal sense as in the present passage.

A few scholars assert that the original text consistently referred to Ham as the offender and as the one cursed and that Canaan is a later addition to the text.[91] But this is pure speculation for which there is no firm support in the ancient texts and versions. This position is rendered completely untenable, moreover, by the statements, "Ham was the father of Canaan," and "Ham the father of." If Ham was the consistent reading of the original text these statements are superfluous and unintelligible. And if someone added Canaan to the text why did he not remove all references to Ham?

Various explanations are offered to account for Canaan being cursed for the offense of Ham. Some find here the working of a principle of retribution: as Noah suffered at the hands of his youngest son, Ham, so Ham is afflicted in the person of his youngest son, Canaan. But nowhere is such a principle enunciated in the Bible nor is an example to be found where the guilty father is passed over and his son punished in his stead.

Others account for the cursing of Canaan on the grounds that one whom God had blessed (Ham in Gen 9:1) could not be cursed. Equally valid is the principle that the innocent should not be cursed for the misdeed of the guilty.

Still others would account for the presence of Canaan in the curse because Canaan was the nearest and best known of Hamitic peoples to the Israelites. Rather, that only Canaan is mentioned in the curse most naturally suggests that all other Hamitic peoples are excluded from it. And if Ham is the guilty party, the text provides no answer as to why only Canaan and not all Hamitic peoples should be cursed.

Finally, it has been maintained that both Ham and Canaan are guilty, that Canaan first saw Noah's nakedness and Ham told his brothers. There are also traditions that either Ham or Canaan (or a lion) rendered Noah impotent (or attacked him homosexually) and that this was what "his youngest son had done to him" (v. 24). But the context indicates that the disrespectful seeing itself was the offense done to Noah.[92] And if both father and son are guilty, why is the father treated as less responsible than the son?

90. Ibn Esra; Redak (cited by Jacob, *Das erste Buch der Tora*, 263); Dillmann, *Genesis*, 307; Surfelt, "Noah's Curse and Blessing," 740.

91. König, *Die Genesis*, 386–387; Heinisch, *Das Buch Genesis*, 186; Junker, *Das Buch der Anfänge*, 35; de Fraine, *Genesis*, 98.

92. "And it is the seeing itself, the looking, that is accounted by the refined sensitivity of the Israelite as something disgusting, especially when it is associated, as it is here, with

A completely different tack is taken by Bassett. On the basis of the usage attested in Leviticus 18 and 20 that to see a man's nakedness may have the idiomatic meaning of having sexual intercourse with his wife, Bassett interprets the passage to mean that Ham committed incest with his mother and that Canaan was cursed because he was the fruit of this illicit union. Bassett thinks that the case of the Reubenites who lost their preeminence among the tribes of Israel because of Reuben's affair with his father's concubine, Bilhah, and the midrashic traditions that Ham's offense against Noah was one of castration (which also has to do with displacing one's father) support his understanding of the passage. In order to maintain this interpretation, however, Bassett has to delete 9:23 as the later addition of a redactor or editor who "missed the idiomatic meaning"[93] of the seeing of Noah's nakedness.

Bassett overstates the case for the sexual implications of nakedness. E. A. Speiser points out on the basis of Gen 42:9, 12 that nakedness in the first instance "relates to exposure" and "does not necessarily imply sexual offenses" (see Gen 2:25; Exod 20:26; 2 Sam 6:20).[94] In a passage that may have been formulated under the influence of Gen 9:18–27, Hab 2:15,[95] drunkenness and nudity are associated with each other without any sexual overtones (see also Lam 4:21).

Furthermore, the proper idiomatic expression for intercourse is to *uncover* the nakedness of another. Except for one instance, "uncover" is consistently the verb of the idiom for intercourse in Leviticus 18 and 20. In Lev 20:17 "uncover" and "see" are used in parallelism to each other, but this usage of "see" is clearly exceptional for the parallelism with "uncover" has to be made explicit. Bassett cites no other passages where to see the nakedness of another means to have sexual intercourse. Nor do the standard lexicons give this as a meaning for *r'h*. Still more damaging to Bassett's argument is the fact that "uncover" and "see" are used in adjoining sentences in Gen 9:18–27 (vv. 21, 22) but there is no effort to relate them to each other and here they clearly are not synonymous. Canaan does not uncover Noah; Noah uncovers himself.[96] In short, Bassett has not established a case

an affront to the dignity of one's father" (Cassuto, *A Commentary on the Book of Genesis*, 151–52). See also Dussaud, "Cham et Canaan," 222.

93. Dussaud, "Cham et Canaan," 233–34, see 237.

94. Speiser, *Genesis*, 61.

95. Cassuto, *A Commentary on the Book of Genesis*, 152.

96. The reflexive nature of the verb in question, *wa-yithgal*, has not always been

for the general usage of the expression to see the nakedness of another as meaning sexual intercourse. Nor does the context in Gen 9:18–27 support such a usage. Quite simply the text states that Noah uncovered himself and Canaan witnessed him in this state.

Not only does Bassett overstate the case, but he is inconsistent. He asserts on the one hand that "the idiomatic interpretation is so firmly established in Leviticus that it should be accepted as the normal one unless some other meaning is demanded by the context" yet maintains that Gen 9:23 was added "by someone who did not understand the idiom"![97] On the one hand, Bassett commits himself to the limited, parochial tradition of Noah's family in that he takes 9:20–27 to be an ethnological tradition "designed to discredit the Canaanites and justify the Israelite and Philistine hegemony over them." The major burden of the paper, on the other hand, is to defend the catholic tradition of Noah's family according to which the sons are Shem, Ham, and Japheth (pp. 234ff.).

Critical to Bassett's position is his assertion that 9:23 is secondary. There is no evidence in the ancient texts and versions to support this claim. No other scholar has found reason to regard only this verse as alien to its context. Rather, the blessing of Shem and Japheth is unintelligible apart from some such meritorious act on their part as reported in verse 23. And if verse 23 is integral to its context it is fatal to Bassett's theory. For, as Cassuto observes, "if the covering was an adequate remedy, it follows that the misdemeanor was confined to seeing."[98] For that matter, verse 22 stands in great tension with Bassett's position. If Ham committed incest with his mother, it is likely that he would come outside and tell his brothers?

There are other flaws in Bassett's interpretation. If Ham's offense was incest it is difficult to see how Noah could curse by name the issue of this union at the time of conception and completely ignore the perpetrators of the deed. There is a persistent and often bitter polemic against the Canaanites in the Old Testament. Had Canaan's origin been an incestuous one it

respected by translators and commentators. But grammatically the verb is a reflexive. Moreover, the context supports a reflexive construction. The heat from the wine would have caused Noah to uncover himself. The verb is translated as a reflexive among others by Rashi, Skinner, *Prophecy and Religion*, 183; König, *Die Genesis*, 384; Jacob, *Das erste Buch der Tora: Genesis*, 260; Leupold, *Exposition of Genesis*, 344, 345; Hughes, *A Critical Study of 'RWR in Gen 9:18-27*, 117; Jerusalem Bible; New Jewish Version (see Orlinsky, *Notes on the New Translation of the Torah*, 80).

97. Bassett, "Noah's Nakedness and the Curse on Canaan," 137.

98. Ibid., 151.

almost certainly would have been exploited (see Gen 19:30–38), but nowhere is there any reference to it. Finally, Bassett's position leaves unsolved the questions that arise in connection with "youngest son" in verse 24.

Almost three hundred years ago a position essentially identical with that of Bassett was put forward by Hermann von der Hardt.[99] It received prompt rebuttal[100] and has since enjoyed the oblivion it deserves.

Unsatisfactory also is the attempt to master the difficulties of Gen 9:18–27 by separating the curse and blessing from the preceding narrative. The following structure is transparent in the text:

Introduction: Noah's vineyard and drunkenness

I. The behavior of Noah's sons

A Canaan's disrespect and shamelessness

B. The respect and piety of Shem and Japheth

99. *Ephemerides philologicae* (Helmstadt, 1696), 43–54. (The pages cited above constitute the second of a series of notes on the Pentateuch by von der Hardt). As Bassett, von der Hardt bases his interpretation on the idiomatic meaning of uncovering the nakedness of another in Leviticus 18 and 20 and thinks incest best accounts for the curse on Canaan and the severity of the curse. Unlike Bassett, von der Hardt retains Gen 9:23 and understands the verse to mean that someone (unidentified) who witnessed Ham and his mother or step-mother reported it to Shem and Japhath outside and they cast their cloak, not over their father but over (literally, the shoulders) the guilty pair (who were sleeping) as evidence of having witnessed the crime, turned and left the scene. When the text says that Shem and Japheth did not see the nakedness of their father it means that they did not violate his wife as did Ham.

100. Calvoer, *Gloria Mosis*, 244–64. In his rather wordy and repetitious reply to von der Hardt, Calvoer maintains that the traditional, literal understanding of Gen 9:20–27 is supported by a critical examination of the text whereas the position of von der Hardt is forced, extreme, does violence to the text, and is not critically established. Calvoer emphasizes that the verb, uncover, is a reflexive, that Noah uncovers himself rather than that he was uncovered by Ham. Verse 23 is treated in great detail. Calvoer shows how von der Hardt takes liberties with the text and how this verse, if understood simply and literally, is in fundamental conflict with the position of von der Hardt. The special emphasis on Canaan is to be accounted for, not because of his incestuous origin, but more plausibly by the Jewish tradition that he was born on the ark (see also Chrysostom). Calvoer also observes that the credibility of von der Hardt's argument is strained by the fact that Ham's mother would have been a very old woman (and we have no evidence that he had a step-mother).

II. Noah's response to his son's behavior

A. Curse on Canaan

B. Blessing on Shem and Japeth.[101]

The two parts of the passage correspond symmetrically and necessarily to each other. And this correspondence is unmarred by literary seams, formal dislocations, or other incongruities.

Those scholars then who defend the unity of Gen 9:18–27 or who maintain that there was only one tradition of Noah's sons have not presented an interpretation that does justice to the text. They are at odds with each other and cannot agree on a common understanding. None of them has taken seriously the conflict between the catholic and parochial conceptions of Noah's family standing in juxtaposition to each other. In short, no satisfactory explanation of Gen 9:18–27 has been given on the assumption that it is organic literary unity speaking with a single voice, nor, on this assumption, is one possible.

IV

From a form-critical point of view, Gen 9:20–27 is an ethnological etiology concerned with the theology of culture and history.[102] The correct understanding of the passage is bound up with the question of the identity of Shem, Japheth, and Canaan and with locating the period of history that corresponds to the conditions set forth in the curse and blessings.

One group of scholars, headed by Gunkel, understand the passage against the broad background of the second millennium BCE. Canaan is taken to embrace the inhabitants of the entire coastal region of Western Asia bordering the Mediterranean Sea. Japheth is identified with the Hittites or possibly northern Sea Peoples. Shem is regarded as a comprehensive designation for the Arameans and Hebrews (Gunkel), the Amorites, Arameans, Hebrews, and Arabs (Procksch), or the Suti and Amurri (Skinner). But the fact that special emphasis is placed on Yahweh, the covenant God of Israel, as the God of Shem (Gen 9:26) precludes so broad a designation for Shem. In Gen 10:15, moreover, the Hittites are regarded as the son of

101. Gunkel, *Genesis*, XXXIV, 78, 79; ct. 81. See also Procksch, *Die Genesis*, 72, 73; Jacob, *Das erste Buch der Tora: Genesis*, 262–63.

102. Gunkel, *Genesis*, XXI; see 80; see Hughes, *A Critical Study of 'RWR in Gen 9:18–27*, ch. II.

Canaan. And relations between the Hebrew patriarchs and the Canaanites as reflected in the book of Genesis are surprisingly devoid of hostility and animosity.[103]

A second group of scholars relate Gen 9:20–27 to the period of the Israelite conquest under Joshua and/or the period of the judges (ca. 1300–1150 BCE). This point of view is developed most fully by D. Neiman.[104] He identifies Shem with Israel, Japheth with Greek Sea Peoples, and Canaan with the Canaanites and argues that Noah's curse and blessing can be pin-pointed to either ca. 1230–1220 BCE or ca. 1190–1180 BCE for on both occasions Israel was in effect allied with the Philistines against the Canaanites. During the decade ca. 1230–1220 the Israelites were invading Canaan from the east and a coalition of Libyans and Greek Sea Peoples was threatening the Delta region of Egypt and Canaan from the west. Some forty years later the Greek Sea Peoples again launched an attack against the Hittites, Canaan, and Egypt while Israel had to defend herself against the Canaanites in the Battle of Tanaach (Judg 4; 5).

Neiman admits that the Hebrews and Greek Sea Peoples were not necessarily working consciously and formally together, but Gen 9:25–27 presupposes a relationship of more than a casual or coincidental nature. If the Hebrews and Philistines were allies in the conquest of Canaan why is there no reference to it in Joshua and Judges? More telling still is the absence of any reproof against the Philistines because they "did not remember the covenant of brotherhood" (see Amos 1:9) when they forced the Danites to relocate (Judges 17–18).

Most scholars relate Gen 9:20–27 to the period of the early Israelite monarchy when the Canaanites were finally subdued, but there is no agreement as to the identity of Japheth nor as to the specific occasion embraced by the curse and blessing. Budde identifies Japheth with the Phoenicians and relates the passage to Solomon's ceding of a number of Galileean towns to Hiram of Tyre (1 Kgs 9:11–13).[105] But it is difficult to see how such a

103. See van Selms, "The Canaanites in the Book of Genesis," 182–213. Cassuto thinks the historical references in Noah's curse and blessing are to the episode of Genesis 14 (*A Commentary on the Book of Genesis*, 168–69)!

104. Neiman, "The Date and Circumstances of the Cursing of Canaan," 127–32. See also Smith, *The Early Poetry of Israel*, 48–49; Pfeiffer, *Introduction to the Old Testament*, 275; Speiser, *Genesis*, 62–63; van Selms, "The Canaanites in the Book of Genesis," 186–87; van Selms "Judge Shamgar," 308; and the note by Grispino in *The Old Testament of the Holy Bible*, Confraternity Version, 23.

105. Budde, *The Religion of Israel to the Exile*, 338–65, 506–15.

minor event could have called forth such an exalted utterance and that it should be attributed to Noah. Budde's position is seriously flawed by the fact that the Phoenicians themselves are Canaanites (see Gen 10:15). Moreover, the Phoenicians did not exercise dominion over the remaining Canaanites. And it is difficult to see how the Phoenician name, Japheth, would have been transferred to the peoples of Greece and Asia Minor as it is in Gen 10:2–5.

Rost thinks the passage originally had to do only with Shem and Canaan and in this form belongs to the early period of David's kingship over all Israel, perhaps shortly after the ark was brought to Jerusalem. Some thirty or forty years later at the time of Solomon's organization of his kingdom into twelve administrative districts, the Japheth speech was added to persuade the remaining Canaanite city-states to become a part of the Israelite kingdom by promising them a share in the rule of the previously conquered territory of Canaan.[106] This position suffers from the fact that the passage is literarily atomized and above all because Japheth is identified with the unconquered Canaanite city-states or their ruling class in the time of Solomon. Moreover, both David and Solomon had little reason to persuade; they had enough power and more to compel.

The most satisfactory solution in the judgment of the writer is to identify Shem with Israel, Canaan with the Canaanites, Japheth with the Philistines,[107] and to understand the curse and blessing as rooted in the historical situation of the first seven and one half years of David's reign when he was king of Judah at Hebron (2 Sam 2:1–11; 5:5). It is frequently raised as an objection to identifying Japheth with the Philistines that the Israelites and Philistines were fierce rivals and enemies and that it is inconceivable that any Israelite would welcome the Philistines to the tents of Shem. This

106. Rost regards the incident of Noah's drunkenness as an independent literary unity that was added to the original nucleus at the same time as the section on Japheth ("Noah der Weinbauer," 174–175). He also follows Procksch (*Die Genesis*, 71, 73; see also Jacob, *Das erste Buch der Tora: Genesis*, 267; Surfelt, "Noah's Curse and Blessing," 741) in understanding the word translated "enlarge" in v. 27 by most authorities as having rather the meaning, "delude, persuade" (176). But the usage of the word in the present context is against this understanding (see Hoftijzer, "Some Remarks on the Table of Noah's Drunkenness," 25 n.7).

107. Japheth is philologically the equivalent of Iapetus, the Titan and father of Prometheus, the primeval ancestor of Hellen, the eponym of the Greek peoples, from among whom came the Philistines. This identification was already suggested by Milton in *Paradise Lost* IV 715–718 (cited by Williams, *The Common Expositor: An Account of the Commentaries on Genesis 1527–1633*, 155).

certainly holds true for most of the relationship between Israel and the Philistines but not for the period of David's kingship at Hebron.

Even before David became king of Judah at Hebron, he was a Philistine subject for one year and four months (1 Sam 27:7). Wearying from the unrelenting pursuit of Saul, David sought refuge with Achish, the ruler of Gath, and in the course of time was given the city of Ziklag as a feudal holding (1 Sam 27:1ff.). Although David dealt deceptively with Achish, he completely won the confidence of his Philistine overlord (1 Sam 27:8ff.; 29:1ff.) and the fact that Achish continued as an independent ruler in the time of Solomon (1 Kgs 2:39) is proof of David's gratitude for the kindness and confidence shown him. As undisputed masters of Israel and Canaan following the defeat of Saul, it would have been only with the consent and approval of the Philistines that David became king of Judah at Hebron. In fact, the Philistines probably continued to regard David as their vassal.

It was only after David became king of all Israel that the Philistines, fearing the Israelites as rivals, turned against David. In two major engagements near Jerusalem, David defeated them (2 Sam 5:17–25; see 8:1; 21:15–22; 23:9–17). No details have been preserved as to how David dealt with the Philistines beyond the fact that they paid tribute (see 2 Sam 8:12) and were reckoned among those acknowledging the sovereignty of Israel's king (1 Kgs 4:24). Yet it is clear that no great encroachment was made on Philistine territory or independence.[108] When one considers the strategic location of Philistia astride the major trade arteries between Europe, Asia, and Africa, the harshness that David was capable of in treating conquered peoples (see 2 Sam 8:2–4, 13–14; 12:31; 1 Kgs 11:15), the fact that he incorporated outright the remaining Canaanite city states adjacent to Philistia into his empire, and filled out the border of the northern tribes to the Mediterranean Sea, this becomes truly remarkable. Indeed, how can it be accounted for except that David felt himself constrained by some such directive as Gen 9:27?

For almost nine years then David was the vassal of the Philistines and even after he defeated them there are strong implications that he treated them with special favor. In short, there was a brief period in Israel's history during which there appears to have been genuine cordiality between the

108. See Alt, "The Formation of the Israelite State," 290 n.133; and Aharoni, *The Lands of the Bible*, 261. Although the western boundary of Judah is drawn to the sea in Josh 15:11–12 (see 2 Sam 24:5–7), this is a theoretical or ideal statement; in actual fact Judah never possessed this territory (Noth, *Das Buch Josua*, 89).

Israelites and the Philistines[109] and Gen 9:20–27, while based on ancient tradition, is most intelligible if it is understood as having been given its present form during this time.[110]

Understood against this background, Gen 9:20–27 addresses itself to the fact that Israel (Shem), whose ancestors were not natives of Canaan, were in process of acquiring this land through conquest. Was this conquest simply a naked act of aggression without any moral justification? And what should Israel's attitude be towards the Philistines (Japheth) who were also bent on conquering the Canaanites? Genesis 9:20–27 justifies Israel's right to displace the Canaanites in their native land on the grounds that there was a basic moral flaw, a perverse sexuality in the character of the Canaanites (see also Gen 13:13; 15:16; see 19; Lev 18:24–30; 1 Kgs 14:24). And Israel is exhorted to accept and to welcome the presence of the Philistines as providentially ordained and to regard them as joint custodians of the land of Canaan.[111]

109. It is perhaps worth noting in this context David's relationship to his Philistine mercenaries. David may have forced them to join him following his victories over them, but however they came into his service they served David well and were loyal in defeat as well as in victory. When David had to abandon Jerusalem because of Absalom's revolt, the Cherethites, the Pelethites, and six hundred from Gath accompanied him. That they chose to do so is clear from Ittai's response to David's invitation to them to return home: "As the LORD lives, and as my lord the king lives, wherever my lord the king shall be, whether for death or for life, there also will your servant be" (2 Sam 15:21).

110. The basic reason for thinking that Gen 9:20–27 in its present form dates not from the time of Noah but David is because it is never cited or appealed to in connection with Israel's efforts to gain the land of Canaan. The promises made to Abraham (Gen 12:1–3, 7), on the other hand, are made use of again and again. Moreover, as Gunkel and others point out, etiologies characteristically presuppose that which they account for.

111. Ancient Jewish tradition interpreted the subject of the statement, "dwell in the tents of Shem" in v. 27 to be God or understood the verse to mean that the Greek language, "the beauty of Japheth," might be used in public worship and for making a written translation of Hebrew Scripture (Bereshith Rabbah 36:8). For an appreciation of "those currents in the history of Jewish thought which were produced or influenced by the contact of Judaism with Greek thought," see Neumark, "The Beauty of Japheth in the Tents of Shem," 5–17. Christian tradition up until the time of Wellhausen, on the other hand, characteristically understood the passage messianically, that is, as a prophecy of the admission of the Gentiles (Japheth) into the Church (the tents of Shem) (see, e.g., Delitzsch, *A New Commentary on Genesis*, 296–98; and Heinisch, *Das Buch Genesis*, 185, 186). Neither interpretation strictly speaking is permitted by the text, but v. 27 is not without typological significance (see Simpson, *The Early Traditions of Israel*, 135).

For the question of the place of Gen 9:20–27 in the larger scheme of the Yahwist epic, see Rendtorff, "Genesis 8:21 und die Urgeschichte des Yahwisten," 69–78; Bruggeman, "David and his Theologian," 156–81; Clark, "The Flood and the Structure of the

Gen 9:20–27 is significant as one of the earliest examples of a theology of culture and history. And its openness to the Philistines is remarkable in any period of history. This passage, however, has nothing to do with Ham or with Black people.

V

The earliest evidence of a racist interpretation of Gen 9:18–27 is found in Bereshith Rabbah, an expository commentary on Genesis utilizing the work of rabbis from the second to the fourth centuries and probably completed in the early fifth century.[112] Alluding to a tradition that Ham castrated Noah, Rabbi Joseph has Noah say to Ham: "You have prevented me from doing something in the dark (cohabitation), therefore your seed will be ugly and dark-skinned."[113] "The descendants of Ham through Canaan therefore have red eyes, because Ham looked upon the nakedness of his father; they have misshapen lips because Ham spoke with his lips to his brothers about the unseemly condition of his father; they have twisted curly hair, because Ham turned and twisted his head round to see the nakedness of his father; and they go about naked, because Ham did not cover the nakedness of his father."[114] And according to Pesahim, 113b of the Babylonian Talmud, "Five things did Canaan charge his sons: Love one another, love robbery, love lewdness, hate your masters, and do not speak the truth."

This view gained no prominence in the ancient world, however, which by and large was free of color prejudice.[115] Moreover, in the Middle Ages

Pre-patriarchal History, 184–211.

112. So Moore, *Judaism*, 1:166.

113. Bereshith Rabbah 36:7–8, in *Midrash Rabbah*, I, 293.

Because the males and females of Noah's family were commanded to enter the ark separately (Gen 6:18) but commanded to go forth together and to be fruitful and to multiply (8:15, 17) it was assumed by early Jewish authorities that men and women were segregated on the ark and that continence was enforced. There are persistent traditions that Ham violated this regulation. For the popular folk tale of Ham's copulation with his wife on the ark current in Europe in the thirteenth century, see Utley, "Noah's Ham and Jensen Enikel," 241–49, and the account of George Best dating from 1578 cited by Jordan, *White Over Black*, 41. Rabbis Hiyya and Levi, on the other hand, maintained that Ham copulated with the dog on the ark and that it was because of this that he became black (Bereshith Rabbah 36:7; Sanhedrian 108b).

114. Ginzberg, *The Legends of the Jews*, I, 169.

115. See the excellent study by Snowden, *Blacks in Antiquity*.

For the history of the interpretation of Gen 9:20–27 before the Middle Ages, see

when the wise men came to be regarded as three, it was apparently with conscious reference to the three sons of Noah, and one of them, Melchoir or Balthasar, was depicted as black.[116] Nevertheless, the racist interpretation of Gen 9:18–27 remained alive[117] and gained new life with the colonial expansion of Europe and the development of slavery in America. Emphasis was now placed on all Black people as being descended from Ham and/or Canaan and by that fact condemned to perpetual servitude because of Noah's curse. While this understanding only became a popular notion in the nineteenth century, it was intellectuals, often within the Church, who "sold" it to an age that found it expedient to exploit it.[118]

Ginzberg, *Die Haggada bei den Kirchenvätern und in der apokryphen Literatur*; Levene, *The Early Syrian Fathers on Genesis*; Kasher, *Encyclopedia of Biblical Interpretation*, vol. 2; Jansma, "Investigations into the Early Syrian Fathers on Genesis," 69–181; Armstrong, *Die Genesis in der Alten Kirche*; Lewis, *A Study of the Interpretation of Noah and the Flood in Jewish and Christian Literature.*

For the period of the Renaissance, see Allen, *The Legend of Noah.*

More general in character are the studies of Charles, "Les noirs, fils de Cham le maudit," 721–39; Allier, *Une énigme troublante*; Perbal, "La race nègre et la malédiction de Cham," 156–77. This latter work inspired articles by McNeill, "Collapse of the Cunard of Cham," 135–137; and by Friedel, "Is the Curse of Cham on the Negro Race?" 447–53. See also Goldman, *In the Beginning*, 501–8; Buswell, *Slavery, Segregation and Scripture*, 64–65 and the bibliography on 93–97; and especially Williams and Brown, *Afro-American Religious Studies*, 71ff., 318–20.

116. See the comment of Beda in his commentary on Matthew at 2:1ff. cited by Charles, "Les noirs, fils de Cham le maudit," 727, Friedel, "Is the Curse of Cham on the Negro Race?," 449, and Toynbee, *A Study of History*, I, 223–24; see Bastide, "Color, Racism, and Christianity," 316.

117. So current in the seventeenth century was the idea that the blackness of Africans was due to a curse (see Calvoer, *Gloria Mosis*, 260 and earlier, Genebrardus, *Chronographiae libri quatuor*, 26–27) that Browne, physician, man of letters, and reporter-at-large for his age, devoted three chapters of his *Pseudodoxia epidemica* to an appraisal of it (*The Works of Sir Thomas Browne*, III, 231–55; see 273–75). See also Davis, *The Problem of Slavery in Western Culture*), 450ff.; and Jordan, *White Over Black*, 17–20, 35–36, 60. It should be noted that there were those who held Ham was white. See Allen, *The Legend of Noah*, 119, 162, and the depictions of Ham in the fifteenth century woodcuts of the Cologne and Lubec Bibles (figures 23 and 24 in Allen's work). More recently, Heras affirms that "the Hamites belong to the white race" and cites three other scholars who share this view ("The Curse of Noe," 67 n.21).

118. See Charles, "Les noirs, fils de Cham le maudit," 732ff.; and Perbal, "La race nègre et la malédiction de Cham," 159ff. Both Charles and Perbal date the modern development of the racist interpretation of Gen 9:20–27 from 1677 with the publication of *Curiosum scrutinum nigridinis filiorum Cham* ("Curious Inquiry into the Blackness of the Children of Ham") by Hannemann at Kiel. They also charge Martin Luther with responsibility, albeit inadvertently, for this development because Hannemann, a Lutheran,

The proper clarification of Gen 9:18–27 was not possible until the composite character of the Hexateuch was established and this was not until the time of Wellhausen in the 1870's. Even so, the interpreter has never been without ample resources for arriving at a non-racist interpretation of the passage. From the fact that the biblical text explicitly identifies Canaan and only Canaan—as the one cursed one may reasonably infer that the other sons of Ham, Kush (Ethiopia), Egypt, and Put (Libya), who are African peoples properly speaking, were not cursed.

Secondly, the immediate context forbids a racist understanding of Gen 9:18–27. Genesis 10 has to do with all the peoples of the world known to ancient Israel and since this chapter immediately follows the episode of Noah's cursing and blessing it would have been most appropriate to express here any prejudicial feelings toward African peoples. Not only are such feelings absent, but all peoples are consciously and deliberately related to each other as brothers. No one, not even Israel, is elevated above anyone else and no disparaging remark is made about any people, not even the enemies of Israel. Indeed, the point of Genesis 10 is that the great diversity and multiplicity of peoples is the fulfillment of God's command to Noah and his sons: "Be fruitful and multiply, and fill the earth" (Gen 9:1). As God inspected his creative work in Genesis 1 and found it good, so in Genesis 10 he approves and rejoices in mankind in all its manifestations.

Had the ancient Israelites been conscious of some taint upon African peoples one would expect Abraham to have alluded to it when he went down to Egypt because of a famine in Canaan. Nor do Abraham and Sarah have any qualms about Hagar because of her Egyptian origin. They are glad to use her to get an heir and so secure through their own efforts God's promise of a great posterity (Genesis 16). While Miriam and Aaron spoke out against Moses because of his Kushite wife, the context clearly shows that what they are really protesting is Moses's authority (Num 12:1ff.).

The prophet Isaiah is very critical of Egypt, which, incidentally was ruled over by an Ethiopian dynasty during the latter part of his ministry,

---

claims Luther as an authority for his position. Actually all that Luther said was that the Scripture depicts Ham in the foulest colors ("foedissimis coloribus depictus," *Luther's Works*, vol. 44, 384). Allier traces the idea of blackness as a curse back to the Jewish rabbis of the third, fourth, and fifth centuries and thinks that Hannemann, who was born in Amsterdam, was influenced in his interpretation of Noah's curse by the Jews he had known there (*Une énigme troublante*, 16–19; see 7 n.1). Allier also emphasizes that not Hannemann alone but many contributed to the popularizing of the ancient Jewish interpretation.

because he wants to dissuade Israel from relying on Egypt in its bid for independence from Assyria. But nowhere does he appeal to some ancient curse. He does make a few disparaging remarks about Egypt's help (see, e.g., Isa 19:11ff.; 30:5, 7; see 18:1ff.), but his point to Judah is: "The Egyptians are men, and not God; and their horses are flesh, and not spirit" (31:3).

It is surely not without significance that Aaron's grandson, who is regarded as the ancestor of the Zadokite priesthood (Exod 6:25; Num 25:6ff.; Josh 22:30; 24:33; 1 Chr 6:4, 50; Ezra 8:2; Ps 106:30), and one of the sons of Eli (1 Sam 1:3; 2:34; 4:11, 17; 14:3) were given the Egyptian name, Phinehas, which means literally, the Nubian. Nor is it without important implications for the understanding of Gen 9:18–27 that the introduction to the prophecies of Zephaniah tells us that his great, great grandfather was (King) Hezekiah and that his father was Kushi, that is, the Ethiopian.

Psalm 87 contains a vision of Zion as the spiritual mother of all men and among these African peoples are explicitly mentioned. Isaiah 19:24–25 anticipates the time when "Israel will be the third with Egypt and Assyria, a blessing in the midst of the earth, whom the LORD of hosts has blessed, saying, 'Blessed be Egypt my people, and Assyria the work of my hands, and Israel my heritage.'"

Simon from the North African city of Cyrene (Luke 23:26) was not regarded as unworthy to bear Jesus's cross. Nor did Philip feel it incumbent upon himself to discuss Gen 9:18–27 with the Ethiopian minister of Candace (Acts 8:26ff.). In short, nowhere in the Bible is there any support for the idea that people of African descent are under a curse. On the contrary, there is much evidence that they were regarded without prejudice and on an equal basis with other people.[119]

While Gen 9:18–27 may well be the most misunderstood and abused passage of the Bible, this is not a reflection on the Bible itself. Rather this misuse and abuse attest to what perversity the human spirit and intellect can sink and with what pains and ingenuity man finds ways to justify to himself and to others his sin.

119. For a more thorough treatment of the African presence in the Old Testament, see Bennett, "Africa and the Biblical Period," 483–500. For a more general approach to a non-racist interpretation of the passage, see Thompson, "The Curse Was not on Ham," 7; Tilson, *Segregation and the Bible*, 23–27; and Maston, *The Bible and Race*, 105–17.

3

Two Black Contemporaries of Jeremiah

It is through scattered, incidental references by and large that we learn of the black African[1] presence in the Old Testament. An exception to this occurs in the time of the prophet Jeremiah where we meet two contemporaries of black African descent.[2] Moreover, the historical and dramatic setting in which each appears is sketched in some detail. Each occupies a clearly defined role in Israelite society. And we are permitted to witness each engaged in sustained, dramatic engagement with his fellow Israelites.

1. Black Africans in the strict sense are designated principally in the Old Testament by the word "Kushite." This term is habitually rendered "Ethiopian" by the Septuagint and Vulgate. English custom has been inconsistent, sometimes reproducing the Hebrew directly, i.e., "Kushite," at other times following the practice of the Septuagint and Vulgate and rendering "Ethiopian." In the English Bible then "Kushite" and "Ethiopian" designate the same people and are synonymous in meaning.

The home of the Kushites or Ethiopians in Old Testament times was not identical with the Ethiopia or Abyssinia of today. There is some uncertainty about the extent of biblical Kush or Ethiopia, but that portion of it most clearly identifiable lay in the southern Nile River valley, beginning at Syene (Aswan) at the First Cataract of the Nile and extending indefinitely to the south. Nubia, a term derived from Arabic and dating from Roman times, is sometimes used to designate this general area. The modern approximate equivalent is the state of Sudan.

2. Actually there is a third black contemporary of Jeremiah, the prophet Zephaniah, but space does not permit an adequate treatment of him at this time. The writer hopes to discuss Zephaniah in some detail in a subsequent article.

I

The best known of these is perhaps Ebed-melek, whose name means literally, "king's servant."[3] Ebed-melek makes his appearance on the stage of history in one of the most traumatic and tragic hours of Israel. The year is 588 BCE, Jerusalem is under siege by the powerful and ruthless Nebuchadrezzar of Babylon. Momentarily the siege has been lifted by the approach of an Egyptian army, for Judah's revolt against Babylon had been encouraged and supported by Egypt (see Jer 21:1–10; 34:1–22; 37:11). Jeremiah accepted the siege of Jerusalem as God's judgment for Israel's sin. This sin, well documented by the prophet, was blatantly reaffirmed when the Hebrew slaves who had been freed at the beginning of the siege were repossessed when the siege was lifted (Jer 34:8–22). Jeremiah steadfastly insisted that the Babylonians would be successful, that the siege would be renewed, that resistance would only lead to the destruction of the city and disaster for the royal house. To prevent needless bloodshed, he even encouraged people to desert to the Babylonians (21:9; see 38:1–3). God was going to use the Babylonian army "to smash the shell in which the nation has attempted to confine His grace."[4]

Jerusalem was deeply divided within itself but dominated by a militant group of nobles who were determined to carry through the revolt. The climate was one in which criticism or opposition to their policies was regarded as treason. Even Zedekiah, a well intentioned but weak and vacillating king, was at the mercy of this party (see Jer 38:5, 14ff.). During the lifting of the siege, as he was leaving the city to attend a family business matter, Jeremiah was accused of deserting to the Babylonians, arrested (37:11–15), and charged with treason by four leading princes who demanded of Zedekiah that he be put to death (38:1–4). While the king did not directly accede to this demand, neither did he resolutely oppose it. He evaded direct responsibility for Jeremiah and at the same time avoided offending the war party by giving them permission (short of execution) to deal with the prophet as they saw fit (38:5). They utilized the king's evasion of responsibility both cleverly and diabolically. Without benefit of public trial and perhaps surreptitiously so as not to antagonize those who held Jeremiah in esteem, they

3. All who served the royal family, from the lowest to the highest capacity, were called the king's servants. There was also a title, "the king's servant." Asaiah bears this title in 2 Kgs. 22:12//2 Chr 34:20, and he is mentioned in connection with Shaphan, the secretary of state, and other notable royal officials.

4. Welch, *Jeremiah*, 211.

placed the prophet in an empty but dank and mirey cistern (38:6). This act could have been defended as a means of solitary confinement taken to silence Jeremiah. In effect, it was a form of execution. For Jeremiah, who was by now an old man (he began his ministry forty years before), would soon have perished from exposure and lack of food.

This malicious scheme was frustrated by Ebed-melek. Somehow (just how we are not told), he learned of what had happened to Jeremiah (38:7). Immediately he sought out Zedekiah who was at the Benjamin gate of the city. The king may have been overseeing preparations in anticipation of a resumption of the siege by the Babylonians. Or he may have been acting in his role as judge, hearing complaints and adjudicating cases from the populace. At any rate, it was in a public setting that Ebed-melek confronts the king, informs him of Jeremiah's fate, and charges the men responsible for it with committing a crime (38:8–9). Given the temper of the time, Ebed-melek took his life in his hands by this act. We know in fact from Jer 39:17 that he lived in fear of reprisal from this moment onward. Incidentally, if Ebed-melek was aware of Zedekiah's inadvertent complicity in what happened to Jeremiah, he had the good judgment not to call attention to it, thereby putting the king on the defensive.

Whereas the king had been intimidated by the aggressiveness of the four nobles (38:4), he feeds upon the courage and sense of right of Ebed-melek and acts to save Jeremiah. He puts Ebed-melek in charge of the rescue mission and places three of his troops under his command (38:10).[5] The manner in which Ebed-melek goes about rescuing Jeremiah reveals another side of his character. He goes to a storeroom and gets some old rags and carefully lets them down into the cistern by rope so as to keep them from becoming scattered and soiled (38:11). Then, so that the rope would not cut his flesh, Ebed-melek instructed Jeremiah: "Put the rags and clothes between your armpits and the ropes" (38:12). Ever so carefully and gently, we can be sure, the old prophet was loosed from the mire of the cistern and drawn to the safety of the court of the guard where he remained until the fall of Jerusalem in July, 587 BCE (38:13). Ebed-melek's courage, dispatch, compassion, and his ability to bring out the best in the king make Jer 38:7–13 "one of the fairest stories in the Old Testament."[6] Moved to save

5. The Hebrew text of Jer 38:10 reads "thirty men," but most scholars, because of grammatical (and practicable) considerations and with the support of one manuscript change one letter and read, "three" (see, e.g., Driver, *Jeremiah*, 233 n.d).

6. Smith, *Jeremiah*, 281.

the life of another and acting without calculation or counting the cost, an otherwise unknown black man emerges "from obscurity to immortality."[7]

Sometime after his rescue, Jeremiah sent a word to Ebed-melek assuring him he would be saved from those who sought his life and would even survive the fall of the city (39:15–18). The basis of Jeremiah's assurance to Ebed-melek is that he trusted in God. The context in which this is spoken fills the word "trust" richly with content. It means, first of all, that Ebed-melek was among those who believed that Jeremiah was God's authentic voice to his people, interpreting the true significance of the events of the time as over against the so-called prophets who were part and parcel of the status quo and who proclaimed peace when there was no peace (see 23:9–40). Only one who was so convinced could have acted with such dispatch and courage, and how precious this "amen" to his life's work must have been to Jeremiah! Secondly, the word trust implies that Ebed-melek was so open to God that he was able to transcend the fears that crippled everyone else and to be the instrumentality for the divine purpose and providence for Jeremiah. Thus, in his personal word to Ebed-melek, Jeremiah singles out the one trait that truly distinguishes him and which is the source of his other virtues, his faith.

Logically, Jeremiah's promise to Ebed-melek (39:15–18) should follow the account of his rescue (38:7–13). Rather, it is placed in a context that tells of the fall of Jerusalem, the capture of Zedekiah near Jericho, his being made to witness the slaughter of his sons, being blinded, and taken captive to Babylon (39:1–7). But Jeremiah's promise to Ebed-melek is placed in its present context for a purpose. It lets us see how the king, who acted without faith, lost his life and the life of his nation, whereas one who did act in faith was saved.

According to most translations of Jer 38:7, Ebed-melek was a eunuch. This may or may not be so, for the Hebrew word in question, *sārîs* (plural, *sārîsîm*), can mean both "officer, courtier" and "eunuch." Actually, *sārîs* is a loan word from the Assyrian *sha rêshi*, "he at the head," i.e., he "who goes before the king, one of his confidential advisors."[8] The Assyrian original also has the specialized meaning of "eunuch."

7. Calkins, *Jeremiah*, 298.

8. De Vaux, *Ancient Israel*, 121.

Since the Greek translation of Jeremiah diverges rather freely from the Hebrew text it is difficult to evaluate the omission of *sārîs* from its rendering of Jer 38:7. Ehrlich's conjecture that the present Hebrew text of 38:7 is a corruption of an original *serîs malkiyyāhû ben-hammelek*, "officer of Prince Malkiah," i.e., Malkiah's personal attendant,

In the Old Testament *sārîs* is found some forty-five times. Potiphar, Pharaoh's captain of the guard (and a married man) is called *sārîs* (Gen 37:36; 39:1). So also are the chief cupbearer and chief baker (Gen 40:2, 7). The attendants of the king are divided into two classes in 1 Sam 8:15: his servants and his *sārîsîm*. In 1 Chr 28:1 all the officials of Israel are broken down into the following categories: the officials of the tribes, the officers of the divisions that served the king, the commanders of thousands, the commanders of hundreds, the stewards of all the property and cattle of the king and his sons, together with the *sārîsîm*, and all the seasoned warriors. It was a *sārîs* that King Ahab sent to fetch the prophet Micaiah ben Imlah (1 Kgs 22:9//2 Chr 18:8) and a *sārîs* who, at the command of the king, restored the house and land of the Shunammite woman (2 Kgs 8:6). The Assyrian and Babylonian armies had a high military or diplomatic officer whose title was *Rabsaris* (2 Kgs 18:17; Jer 39:3, 13). At the time of the fall of Jerusalem the Israelite men of war were commanded by a *sārîs* (2 Kgs 25:19//Jer 52:25).

That a *sārîs* might be a person of great wealth and high social position is illustrated by the example of Nathan-melek,[9] who had a dwelling in the immediate vicinity of the temple (2 Kgs 23:11). This is further confirmed by the fact that those who belonged to the class of *sārîs* were marked for deportation by the Babylonians (Jer 29:2; 34:19; 2 Kgs 24:12, 15). It was the Babylonian policy to exile only the leaders of a conquered people.

In all the instances cited above, the proper meaning of *sārîs* would seem to be "officer, courtier." These examples of its usage show that in range and flexibility of meaning it is somewhat like the English word, "lieutenant."

The clearest instance in which *sārîs* means "eunuch" is Isa 56:3, 4. This also seems to be the meaning in Est 1:10, 12, 15; 2:3, 14, 15, 21; 4:4, 5; 6:2, 14; 7:9; and Dan 1:3, 7, 8, 9, 10, 11, 18. (Almost half of the occurrences of *sārîs* in the Old Testament are found in these two books.) It may be observed that all these passages belong to a time much later than that of Jeremiah. Also, in the case of Esther and Daniel the setting in which these officials function is a non-Israelite one. Perhaps 2 Kgs 20:18 and the parallel

is too speculative and has justly found no support (*Randglossen zur Hebräischen Bible*, IV, 339).

9. It is intriguing to note that Ebed-melek and Nathan-Melek share a name compounded with *melek* and both are designated as *sārîs*. They may be contemporaries; at most a generation separates them. Nathan-melek is mentioned in connection with King Josiah's reform of 622 BCE. As indicated above, the episode in connection with which Ebed-melek makes his appearance is dated to 588. Are the two related in some way?

in Isa 39:7 should be included with these passages, for they anticipate the fate of Hezekiah's sons in the Babylonian court.

Although *sārîs* in the sense of "eunuch" is attested primarily in material dating from a much later period than Jeremiah and most frequently in a non-Israelite setting, there are a few passages earlier than and contemporary with Jeremiah where it may have this meaning. "Eunuch" may be the proper meaning of the term in 2 Kgs 9:32, for the *sārîsîm* who threw Jezebel out the palace window were in the palace with her when Jehu drove up. And because they are mentioned in connection with the women and children, the *sārîsîm* in Jer 41:16 may be eunuchs. But not enough detail is given in these two passages to make a definitive judgment. Actually, there is no firm evidence that Israelite monarchs ever employed eunuchs to oversee their harems. Such a person would automatically be excluded from the Israelite congregation (Deut 23:1; Lev 21:17–21). With the strict sexual morality that characterized ancient Israel, one wonders if there would have been any need for eunuchs.

With a word such as *sārîs* the context is all important in determining its proper meaning. In the case of Jer 38:7, two considerations have been adduced to support the meaning "eunuch." The statement, "who was in the king's house," that follows the reference to Ebed-melek has been understood in the sense that Ebed-melek was attached to the royal palace. But this statement need mean no more than that Ebed-melek was in the palace of the king at the time he heard what had happened to Jeremiah, and this detail is related to explain why he had to seek out the king at the Benjamin gate. Secondly, the fact that Ebed-melek knows where to find the old rags to protect Jeremiah from the rope (38:11) has been taken as proof of his familiarity with and custody over domestic matters of the palace. But this is hardly decisive, for who would not have known the location of this storage room?

If Ebed-melek was a practicing Israelite, as Jeremiah's promise to him suggests, he could not have been a eunuch, for Israelite law prohibited such from the congregation. Moreover, if Ebed-melek was a eunuch and his duties confined to the care of the harem or the queen-mother, one wonders if he would have known much about Jeremiah, especially enough to risk his life, or for that matter, if Zedekiah would have placed three of his troops under his command (38:10). And it is not without significance that of the five instances in which *sārîs* is found in Jeremiah, in three of these the context strongly supports the meaning, "officer, courtier" (29:2; 34:19; 52:25).

Because of the ambiguity of *sārîs*, certainty perhaps cannot be claimed for its meaning in Jer 38:7. In the judgment of the writer, probability favors the meaning "officer, courtier." This is also the judgment of the translators of the Jewish Version, the Confraternity Version, the New American Bible, the Living Bible, and Monsignor Knox.[10] With regard to the spiritual manhood of Ebed-melek, however, no question arises. On that shameful day of Jeremiah's intended execution in 588 BCE, he towers above all others, including King Zedekiah, in spiritual stature. Indeed, is this not the reason why Ebed-melek is so expressly and emphatically identified as "the Ethiopian" (four times! 38:7, 10, 12; 39:16)—to emphasize the prophet's utter abandonment by his fellow countrymen?

II

The second black contemporary of Jeremiah was Yehudi ben Nethaniah ben Shelemiah ben *Kushi*. He makes his appearance in connection with an incident that is precisely dated to December 604 BCE. This, too, was an occasion fraught with destiny. The king of Judah at this time was Jehoiakim, an opportunistic, evil, and arrogant man (see 2 Kgs 23:34–24:6; Jer 22:13–19; 21:11–14). The previous year, 605, had witnessed one of those moments in which one chapter of Near Eastern history was brought to a close and a new one opened. That turning point was the battle of Carchemish which brought the final end to the Assyrian empire and decided the rivalry between Egypt and Babylon for hegemony over Palestine and Syria in favor of Babylon.

Early, if not from the beginning of his ministry, Jeremiah was given to see that Jerusalem and Judah were threatened by a foe from the north (Jer 1:13–16; 4:5—6:26). But he understood this as embraced within the providence of God. It was part of the tearing down and plucking up that was necessary in order to build and to plant (1:10). It was spiritual surgery necessitated by the critical spiritual illness of the nation. With the Babylonian victory at Carchemish the foe from the north became historical reality for Jeremiah. It meant that for the covenant people the hands of the clock of her physical and spiritual destiny were poised at twelve.

10. So also the Targum; Freedman, "Who Is Like Thee?," 254; Blank, *Jeremiah*, 54, 211. Volz has not been able to make up his mind and simply transliterates: *ein Saris* (*Jeremia*, 336).

In one final appeal to his people, Jeremiah gathers together a selection of sermons he had preached from the beginning of his ministry—the fruit of some twenty-three years of labor—and had his close friend, Baruch, write them down at his dictation (36:2–4). The contents of this scroll are generally thought to be the "first edition" of what is now Jer 1–25. In favor of Jeremiah 25 forming the conclusion of the collection is the fact that it is dated to the same year as the writing of the scroll (25:1; 36:1), identifies Nebuchadrezzar as the instrument of God's judgment (25:9; see 36:29), and refers to "everything written in this book" (25:13). Although he was debarred from the temple at this time (36:5), Jeremiah does not let this silence him. Perhaps recalling the dramatic and powerful impact of the reading of the law book at the time of the Deuteronomic reformation, he commissions Baruch to do a public reading of his sermons. The reason for Jeremiah's exclusion from the temple is not given, but it may well have resulted from the clash between him and Pashhur recorded in ch. 20.

While this collection of sermons was prepared in the fourth year of Jehoiakim (36:1), i.e., 605 BCE, it was not immediately read in public by Baruch. Rather, Jeremiah waited for the next solemn occasion on which, due to some national distress or emergency, the people should call a fast day. On such an occasion, when citizens throughout the land had gathered to the temple in Jerusalem and were in a sober and penitent mood, Jeremiah hoped his words would reach their hearts. Even at this late hour there was still hope (36:3, 6–7). Through his prophet, God "wants to be enabled to pardon."[11]

Such an occasion presented itself in the ninth month of the fifth year of Jehoiakim (36:9, 22), i.e., in December 604 BCE. We are not told what precipitated this fast day, but we know that in this very same month the Babylonian army destroyed the near-by Philistine city of Askelon.[12] This coincidence, plus the fact that the king's cabinet was in session during the fast, makes it probable that the presence of the Babylonian army in the Philistine plain occasioned the fast.

11. Blank, *Jeremiah*, 26.

12. Wiseman, *Chronicles of Chaldean Kings (626–556 B.C.) in the British Museum*, 68–69; Bright, *Jeremiah*, 182.

Other scholars think that the later custom attested in the Mishnah (Taanith 1:5) of fasting if there had been no rain by the first day of Kislev (the ninth month) may have been in effect in the time of Jeremiah and that the fast was occasioned by the absence of rain.

In what must have been the most memorable day of his life, Baruch read the collection of Jeremiah's sermons before the great assembly gathered in the courtyard of the temple from the balcony of the chamber of Gemariah, the son of Shaphan (36:10).[13] We are not told of the response of the multitude, but the very absence of any reference to a protest by the priests and prophets who at the time of the temple sermon had demanded that Jeremiah be executed (7:1–15; 26), suggests that those keeping fast were profoundly moved. This impression is strengthened by the fact that the son of Baruch's host, Micaiah, went immediately and interrupted the session of the king's cabinet (36:11–13). Upon hearing Micaiah's report, the royal ministers of state broke off their meeting, had Baruch brought before them, and heard for themselves the words of the scroll. Sensing in these sermons a divine ultimatum to the nation, they were deeply distressed and prepared immediately to consult the king (36:14–16).

After establishing that the words of the scroll were in fact the words of Jeremiah and were drawn up at his request (and were therefore addressed to the crisis then confronting the nation) and after prudently advising Baruch and Jeremiah to hide themselves,[14] they reported the matter to the king and his immediate entourage (36:17–20). For the third time that day the words of Jeremiah were read, but this time after three or four columns were heard, Jehoiakim would cut off the scroll and burn it in the fire by which he warmed himself on that December day (36:21–23). The author of Jeremiah 36, perhaps recalling Josiah's response to the reading of the law book (2 Kgs 22:11ff.), recoils in horror, for the deliberate contempt and defiance of Jehoiakim and his inner circle (36:24) was not only blasphemous but it sealed the doom of the nation.

13. Shaphan was secretary of state under King Josiah (2 Kgs 22:3ff.). This prestigious family lent its moral and material support to Jeremiah on more than one occasion. Had not Shaphan's son, Ahikam, intervened following Jeremiah's temple sermon, the prophet almost certainly would have lost his life (Jer 26:24). Jeremiah and Baruch may have asked Gemariah's permission to read the scroll from the balcony of his house to avoid another mob scene like that following the temple sermon. That Gemariah consented to this says much for his courage and sense of integrity. It is a mark of his thoughtfulness and courtesy that he leaves his son, Micaiah, in his absence to serve as host to Baruch.

14. This advice shows that these nobles knew well how to anticipate the response of the king. One of them, Elnathan ben Achbor (Jer 36:16), had in fact been instrumental in extraditing the prophet Uriah from Egypt, whom Jehoiakim subsequently executed (Jer 26:20–23). The fact that Elnathan is one of the few who protests the burning of Jeremiah's scroll (36:25) suggests that in the matter of Uriah he was simply acting under orders.

Upon the completion of the reading and destruction of the scroll, Jehoiakim orders the arrest of Baruch and Jeremiah, "but the LORD hid them" (36:26). Later Jeremiah re-dictated the scroll, included in it a personal oracle of judgment against Jehoiakim (36:27–31), and added to the original scroll "many further words of the same sort" (36:32).

The eyewitness account in Jeremiah 36 lets us know the names of the principal personalities involved and gives us fleeting glimpses of them in action. Of these, Jeremiah, even in his absence, looms largest and next to him Baruch. Among the king's cabinet ministers are Elishama the secretary, Delaiah ben Shemaiah, Elnathan ben Achbor, Gemariah ben Shaphan, and Zedekiah ben Hananiah (36:12). Then there is the defiant Jehoiakim and those who identify most closely with him, Prince Jerahmeel, Seraiah ben Azriel, and Shelemiah ben Abdeel (36:20–26). Even Micaiah, the son of Gemariah, is named (36:11). Also among those identified personally is Yehudi ben Nethaniah ben Shelemiah ben *Kushi* (36:14, 21, 23). That is, among the participants on that fateful day in December in 604 BCE was a black man.

There are two unusual features about the identification of Yehudi. He alone has his ancestry given to the fourth generation. And his name means literally "Jew" whereas the name of his great-grandfather means "Ethiopian."[15] These peculiarities have given rise to the most diverse explanations.

A long-standing explanation is that they answer to the requirement of Deut 23:7–8 that only Egyptians (and Ethiopians) of the third generation could "enter the assembly of the LORD." Kushi's name (construed as a gentilic) shows that he was an Ethiopian, the names of his son and grandson (which are compounded with Yahweh) show that they were followers of Yahweh, while Yehudi's name (construed as a gentilic) indicates that he has

15. This type of name, calling attention to one's place of origin, people, or tribe, though used sparingly, is well attested as a proper name in the Old Testament. "Judith" in Gen 26:34 is the feminine form of Yehudi and means literally, "Jewess." King Menahem's father was Gadi, i.e., a Gadite (2 Kgs. 15:14). "Buzi," i.e., Buzite, is twice attested as a proper name (Ezra 1:3; Job 32:2, 6). Also "Hachmonie" (1 Chr 27:32) refers to a Hachmonite, as 2 Sam 23:8 and 1 Chr 11:1 make clear (see Noth, *Die israelitischen Personennamen*, 232). Kushi as a proper name is also attested in an inscription from Ipsambul (cited by Schwally, "Das Buch Ssefanjâ," 167).

A few scholars, among them Schwally, suggests that the proper name Kushi does not designate literally a Kushite. The best proof to the contrary is the pains certain scholars go to in order to discount or to disprove that Kushi was an African.

become a full-fledged Israelite.[16] On the other hand, the name Kushi has been explained on the supposition that his father, a native Israelite, was on a mission to Ethiopia at the time of his birth. Yehudi is accounted for as a name given to celebrate his father's return from abroad or to distinguish him as the son of a native Israelite mother in contrast to his half-brothers who were born to non-Israelite women.[17] Or the African ancestry of Yehudi has simply been dismissed as an unnecessary supposition "since the prophet Zephaniah had a father named Kushi (Zeph 1:1) who was of pure Hebrew lineage."[18]

A surprisingly large number of scholars find the unusually long genealogy of Yehudi so exceptional that they change the text to get two personalities. Yehudi ben Nethaniah *and* Shelemiah ben Kushi.[19] In a variation on this, Volz thinks 36:14 refers only to "Nethaniah ben Shelemiah, the Ethiopian," who is distinct from and bears no relation to the Yehudi of 36:21, 23.[20] A goodly number of scholars assume (because of his African background?) that Yehudi was merely a messenger or petty official, a clerk.[21]

Actually the law of Deut 23:7 does not mention Ethiopians; it "applies only to the posterity of the Edomites and Egyptians" and "was based on

16. Hitzig, *Der Prophet Jeremia*, 302; Graf, *Der Prophet Jeremia*, 444; Giesebrecht, *Das Buch Jeremia*, 198; Condamin, *Le Livre de Jérémie*, 261; Bewer, *Jeremiah*, II, 37.

17. Duhm, *Das Buch Jeremia*, 292. Duhm does allow as an alternative that Kushi's mother could have been an Ethiopian.

18. Freedman, "Who Is Like Thee?," 243.

19. The first to propose this was Cornill, *Das Buch Jeremia*, 390–391. Among those who follow Cornill are: Nötscher, *Das Buch Jeremias*, 261; Steinmann, *Le Prophète Jérémie*, 187, 188; Leslie, *Jeremiah*, 179, 180; Hyatt, "The Book of Jeremiah," 1066 ("This may be correct"); Rudolph, *Jeremia*, 212; Weiser, *Das Buch des Propheten Jeremia*, 321; Blank, *Jeremiah*, 28; Lamparter, *Prophet wider Willen*, 367 n.4.

This change is recommended in the critical apparatus of Kittel's *Biblia Hebraica* and *Biblia Hebraica Stuttgartensia* and is incorporated in the translation of the *Jerusalem Bible*.

20. Volz, *Jeremia*, 324, 325–26 n.i. Volz assumes that after the first reference to Baruch in 36:14 there followed "ben Neriah" (as after the second reference in this verse) and that this was carelessly written giving rise to the mistaken reading, "Yehudi." By a lesser authority such textual criticism would be regarded as absurd.

21. So, e.g., Graf, *Der Prophet Jeremia*, 444; Duhm, *Das Buch Jeremia*, 292; Peake, *Jeremiah and Lamentations*, II, 156, Streane, *Jeremiah together with The Lamentations*, 223; Binns, *Jeremiah*, 272; Condamin, *Le Livre de Jérémie*, 261; Steinmann, *Le Prophète Jérémie*, 188; Weiser, *Das Buch des Propheten Jeremia*, 321 n.4; Cunliffe-Jones, *Jeremiah*, 218; Rudolph, *Jeremia*, 212; Heller, "Zephanjas Ahnenreihe," 102, who thinks it probable that Yehudi was the descendant of a freed slave.

grounds which did not permit of its application to other nations."[22] Those who change the text of Jer 36:14 to get two different individuals do so without the benefit of any support from the ancient texts and versions; such a change is required only by one's presuppositions. A quite simple explanation of Yehudi's genealogy lies readily at hand; its very obviousness must be the reason it has been overlooked. Had not Yehudi been provided with an extended genealogy it would have been easy to confuse him and his ancestors with other personalities in the book of Jeremiah.

Among those the king delegates to arrest Baruch and Jeremiah is a certain Shelemiah (36:26). That he is further identified as the son of Abdeel indicates that the author of Jeremiah 36 is concerned to avoid confusing this Shelemiah with the grandfather of Yehudi. In Jer 37:13 we meet Irijah ben Shelemiah. Again to avoid confusion it is pointed out that this Shelemiah was the son of Hananiah. In Jeremiah 40 and 41 we encounter another Nethaniah, the father of Ishmael. Are Yehudi and Ishmael then first cousins? No; for we learn from Jer 41:1 that Nethaniah, the father of Ishmael, was the son of Elishama. Had not Yehudi's ancestry been traced back as far as it is much confusion would have arisen concerning the relationship of these personalities. It is this concern that necessitated the inclusion of Yehudi's great-grandfather, Kushi. This is all the more reason the name should be taken seriously as designating an African. Those who attempt to explain this away or to dismiss it expresses a concern not shared by the author of Jeremiah 36.

At first glance it is possible to understand Yehudi as being a subordinate official. The king's ministers send Yehudi to bring Baruch before them (36:14), Jehoiakim sends Yehudi to get Baruch's scroll that had been left in the chamber of Elishama (36:21), and it was Yehudi who read the scroll to the king (36:21, 23). But far from indicating that Yehudi was merely a messenger or petty official, the role he plays means that he was the most trusted and respected man on the scene. Skinner is undoubtedly correct in discerning a "cleavage between the king with his immediate *entourage* and the high officials who conducted the business of state."[23] The fact that

22. Keil, *The Prophecies of Jeremiah*, II, 99.

23. Skinner, *Prophecy and Religion*, 238. Whereas the cabinet ministers had treated Baruch courteously and invited him to sit as he read (Jer 36:15), the king sits and keeps them standing as he hears the scroll (vv. 21, 22). Three of the cabinet ministers urge Jehoiakim not to burn the scroll (v. 25), but the king's immediate *entourage* joined him in showing no fear of Jeremiah's words (v. 24). The king's attitude is perhaps most revealingly disclosed, as Erbt observes, by the fact that he charges, not the cabinet ministers,

Yehudi is called upon by the ministers of state and the king means that he has the trust and respect of both. This says a good deal about his personality and character. It means that he was one who transcended party strife.

The fact that Yehudi reads Jeremiah's sermons to Jehoiakim indicates, not his subordinate position, but the high regard with which he was held by the king. At the time of the reform of King Josiah it was none other than Shaphan the secretary of state who read the newly discovered book of the law to the King (2 Kgs 22:10). Indeed, the most natural supposition concerning Yehudi is that he is not only of African ancestry, but one of the royal officials comprising the king's cabinet.[24] In Jer 37:3 and 38:1 there is reference to Jehucal ben Shelemiah. This Shelemiah is not further identified (as is the one in 37:13). Is he the same Shelemiah as the grandfather of Yehudi? The fact that he is not distinguished from Yehudi's grandfather favors this identification. If so, it would confirm the high position of Yehudi, for Jehucal, as is clear from both contexts in which he appears, belongs to one of the most prominent and influential families in Jerusalem.[25]

There is a certain symbolic significance in the fact that this genealogy begins with Kushi ("Ethiopian") and ends with Yehudi ("Jew"). This sequence expresses the genius of the African to adopt an alien culture and religion and, without giving up his own heritage, to exemplify the best in them.

III

Why is it that it is only in the time of Jeremiah that we are able to identify two or more black men who were contemporaries? And why are they all

but those present with him in the winter palace to arrest Baruch and Jeremiah (*Jeremia und seine Zeit*, 8).

24. So far as I am aware, Giesebrecht (*Das Buch Jeremia*, 198) is the only one to admit this possibility. Calvin infers from his genealogy that Yehudi "was a man of some eminence" (*Jeremiah and The Lamentations*, IV, 339). Calkins thinks Yehudi was Jehoiakim's scribe (*Jeremiah*, 185).

Those who divide the genealogy in Jer 36:14 so as to get two persons tend to regard the first, i.e., the one of African ancestry, as a messenger, but Yehudi as a royal official (Lamparter) or Jehoiakim's adjutant (Volz).

25. To be sure, in Jer 38:1–4 Jehucal (here spelled Jucal) is among those who demand that Jeremiah be executed. Whereas Yehudi appears to be one who was above party strife, Jehucal clearly belongs to those who favor the revolt against Babylon. If Jehucal is Yehudi's uncle, it would not be the first time in which those so related have differed in personality and persuasion.

closely associated with the royal house of Judah? The answer to these questions undoubtedly lies in the fact that a century before the time of Jeremiah Judah was the ally of Egypt, which at that time was ruled by an Ethiopian dynasty. Isaiah refers to what may have been the first negotiations leading to this alliance in the following words:

> Ah, land of whirring wings
> which is beyond the rivers of Ethiopia;
> which sends ambassadors by the Nile,
> in vessels of papyrus upon the waters!
> Go, you swift messengers,
> to a nation, tall and smooth,
> to a people feared near and far,
> to a nation mighty and conquering,
> whose land the rivers divide. (Isa 18:1–2)

Isaiah goes on to express his disapproval of the alliance but his admiration for the Ethiopians is a valuable testimony regarding the Israelite attitude toward black people. In spite of Isaiah's opposition, the alliance was formed and following the death of Sargon in 605 BCE, Hezekiah, one of Judah's best and wisest kings, cast his fortune and his sacred honor with Egypt and Ethiopia in revolt against Assyria (2 Kgs 18:13—19:37). This alliance by necessity required sustained contacts between the two peoples. The sharing of a common destiny in opposition to Assyria would inevitably have engendered many deep and abiding friendships and intermarriages over the years.

It is this alliance that best accounts for the two black contemporaries of Jeremiah who are also closely associated with the royal house of Judah. The roles these men play show that from the beginning (as is clear from Isaiah 18), there was mutual respect on the part of the two allies and that black Africans were welcomed into and participated in Israelite life at all levels.[26] One may legitimately infer that the black presence in ancient Israel, which is there from the beginning, was greatly enriched by the alliance between

26. The alliance between Judah and the Ethiopian dynasty of Egypt was initiated approximately a century before the appearance of Yehudi in Jeremiah 36. Yehudi's great-grandfather must have become an Israelite citizen soon after the alliance was formed. That close relations continued between the two peoples is documented by the fact that Zephaniah, who carried out his prophetic activity ca. 630 BCE, was the son of a man named Kushi (Zeph 1:1) and by the presence of a significant number of Israelite refugees in Egypt and Ethiopia during and after the Exile (Isa 11:11).

Judah and the Ethiopian dynasty of Egypt in the latter part of the eighth century BCE. Is not the conclusion inevitable that there were many more black contemporaries of Jeremiah—and the other prophets—whom chance did not choose to identify or to include in the biblical record?

4

Was Amos a Racist?[1]

Although his prophecy consists of only nine chapters and, therefore, is grouped with the minor, i.e., shorter prophetic books, Amos of Tekoa unquestionably belongs among the greatest of the prophets of Israel. Before him no one had shown such sensitivity to the evil of a whole society and proclaimed so powerfully its incompatibility with the destiny of God's covenant people. The first of the prophets whose words were preserved separately in written form, Amos profoundly shaped the prophetic movement and left a collection of sermons and narratives that belong to the classics of our faith. Yet among these is a passage that may be understood in a racist sense. Speaking as the herald of God in 9:7, Amos asks: "Are you not like the Ethiopians to me, O people of Israel?" For all his greatness, was Amos a racist?

Approximately half of the authorities consulted in this study answer this question affirmatively.[2] Characteristically, those scholars who take

1. *Editor's note*: The language in this article has been updated to include gender inclusive language as the author undoubtedly would have used if he were writing today.

2. Among these are: Keil, *The Twelve Minor Prophets*, 1. 327; Pusey, *The Minor Prophets*, 333; Wolfendale, *A Homiletical Commentary on the Minor Prophets*, 326; von Orelli, *The Twelve Minor Prophets*, 151; Driver, *Joel and Amos*, 219; Wellhausen, *Die kleinen Propheten*, 94; Marti, *Dodekapropheten* 1, 223; Harper, *Amos and Hosea*, 192; Hoonacker, *Les douze petits Prophètes*, 280; Horton, *The Minor Prophets*, 172; Edghill, *Amos*, 90; Desnoyers, "Le Prophète Amos," 230; Nowack, *Die kleinen Propheten*, 166; Orchard, *Oracles of God*, 46; Robinson, "Amos," 783; Sutcliffe, *Amos*, 74; Nötscher, *Zwölfprophetenbuch*, 75; Schumpp, *Das Buch der zwölf Propheten*, 141; Maag, *Text, Wortschatz und Begriffswelt des Buches Amos*, 59, 160; Laetsch, *The Minor Prophets*, 188; Heschel, *The Prophets*, 33; Ullendorff, *Ethiopia and the Bible*, 14; Bič, *Das Buch Amos*, 183; Hammershaimb, *Amos*,

this position simply assert that the reference to Ethiopia is contemptuous and that Amos' audience would have been offended by the comparison. The logic of their thinking, never explicitly stated, seems to be as follows: It is well known that the Philistines and Syrians, with whom Israel is also compared in 9:7, had been mortal foes of Israel, and the mere mention of them would evoke bitter feelings. If this was true for the Philistines and Syrians, it must also be true for the Ethiopians. Since there was no history of enmity between the Ethiopians and the Israelites, the offense of the comparison must lie in the color of the Ethiopians. For a few, the offense is stated to be because the Ethiopians were descended from the "wicked" and "accursed" Ham; for others, because the Ethiopians were assumed to be "heathen" and "uncivilized," or because they were frequently enslaved.

In order to evaluate these judgments, the passage in question must be examined in both its immediate and larger contexts. The complete unit reads as follows:

> "Are you not like the Ethiopians to me,
> O people of Israel?" says the LORD.
> "Did I not bring up Israel from the land of Egypt,
> and the Philistines from Caphtor and the Syrians from Kir?
> Behold, the eyes of the Lord GOD are upon the sinful kingdom,
> and I will destroy it from the face of the ground." (Amos 9:7–8a)[3]

134; see Mays, *Amos*, 157. The comparison with Ethiopia is so unthinkable to Ehrlich that he avoids it by translating: "Do you not conduct yourselves towards me as the Kushites?" (*Randglossen zur Hebräischen Bible* 5, 254). This is a forced translation and has elicited virtually no support.

Apparently the first to affirm that the color of the Ethiopians was not offensive to the Israelites of Amos' day were: Guthe, *Der Prophet Amos*, 46 and Budde, "ZuProphete Text und Auslegung des Buches Amos," 109. See Snaith, *Amos, Hosea and Micah*, 49, but see his *Notes on the Hebrew Text of Amos, Part II: Translation and Notes*, 141.

3. A few scholars take 9:7 as a complete unit or as a fragment of a larger unit. See Löhr, *Untersuchungen zum Buch Amos*, 30–33); Duhm, "Anmerkungen zu den Zwölf Propheten," 17; Koehler, *Amos*, 30; Gressmann, *Die älteste Geschichtsschreibung und Prophetie Israels*, 357; Maag, *Text*, 58–59; Robinson, *Die Zwölf Kleinen Propheten: Hosea bis Mica*, 106; Amsler, *Osée, Joël, Abdias, Jonas, Amos*, 241–42; Weiser, *Das Buck der zwölf kleinen Propheten*, 200. Earlier, Weiser had joined 9:7 to 9:1–4 in his *Die Prophetie des Amos*, 46ff.). See also Sellin, who joins 9:7–10 to 3:1–2, making 9:7 precede 3:2 and 9:8 follow (*Das Zwölfprophetenbuch*, 174). Wolff, on the other hand, thinks 9:7 may be composed of two originally independent speeches (*Dodekapropheton 2: Joel und Amos*, 396). Following Amsler, Rudolph argues forcefully for understanding 9:7 as a complete unit (*Joel–Amos–Obadja–Jona*, 272–73).

It is best, however, with the majority of modern scholars to include 9:8a with 9:7.

From the information given in the superscription to the book of Amos (1:1), and from the picture of contemporary society reflected in his prophecies, it can be determined that Amos was active as a prophet ca. 750 BCE. This was some 600 years after the Exodus from Egypt and almost 200 years after the division of the tribes into two separate kingdoms following the death of Solomon. The period from the death of Solomon to the appearance of Amos is the most disappointing chapter in the history of the covenant people. Those who had been called to be a kingdom of priests and a holy nation, God's instruments of blessing to all the families of the earth, had lost their sense of mission and seriously compromised their destiny. On the one hand, the two Israelite kingdoms wasted their time and substance in rivalry and warfare, first with each other and then with the Aramean kingdom of Damascus. Secondly, the northern kingdom so opened itself to Canaanite culture and religion that it lost its distinctive identity. By 750 BCE the light of the northern kingdom was no longer visible and its salt had lost its savor.

It is against this background of almost 200 years of wasted opportunity that God, through Amos, shatters the oblivion and complacency of the people by announcing the end of the northern kingdom. Confronted with this message, the people appeal to their special relationship to God through the covenant. Reading between the lines of the book of Amos, it is only too clear that the royal service to which Israel was called through the covenant had been subverted into a sense of privilege, protection, and favoritism. In a terse, explosive oracle in 3:1–2, Amos attacks this thinking. True, he agrees, they had enjoyed a unique relationship to God through the covenant, but that meant that they were the more responsible—and the more liable to God's judgment. "You only have I known of all the nations of the earth; therefore I will punish you for all your iniquities."

The passage referring to the Ethiopians (9:7–8a) is a companion piece to 3:1–2. The fact that Amos has to deal with this subject a second time is proof of how deep-seated was the feeling of privilege and protection and how hopelessly corrupted was the true understanding of the covenant. The word in 9:7–8a is designed to deal with this self-deception once and for all.[4] Amos formulates his thought by means of two questions and an

Otherwise, 9:8a stands isolated, and the point of the comparisons in 9:7 is not clear. 9:8b flatly contradicts 9:8a as well as 9:1–2, and is widely regarded as stemming from the disciples of Amos who adapted his word to their own time and situation.

4. This passage should also be seen in relation to the vision in 9:1–2, which has the purpose of reinforcing the massage of the end of the nation against the protests of the

affirmation. The questions are: (1) "Are you not like the Ethiopians to me, O people of Israel?" and (2) "Did I not bring up Israel from the land of Egypt, and the Philistines from Caphtor and the Syrians from Kir?" These questions are rhetorical. The context indicates that they can only be answered affirmatively. But what is their logic? What awareness is the prophet seeking to awaken by means of them?

The thrust of Amos' questions is most transparent in the last one. Here, that remarkable act of providence in the history of Israel, the liberation from Egyptian bondage, is placed in juxtaposition to the migration of the Philistines from Caphtor and the Syrians from Kir. Why, of all peoples, does Amos choose precisely the Philistines and Syrians? The answer must lie in the fact that the one thing Israel has in common with the Philistines and Syrians is shared possession of the promised land. While Israel claimed all the territory from the Brook of Egypt to the Euphrates and from the Mediterranean Sea to the Transjordan Plateau (see Num 34:1–12; Ezek 47:13–20), in actual fact she had to concede significant portions of this territory to the Philistines and the Syrians. Moreover, this state of affairs was the result of the bitterest rivalry. As a result of it, Israel was very nearly overcome by the Philistines in the time of Saul and by the Syrians some two generations before Amos. While the Philistines and Syrians had long since been reduced to shadows of their former selves by the time of Amos, the memories of the atrocities suffered at their hands were still painfully alive. In his famous sermon in 1:3—2:16, Amos draws upon these memories and places the Syrians and Philistines at the head of the peoples he condemns as a prelude to condemning Israel.

The affirmative answer required by Amos' question is both an acknowledgment and a confession that the providence of God embraces all peoples, including the bitterest rivals and enemies of Israel. And Amos could not have chosen a more delicate issue to relate this affirmation to, the possession of the promised land. Contrary to the opinion of some scholars, Amos does not mean to suggest that because of Israel's failure in the covenant, the liberation from Egyptian bondage and the gift of her portion of the land have been reduced to "secular" events, of no more significance than the migrations of the Philistines and Syrians. Such a thought is akin to the presuppositions of Amos' audience, namely, that God acts exclusively in the history of Israel. Rather than reducing Israel's Exodus and Conquest

---

people and possibly of overcoming self-doubt on the part of Amos.

to secular events, Amos raises the life stories of the Philistines and Syrians to sacred events. Here, indeed, is a high watermark in the Old Testament.

Against this background we are in a better position to deal with the first question Amos puts to his audience: "Are you not like the Ethiopians to me, O people of Israel?" Now the Ethiopians were not, nor had they ever been, enemies of Israel. Nor did they share in the possession of the promised land, as did the Philistines and Syrians. Why, then, the choice of the Ethiopians from among all the peoples known to the prophet?[5] Is the comparison for the sake of demeaning Israel? Is there any truth in the rather widely shared assumptions that the Ethiopians were scorned because they were frequently enslaved, that their color was offensive, or that they were regarded as heathen and uncivilized?

A little more than a generation after Amos, Isaiah generously expresses his admiration for the Ethiopians (Isa 18:1–2). How could they be regarded with contempt in the time of Amos but admired in the time of Isaiah? Since Amos does not mention Ham or the color of the Ethiopians, the only way the comparison could be offensive is for the terms "Ethiopia" and "Ethiopian(s)" to have had bad connotations in Israelite usage. There is absolutely no evidence of this in the Old Testament. The only connotation that can be established for Ethiopia is that it was thought of as a distant (Est 1:1; 8:9) and wealthy land (Isa 43:3; 45:14; Job 28:19).[6] Contrary to the interpretation of Gen 9:18–27 that was developed to justify slavery, this passage does not speak of a curse on Ham (and African peoples in general). It was Canaan and his descendants whom Noah cursed (v. 25) because of sexual perverseness, a trait for which the Canaanites were notorious. Slavery was a fate to which peoples of the ancient Near East fell victim indiscriminately. After all, Israel began her existence in slavery and continued to be raided for slaves until not long before the time of Amos (Amos 1:6, 9).

5. A few scholars maintain that the logic of the question about the Ethiopians is akin to that concerning the Philistines and Syrians. Some older scholars, under the erroneous assumption that the home of the Kushites was originally Arabia, think the question alludes to the migration of the Kushites from Arabia to Africa. See Farrar, *The Minor Prophets*, 67; Henderson, *The Twelve Minor Prophets*, 178; Cowles, *The Minor Prophets*, 153; Mitchell, *Amos*, 170. More recently van Wyk argues that the point of the question is that just as Israel was delivered from Egyptian bondage, so were the Ethiopians ("The Kushites in Amos 9:7," 38–45). But the prophet asks not one but two questions, and he has more than one point to make.

6. The remoteness of the Ethiopians was also prominent in Greek thought. See the discussion of Snowden, *Blacks in Antiquity*, 101–2 and 279 n.2. On the wealth of Ethiopia, see Hansberry, *Pillars in Ethiopian History*, 50.

The only passage in the Old Testament where the color of the Ethiopians is mentioned is Jer 13:23. When the prophet asks, "Can the Ethiopian change his skin or the leopard his spots?" he is not implying that the Ethiopian is dissatisfied with the color of his skin and wants to change it (or the leopard his spots). Jeremiah asks these questions to make vivid how difficult it is for one for whom sin has become second nature to change his behavior. In a part of the world where peoples of Europe, Asia, and Africa freely mixed and mingled and where most were probably people of color, the idea that the color of the Ethiopians was offensive to the Israelites is most unlikely.

Ironically, we have more cultural artifacts from the Ethiopians, roughly contemporary with Amos, than we do from the Israelites of his day. Both peoples were debtors in the realm of culture, the Israelites especially to the Canaanites and Phoenicians, the Ethiopians to the Egyptians. The narrative of the initial Ethiopian conquest of Egypt by Piankhi (or, Peye[7]), ca. 730 BCE, is widely esteemed as one of the finest examples of literature and historiography from the ancient world. One eminent authority considers it to be "the clearest and most rational account of a military expedition which has survived from ancient Egypt."[8] Because of its vividness and detail, it is, in fact, "one of the most interesting ancient historical inscriptions that exists in any country."[9] And the remarkably realistic sculptures of Mentemhet, governor of Thebes during the latter period of the Twenty-fifth Dynasty, belong in any history of Egyptian plastic arts.[10] With these may

7. See Priese, "Nicht-ägyptische Namen und Wörter," 166–75.

8. Breasted, *A History of the Ancient Egyptians*, 370. See Breasted's fuller statement in which he also praises the literary merits of this narrative in his unabridged work, *A History of Egypt*, 545. Piankhi's stele recording his campaign was discovered in 1862 at Napata and in 1864 taken to Cairo, where it is now housed in the Museum of Egyptian Antiquities. The complete text of the campaign is translated by Breasted in his *Ancient Records of Egypt* 4, 406–44. Additional bibliography on the text is given by Kitchen, *The Third Intermediate Period in Egypt*, 346 n.699. This work is also an excellent source for the chronology and political history of the Twenty-fifth (Ethiopian) Dynasty, which ruled Egypt from ca. 730 to 663 BCE (see 138ff., 362ff.). For the iconography of the Twenty-fifth Dynasty, see Leclant, "Kushites and Meroites," 89–132.

9. Hall, *Cambridge Ancient History* 3: *The Assyrian Empire*, 273. For other admiring estimates of the account of Piankhi's conquest, see, e.g., Budge, *The Egyptian Sudan* 2, 11; Gardiner, "Piankhi's Instructions to His Army," 219; Scharff and Moortgat, *Aegypten und Vorderasien im Altertum*, 177–78; Wilson, *The Culture of Ancient Egypt*, 293; von Zeissl, *Aethiopen und Assyrer in Aegypten*, 10; Wolf, *Kulturgeschichte des Alten Aegypten*, 413.

10. See Wreszinski, "Eine Statue des Monthemhêt," 10–18; Bosse, *Die menschliche Figur in der Rundplastik der ägyptischen Spätzeit*, 83–88, 95–99; *Encyclopedia of World*

be compared the Elohist epic, dating from ca. 750 BCE or earlier, and the ivory carvings found at Samaria, belonging to the period approximately a century before the time of Amos.[11] However one decides between the two cultures, the Ethiopians cannot be regarded as uncivilized.

Nor is there any basis for the notion that the religion of the Ethiopians (essentially at this time that of Egypt) was primitive and crude. After all, Amos himself felt that the Egyptians as well as the Assyrians would be shocked by the behavior of the Israelites (3:9). The inscriptions of the Ethiopian monarchs of the Twenty-fifth Dynasty are replete with expressions and deeds of personal piety. They were most generous in their support of the priesthoods and temples. Significantly, there is a conspicuous decline in military scenes from the temple decorations of the Twenty-fifth Dynasty. It is not without reason that the Greeks and Romans thought of the Ethiopians as blameless, as exemplars of justice, and as those whose offerings were most pleasing to the gods.[12]

In a word, there are no grounds whatsoever for Amos' audience to take the comparison with the Ethiopians as demeaning. Taking this into account, and given the logic of the choice of the Philistines and Syrians, the choice of the Ethiopians (rather than, for example, the Arabs or Egyptians) is best explained because they were one of the most distant and different people known to the Israelites.[13] By the comparison with the Ethiopians, Amos says to Israel, in effect: "Think of the most distant and different people you can imagine; they are just as near and dear to God as you are." This is not to deny the covenant relationship and Israel's special place in

---

Art 4, plate 386.

For funerary furniture, jewelry, and small objects of the Twenty-fifth Dynasty, see Smith, *Ancient Egypt as Represented in the Museum of Fine Arts, Boston*, 165ff.

For a more general treatment of art and culture, see Kees, *Aegyptische Kunst*, 68–70; Leclant and Yoyette, "Notes d'histoire et de civilisation éthiopiennes," 1–39; von Zeissl, *Aethiopen und Assyrer*, ch. 9.

11. Jack, *Samaria in Ahab's Time*; Crowfoot and Crowfoot, *Early Ivories from Samaria*; McCown, *The Ladder of Progress in Palestine*, 196–98; Wright, "Samaria," 67–78; Kenyon, *Royal Cities of the Old Testament*, 71ff.

12. See Snowden, *Blacks*, 144–50, 181.

13. The following statement, while based on a study of Graeco-Roman sources, is nevertheless pertinent to the present study. "The Negro's blackness was merely *different* from the white man's whiteness. Such was the basic significance of the color of skin in Graeco-Roman thought—whether mentioned in anthropological theories, in philosophical reflections, or in spiritual imagery" (Snowden, "Ethiopians and the Graeco-Roman World," 31).

God's purpose. It is an affirmation that all people are embraced in his love and purpose.[14] Again Amos lifts our spirits in a breathtaking vision of the universality of God and the fellowship of all humanity that transcends all barriers.

The logic of the two questions in Amos 9:7, then, is that the God to whom Israel is bound by covenant and by whom her history has been decisively shaped is the God of *all* people. All are as near and dear to him as Israel. All are embraced within his purpose and providence. From this it follows that God is no respecter of persons, that he is without partiality or favoritism to anyone. This is the point of Amos' affirmation in 9:8a (see also Amos 1:3–2:16; 5:18). Specifically, Israel can expect no special treatment. "The eyes of the Lord GOD are upon the sinful kingdom," whoever it may be; it he will "destroy from the surface of the ground" (9:8a).

This affirmation seems exceedingly harsh to modern ears. If one could discuss the matter with Amos, he would probably allow that it is not so much a matter of God destroying man as it is of man destroying himself. At the heart of the preaching of Amos (and of the prophets in general) is the conviction that the most powerful force shaping the destiny of man is morality. This conviction was every bit as real to Amos as the law of gravity is to modern man. For the prophet, the very foundations of the universe are shaken by man's sin. Sin is the carcinogen of the human spirit. But in biblical thinking, sin is never impersonal. And in the end, Amos would probably insist on his wording to make the point that behind the requirements of morality stands a Person, and that these requirements presuppose and require a relationship to this Person.

Far from being racist, Amos 9:7 is one of the soaring passages of the Bible, luminous with the truth of the universal love of God and the fellowship of all humanity. For all their grandeur, Amos does not treat these ideas

14. The following is a partial listing of those who share this understanding of this passage: Davidson, "The Prophet Amos," 177, 178; Löhr, *Untersuchungen*, 30–33; Cripps, *Amos*, 262–64; Calkins, *The Modern Message of the Minor Prophets*, 26; Pfeiffer, *Introduction to the Old Testament*, 580, 581; Bewer, *The Twelve Prophets* 1, 33; Lods, *Histoire de la Littérature Hébraique et Juive*, 240; Procksch, *Theologie des Alten Testaments*, 168–69, 170, 511, 579; Neher, *Contribution a l'étude du prophétisme Amos*, 141; James, *Personalities of the Old Testament*, 221–22; "Amos," *The Seventh-Day Adventist Bible Commentary*, 982; Myers, *Hosea, Joel, Amos, Obadiah, Jonah*, 147; Marsh, *Amos & Micah*, 71; Smart, "Amos," *I*, 120; Gottwald, *All the Kingdoms of the Earth*, 112; Robinson, *Die Zwölf kleinen Propheten*, 106; Amsler, *Amos*, 241–42; Weiser, *Zwölf kleinen Propheten*, 200–201; Wolff, *Joel und Amos*, 398–99; Hauret, *Amos et Osée*, 112–13; Beck, *Gottes Traum: Eine menschliche Welt Hosea-Amos-Micha*, 71.

as something novel, nor, indeed, were they. The truth that Amos states so succinctly and powerfully belonged to the heritage of his faith and was first given expression centuries before by the author of the Yahwist epic.[15] Since Amos makes no effort to justify or defend what he says in 9:7, it is likely that he presupposes knowledge of its truth based on Israel's ancient epic. The inner appropriation of this truth, however, cannot be taken for granted, and Amos—and we—must ever internalize and reaffirm it. Taken together, Amos's two questions in 9:7 are the equivalent of Paul's affirmation that God has "made from one every nation of men to live on all the face of the earth" (Acts 17:26). By deliberately choosing the Philistines and Syrians, with whom there was a history of enmity, and the Ethiopians, who were remote and different, Amos gives content and substance to his statement that prevents it from being reduced to a pious platitude.

The message of Amos 9:7–8a still challenges us today. We give lip service to the fatherhood of God and the fellowship of all humanity, but in actual practice many of us are shockingly provincial. And how often do we assume that our group is special in God's sight, and that he will make allowances for our foolish and wayward ways? Amos's words in 9:7–8a still ring out clearly and sharply, challenging us to enlarge our awareness of God's love and providence, and warning us against presuming on his indulgence.

15. There is a fairly broad consensus that the Yahwist epic dates from ca. 950 BCE. Its universalism is astounding. It begins, not with the call of Abraham, the father of Israel, but with creation. Gen 2:4b—11:9 traces the early history of humanity, noting that progress in culture is paralleled by increasing alienation from God and each other. With the episode of the tower of Babel, humanity's alienation has become universal and it is precisely against this background that God calls Abraham (and Israel) to be his redemptive agent to all the families of the earth (Gen 12:1–3). Also within the Yahwist epic is the remarkable blessing of Noah, "God enlarge Japheth (the Philistines?), and let him dwell in the tents of Shem (Israel)" (Gen 9:26). Was this passage in the back of Amos's mind as he formulated his questions about the Philistines and Syrians?

5

The African Roots of the Prophet Zephaniah[1]

Standing at the beginning of each of the prophetic books of the Old Testament and serving in effect as a title page is a verse or two that identify the author, give pertinent information about him, and affirm the content of his work to be the Word of God. The kind and amount of information about the prophet varies. In the case of Zephaniah we are told only about his ancestry and that he was active during the reign of King Josiah (640–609 BCE). The information concerning Zephaniah's family is unique, however, in that, alone among the prophets, his ancestry is traced back through four generations. His father was Kushi, his grandfather Gedaliah, his great-grandfather Amariah, and his great-great-grandfather Hezekiah. Normally only a prophet's father's name is given. Only in the case of Zechariah is a prophet's genealogy traced back more than one generation, but only his father and grandfather are named.

The most plausible inference from the exceptional character of Zephaniah's genealogy is that the last named member, Hezekiah, was a person of unusual significance. If this inference is valid, it inevitably follows that this Hezekiah was none other than the king by that name who, according to the generally accepted chronology, reigned from 715–687 BCE.[2]

1. This article is dedicated to my good friend and colleague, Dr. Leon E. Wright, Professor Emeritus of New Testament at the Howard University School of Religion, in commemoration of the completion of thirty-three years of distinguished service at the School of Religion.

2. Albright, "Chronology of the Divided Monarchy," 16–22.

Two major objections have been raised against this identification. First, it is noted that the text of Zeph 1:1 does not explicitly call the Hezekiah of Zephaniah's ancestry King. Secondly, some feel the identification is impossible on chronological grounds. Whereas there are four generations from Zephaniah's ancestor, Hezekiah, there are only three from King Hezekiah through his successors on the throne—Manasseh, Amon, and Josiah. Moreover, the time between King Hezekiah (715–687 BCE) and Zephaniah, who is generally regarded as being active ca. 630 BCE, is extremely short for four generations.

One has only to observe the pattern of marriages in the royal house of Judah, contemporary with Zephaniah, however, to become aware that early marriage and the begetting of children at a youthful age were not uncommon.[3] Amon became a father when he was sixteen (2 Kgs 21:19; 22:1), Josiah at fourteen (2 Kgs 22:1; 23:36), and Jehoiakim at eighteen (2 Kgs 24:8). If it is assumed on the basis of this analogy that Amariah, Gedaliah, and Kushi became fathers when each was sixteen (the average age for Amon, Josiah, and Jehoiakim) and that Zephaniah was about twenty years old when he began his ministry, this would place the birth of Amariah at ca. 698 BCE. This correlates nicely with the date of the birth of Manasseh (presumably the older brother of Amariah) who, according to the chronology of Albright, would have been born in 699 BCE. The discrepancy in generations is readily accounted for by the fact that Manasseh did not become the father of Amon until he was forty-five years old (2 Kgs 21:1, 9). On chronological grounds there is no reason why the two contemporaries, Josiah and Zephaniah, cannot have been descended from King Hezekiah.

To the objection that the Hezekiah of Zephaniah's ancestry is not explicitly identified as king, it may be replied that a greater problem is posed if he were not the king by that name. The memory of King Hezekiah would certainly have been alive in the time of Josiah and Zephaniah. If the Hezekiah of Zephaniah's ancestry were not King Hezekiah, it would have been incumbent upon the author of Zeph 1:1 to distinguish the two Hezekiahs in order to avoid misunderstanding and the displeasure of the Davidic dynasty, especially since Zephaniah is highly critical of Jerusalem and the royal house (see 1:8–9, 10–11, 12–13, 3:1–8).

It may be that "king" is omitted before Hezekiah's name merely on stylistic grounds. Josiah is called king at the end of Zeph 1:1 and the author of this verse may have thought it infelicitous to use this title twice in so short a

3. See Gray, "The Royal Ancestry of Zephaniah," 77.

compass. More likely "king" is omitted to avoid the suggestion that Zephaniah's authority derived from his royal ancestry or that he should receive special consideration because of it. The first thing said about Zephaniah is that he was the recipient of the word of God. Only this constitutes his authority and makes his message deserving of attention and worthy of being preserved. In short, there is nothing that prevents the identification of the Hezekiah of Zephaniah's ancestry with King Hezekiah. And this identification best accounts for the exceptional character of Zephaniah's genealogy.

Another unique feature of Zephaniah's genealogy is the name of his father, Kushi. All the other names are compounded with Yahweh, the name of the covenant God of Israel, and are obviously Israelite names. Kushi stands completely apart in this series. As in the case of Gadi, King Menahem's father (2 Kgs 15:14), Hachmonie (1 Chr 27:32; see 2 Sam 23:8; 1 Chr 11:1), and Buzi, the father of Ezekiel (Ezek 1:3; see Job 32:2, 6; Jer 25:32), it is a gentilic that has become a proper name. Just as Buzi transparently designates a man of Buz, or a Buzite, so Kushi inevitably suggests a man of Kush, or a Kushite. Was Zephaniah not only of royal but also of Ethiopian ancestry?[4]

Most scholars ignore this question, or if they deal with it at all, answer it in the negative. Of the efforts to discount the implication of Zephaniah's father's name, the most widely accepted interpretation is that the names of Hezekiah, Amariah, and Gedaliah are later additions to the text of Zeph 1:1. These good Israelite names were supplied in generous quantity to the genealogy of Zephaniah to show that the prophet, in spite of his father's name, was of pure Judaean stock.[5]

The names of Hezekiah,[6] Amariah, and Gedaliah, however, are missing from no ancient text or version. Moreover, is it credible that descendants of King Hezekiah and Zephaniah would have permitted someone to invent and add members to the family tree? This position is credible only on the assumption that the name Kushi would have been offensive to an ancient Israelite. Isaiah's transparent admiration for the visiting

4. Ethiopia/Kush is here used in its biblical sense of that portion of the Nile valley south of Syene, modern Aswan (see Ezek 29:10), corresponding roughly to the modern state of Sudan.

5. Sellin, *Das Zwölfprophetenbuch*, 371. About a dozen scholars have adopted Sellin's position without elaboration. For an attempt to strengthen and gain wider currency for it, see Heller, "Zephanjas Ahnenreihe," 102–4.

6. Syriac spells Hezekiah's name with an "l" instead of a "z," but this is universally regarded as an error of transmission rather than evidence of a different name.

Ethiopian diplomats in Isa 18:1–2 is proof to the contrary.[7] Had Kushi been an embarrassment to the author of Zeph 1:1, he simply would have omitted Zephaniah's genealogy altogether. As the books of Amos, Micah, Nahum, Habakkuk, Obadiah, Haggai, and Malachi demonstrate, it was not mandatory to include a prophet's genealogy in the superscription to his work.

One interpreter thinks he can prove that Zephaniah's father's name does not imply Ethiopian ancestry. He accepts all the names of Zephaniah's genealogy as genuine but maintains that Kushi was a common name in the time of Zephaniah and has nothing to do with national origins. For example, a certain Kushi from the Assyrian province of Harran is known to have had a father and brother with genuine Aramaic names. "This decidedly proves that we cannot regard him as an Egyptian or an Egyptian captive."[8] In another instance, a Kushi from Abu Simbel demonstrates the ability to write Phoenician. From this it is concluded that he cannot have been of Ethiopian origin.[9]

For this argument to be valid, all Ethiopians would have to have been confined to their homeland with none ever becoming resident in other lands. The truth is that Ethiopians were scattered throughout the Near East and the Mediterranean world. This came about initially because of their being used as mercenaries by the principal powers of the ancient world: Egypt. Israel, Phoenicia, Greece, Persia.[10] Not only did Ethiopians fight in

7. Contrary to the widespread notion, based on Gen 9:18–27, the Old Testament knows nothing of a curse on African peoples. It was Canaan, not Ham, whom Noah cursed. Gen 9:18–27 has nothing to do with race but accounts for Canaan's loss of her land to the Israelites and Philistines because of sexual perversity. (See the writer's articles reprinted in this volume, "The Curse That Never Was" (Gen 9:18–27)," [ch. 2 in this volume]; and, "Was Amos a Racist?" [ch. 4 in this volume].

8. Lipiński, review of Kapelrud, *Zephaniah: Morphology and Ideas*, 689. See Schwally, "Das Buch Ssefanâ," 167; Lippi, *Sophonias*, 73; Rudolph, *Micha-Nahum-Habakuk-Zephanja*, 259.

9. Ibid.

10. Ethiopian troops were an important factor in expelling the Hyksos from Egypt and in achieving Egypt's great imperialistic expansion during the Eighteenth Dynasty. See Steindorff and Seele, *When Egypt Ruled the East*. 27–28; Du Bois, *The World and Africa*, 117, 125–130. Woodson, *The African Background*, 27; Copher, "The Black Man in the Biblical World," 7–16. Ethiopians continued to form a principal component of the armies of Egypt in their Palestinian campaigns. They participated in Shishak's raid against Judah in the fifth year of Rehoboam, ca. 918 BCE (2 Chr 12:3) and they fought in the army of Pharaoh Necho at Carchemish in 605 BCE (Jer 46:9; see Ezek 30:5).

The role Ethiopian troops played in the armies of Egypt evidently led to their being sought as mercenaries elsewhere. It is well-known that David's army was made up of men

the armies of these powers, they were also stationed in various parts of the world as occupation forces or in military colonies.[11] Perhaps the most germane example of such use is the presence of an Ethiopian colony of mercenaries at Gerar in southern Palestine from the tenth to the eighth centuries BCE. This colony was probably first established by Pharaoh Shishak following his invasion of Palestine ca. 918 BCE (see 2 Chr 12:3) as a buffer between Egypt and Judah.[12] We know from 1 Chr 4:39–41 that they were not displaced until the time of Hezekiah. In the meantime, Egypt had lapsed into profound weakness and had given up imperial aspirations. Thus, the Ethiopian mercenaries were left to themselves and became in effect permanent residents. The author of 1 Chr 4:40 credits them with making Gerar into a land with "rich, good pasture . . . quiet, and peaceful; for the former inhabitants there belonged to Ham." Since David's Kushite runner (2 Sam 18:19–33) and Ebed-melech (Jer 38:7–13; 39:15–18) presumably spoke Hebrew, it is entirely credible to find in Harran and Abu Simbel men of Ethiopian ancestry whose native tongue had become Aramaic and Phoenician.

Finally, there are those who assume that Kushi was of pure Israelite stock and that the only comment his name calls for is an explanation for the choice of it. It has been suggested that Kushi was selected to express identification with Egypt and opposition to Judah's collaboration with Assyria during the reign of Manasseh,[13] or sympathy with the ruling

of diverse national origins, such as Philistines and Hittites. It is not likely that the one Kushite who is mentioned by chance (2 Sam 18:21–32) is exhaustive of the Ethiopian presence in his army. Troops from Put (either Punt on the African coast of the Red Sea or Libya, so LXX) were in the army of Tyre (Ezek 27:10), and the mythological army of Gog consists mainly of Kushites and men from Put (Ezek 38:5; see Isa 66:19). For the presence of Ethiopian troops in Crete, Greece, Persia, and Rome, see Beardsley, *The Negro in Greek and Roman Civilization*; Snowden, *Blacks in Antiquity*, 121–29. See also Snowden, "Ethiopians and the Graeco-Roman World," 14, 16–17, 20, 25, 26, 28.

11. From Tell el-Amarna Letter 287 we know that Ethiopian troops were stationed in the vicinity of Jerusalem in the first half of the fourteenth century BCE. See Pritchard, ed., *ANET*, 488. Ethiopian troops were also among the occupation forces of Cyprus under Amasis from 568–525 BCE. See Snowden, *Blacks in Antiquity*, 122–23.

12. See Albright, "Egypt and the Early History of the Negeb," 146. The presence of this Ethiopian colony explains the reference in 2 Chr 21:16 to the Philistines and Arabs "who are near the Ethiopians." Zerah the Ethiopian and his army who fought against King Asa, Rehoboam's grandson (2 Chr 14:9–15; see 16:8), are probably from this colony, for the battle culminates at Gerar.

13. Smith, *The Twelve Prophets* 2, 46. *See also* Bewer, *The Twelve Prophets* 2, 9; Paterson, *The Goodly Fellowship of the Prophets*, 98.

Ethiopian dynasty when Egypt fell to the Assyrians in 663 BCE,[14] or that Zephaniah's father "had an unusually dark complexion."[15] The diversity of these explanations illustrates the subjective and inconclusive nature of this approach.[16]

The efforts to deny the possibility of Ethiopian ancestry to Zephaniah are not convincing. While the name Kushi of itself does not by necessity require the assumption of African origins, this is certainly its immediate and natural implication. When one takes into consideration the fact that Judah and the Twenty-fifth (Ethiopian) Dynasty of Egypt were allies in revolt against Assyria not long before the birth of Zephaniah's father, this implication is powerfully reinforced.

The dominant factor shaping the political life of the entire ancient Near East during the generation prior to this revolt was Assyrian imperialism. Under the able and aggressive leadership of Tiglath-pileser III (745–727 BCE), Assyria, after a half century of weakness and inactivity, was fired with zeal to realize her ancient dream of world conquest and began relentlessly to expand her borders. By 735 Tiglath-pileser was able to invade and subdue Urartu, Assyria's principal rival. With this triumph the balance of power swung decisively in Assyria's favor and her shadow now fell ominously across all Syria and Palestine. In a desperate gamble, whose outcome could only be disaster, the northern Israelite state and Syria tried to organize a coalition to stop the Assyrian advance (734–732 BCE). Judah voluntarily submitted and became Assyria's vassal. Assyria's yoke was heavy, however, and her subjects restive. The remnant of the northern Israelite state rebelled ca. 725, and in retaliation, the Assyrians extinguished what remained of her political life. Although it was futile, a number of Syrian and Palestinian states rebelled again in 720 BCE only to be cruelly suppressed by Sargon II of Assyria (722–705 BCE).

14. Taylor, "The Book of Zephaniah," 1009 n.5.

15. Edens, "A Study of the Book of Zephaniah," 75–76; Kapelrud, *The Message of the Prophet Zephaniah*, 44. See Harrison, *Introduction to the Old Testament*, 939.

16. Among the authorities consulted in this study only six take seriously the implication of Kushi's name, but none has gone into this matter in detail. These are: Bentzen, *Introduction to the Old Testament* 2, 153; Eaton, *Obadiah, Nahum, Habakkuk, Zephaniah*, 121; Kraeling, *Commentary on the Prophets* 2, 260; Copher, "Black Religious Experience and Biblical Studies," 185, 186; Bennett, "Africa and the Biblical Period," 498; Watts, *Joel, Obadiah, Jonah, Nahum. Habakkuk and Zephaniah*, 153. See Gerleman, *Zephanja*, 2; and Keller, *Michée, Nahoum, Habacue, Sophonie*, 187 n.2, who positively evaluate the name, but do not pursue the question of the Ethiopian ancestry of Zephaniah.

It is against this background that the Twenty-fifth Dynasty came to power in Egypt.[17] Since ca. 1200 BCE. Egypt had been in decline and her strength dissipated by the rivalry of petty delta princes. The first assertion of genuine strength in centuries came with the suppression of the delta princes by the Ethiopian Piankhi (or, Peye[18]), ca. 730 BCE. He made no effort, however, to exercise rule over all Egypt. This was first achieved by his successor, Shabako ca. 715 BCE.

The reunification of the Nile valley and the resurgence of power under the leadership of Shabako must have stirred hope throughout Palestine and Syria. Syro-Palestinian aspiration also coincided with the self-interest of the Twenty-fifth Dynasty, for an independent Palestine and Syria would serve as a buffer between Egypt and Assyria. Shabako's reconquest of Egypt ca. 715 BCE may well have been followed by a diplomatic initiative in Palestine of which Isaiah 18 is the witness. For this passage seems to reflect the first flush of Shabako's triumph with its reference to Ethiopia–Egypt as "a people feared near and far, a nation mighty and conquering" (v. 2). In any case, there was open revolt again in Palestine in 712, centering in Ashdod, and from Isa 20 we know that it was supported by the Twenty-fifth Dynasty (see "Ethiopia, their hope," v. 5). But because of Isaiah's vigorous and dramatic opposition, the revolt was confined to Ashdod and Shabako wisely refrained from intervening.

When the heavy hand of Sargon came to rest in death in 705 BCE, the suppressed peoples throughout his empire, from Babylon in the East to Phoenicia in the West, grasped the torch of freedom and revolted. Against the strong opposition of Isaiah, Hezekiah committed Judah to this general uprising.[19] It is not unlikely that there was some planning and cooperation among the rebels. The embassy of Merodach-baladan of Babylon most likely belongs to this time (see 2 Kgs 20:12–19//Isa 39). It is probable that Hezekiah's revolt was coordinated with that of Luli, King of Tyre and Sidon,

17. For the iconography and history of the Twenty-fifth Dynasty, see Leclant, "Kushites and Meroïtes," 89–132; Breasted, *Ancient Records of Egypt* IV, 406–73; Janssen, "Que sait-on actuellement du Pharaon Taharqa?," 23–43; von Zeissl, *Aethiopien und Assyrer in Aegypten*; Gardiner. *Egypt of the Pharaohs*, ch. 12; Kitchen, *The Third Intermediate Period in Egypt* (1100–650 BCE), chs. 9, 10, 11, 22, 23.

18. See Priese, "Nicht-ägyptische Namen und Wörter," 166–75.

19. See Hallo, "From Qarqar to Carchemish," 34–61; Tadmor, "The Campaigns of Sargon II of Assur," 22–40, 77–100; Rowley, "Hezekiah's Reform and Rebellion," 395–431; Donner, *Israel unter den Völkern*, and "The Separate States of Israel and Judah"; Childs, *Isaiah and the Assyrian Crisis*; Bright, *A History of Israel*, ch. 7; Huber, *Jahwe, Juda und die anderen Völker beim Propheten Jesaja*.

and undertaken with the support of the Philistine city-states of Ashkelon and Ekron, which were also among those revolting.[20] Above all, this life-or-death venture was based upon a firm alliance between Judah and Egypt (see Isa 30:1–5; 31:1–3; 2 Kgs 19:9//Isa 37:9).

This alliance by necessity would have required numerous visits, exchanges of personnel, strategy sessions (see Isa 29:15), and exchanges of goods and supplies (see Isa 30:6–7). If the conspiracy began soon after Sargon's death, as it is most natural to assume, these relations would have continued over a period of some four or five years, i.e., from 705 to 701 BCE when effective resistance was ended with the Assyrian victory over the Egyptian army under the leadership of Tirhaqa at Eltekeh in northern Philistia.[21] (This is approximately the length of America's involvement in World War II.) One has only to recall the many deep and lasting relationships established between America and her allies during this time to appreciate what could have happened between Judah and the Ethiopian dynasty of Egypt.

That their common destiny for good or for ill did in fact forge special bonds of friendship between Israelites and Ethiopians seems to be confirmed by the presence of two men of Ethiopian ancestry in Judah in the time of Jeremiah, approximately a century after the revolt under Hezekiah. One of these is a certain Yehudi ben Nethaniah ben Shelemiah ben Kushi (Jer 36:14, 21, 23). The four generations of his ancestry fit naturally into the framework of a century and would allow for Yehudi's great-grandfather, Kushi, to have entered Israelite society in the time of Hezekiah. Yehudi, moreover, is almost certainly a member of King Jehoiakim's cabinet.[22] This is further evidence of close ties between the royal house of Judah and the Twenty-fifth Dynasty.

The second Ethiopian from the time of Jeremiah is Ebed-melech. He, too, is closely associated with the royal house of Judah. The nature of this relationship has been obscured by the unfortunate translation of *sārîs* in Jer 38:7 as "eunuch." A careful study of the usage of the term and the context in Jer 38:7 favor the translation, "officer."[23]

20. See Donner, "The Separate States of Israel and Judah," 446–47.

21. For a reconstruction of this battle, see Kitchen, *The Third Intermediate Period*, 383–86.

22. See the writer's article, "Two Black Contemporaries of Jeremiah," 101–8, also included in this volume, ch. 3.

23. Ibid., 95–101.

The incidental, chance references to Yehudi and Ebed-melech suggest the existence of a larger presence of which they are representative, a presence most naturally accounted for by the alliance between Judah and the Ethiopian dynasty of Egypt. At least, the presence of two men of Ethiopian ancestry with close ties to the royal house of Judah in the time of Jeremiah, which is virtually the same as that of Zephaniah, makes the existence of another such man, especially one with the name Kushi, completely credible.

Since Zephaniah's ancestry is traced in an unbroken line on his father's side to Hezekiah, it is most natural to think of Kushi's mother (Gedaliah's wife) as an African. If this were the case, still it would have been Gedaliah who named his son Kushi, for it was the custom at this time for the father to name the children.[24] That Gedaliah broke with the family tradition of names compounded with Yahweh, a significant departure for one related to the royal house of Judah,[25] is most intelligible on the assumption that his son was of Ethiopian ancestry and that he affirmed this ancestry with pride.[26]

The plausibility of Zephaniah's royal and African ancestry is supported, finally, by the prophet's preaching. It has long been noted that Zephaniah's familiarity with the royal establishment of Judah suggests a connection with the royal family. It is not so much his familiarity with the royal house that supports this inference as his criticism of it (see 1:8–9; 3:3). The climate was such when Zephaniah began his ministry (ca. 630 BCE) that criticism of the royal establishment was highly dangerous. King Manasseh had ruthlessly suppressed those who opposed his paganizing policies (2 Kgs 21:16). For two generations (since the end of Isaiah's ministry, ca. 700 BCE) no prophet had been able to speak out in Judah. At this time in history, possibly only one of royal blood could have pronounced judgment against the state and the royal house and survived.

Considering the small number of Zephaniah's sermons that have been preserved, his preaching exhibits an unusual interest in Ethiopia. In an

24. Herner, "Athalja," 141.

25. See Gray, *Hebrew Proper Names*, 262 n.1.

26. If it is from Gedaliah's wife that Zephaniah's Ethiopian ancestry is to be traced, this means that Kushi was born a generation after the end of the alliance between Judah and Egypt in 701 BCE. Kushi's mother could have been born to an African family, possibly belonging to the diplomatic staff stationed in Jerusalem during the alliance that became resident in Judah following the defeat by Assyria. That some Africans did opt to reside in Judah after the end of the alliance is confirmed by the presence of Yehudi and Ebed-melech in the time of Jeremiah.

oracle against the nations reminiscent of Amos 1–2, Zephaniah announces judgment against nations selected to represent the four cardinal points of the compass in relation to Judah: Philistia to the west, Moab and Ammon to the east, Ethiopia to the south, and Assyria to the north (2:4–15). But Egypt, especially as a counterpoise to Assyria, is the more natural representative of the southern point of the compass. Why Ethiopia?

The burden of Zephaniah's message is an imminent, cosmic day of Yahweh (classically expressed in 1:14–16),[27] which in the first instance is directed against Israel. A message of judgment has no season in which it is at home and the one who bears it commands no welcome. One can readily imagine the resentment of such a message from one of Ethiopian origins if the judgment did not also include this side of his family. Zephaniah's selection of Ethiopia rather than Egypt in 2:12 is best accounted for as a conscious effort to avoid such resentment.

Just as striking as the inclusion of Ethiopia for judgment in 2:12 is the singling out of her for salvation in 3:10.[28] In a few broad strokes, 3:9 sketches a vision of the conversion of "the peoples" (none of whom is named), who are given a pure lip so that they may serve God with one accord. Although succinct in the extreme, this picture is nevertheless complete. All nations are comprehended in it. Yet Zephaniah cannot refrain from making reference to one particular people. "From beyond the rivers of Kush, my suppliants, the daughter of my dispersed, shall bear my offering." There is

27. As is well known, this text inspired the famous medieval hymn, *Dies irae, dies ilia* ("Day of Wrath, O Day of Mourning.") This hymn is attested in manuscripts dating from the middle of the thirteenth century CE. Both words and music are popularly attributed to Thomas of Celano, a disciple and biographer of St. Francis. It was one of the most widely known hymns of the Middle Ages and the most frequently translated into the English language. It forms part of the Office for the Dead and Requiem Mass in the Catholic Church and is a staple for the Advent season among major Protestant denominations. This hymn is proof of the poetic power and spiritual depth of Zephaniah and a living memorial to the prophet. See Clop, "La prose 'dies irae' et l'ordre des Frères Mineurs," 46–53; Kulp, "Der Hymnus Dies irae, dies ilia," 256–63.

28. Since Stade's note in 1889 (*Geschichte des Volkes Israel*, 1:644–45 n.3) and Schwally's article of 1890 ("Ssefanjâ," 230ff.) it has been fashionable to question all or most of ch. 3. The arguments against the authenticity of 3:9ff. tend to be based on the presupposition that a prophet of judgment cannot also be the bearer of a message of salvation, or that the ideas expressed here belong to a later age than that of Zephaniah. These judgments are no longer as widely shared as they once were. Suffice it to say that there is a growing tendency to accept the authenticity of 3:9–10 (and most of ch. 3), and it is accepted by this writer. See, e.g., Keller, *Michée, Nahoum, Habacue, Sophonie*, 210–11; Sabottka, *Zephanja*, 115–22; Kapelrud, *The Message of the Prophet Zephaniah*, 37–38; Rudolph, *Micha-Nahum-Habakuk-Zephanja*, 294–97.

a significant difference in the way Ethiopians are referred to in comparison with other peoples. Whereas the peoples in general must have their lips purged so that they can worship and serve God, there are already those who worship and serve him in Ethiopia.

The explanation of this remarkable statement must again lie in the alliance established between Judah and the Ethiopian dynasty of Egypt in the time of Hezekiah. That is, in the course of the exchange between the two peoples necessitated by the alliance an appreciable number of Ethiopians must have become worshippers of Yahweh. It is not unlikely that some Israelites sought refuge in Ethiopia following the defeat by Assyria in 701 BCE (see Isa 11:11). If so, this would account for the otherwise awkward and difficult twofold reference to the pilgrims from Ethiopia as "suppliants" (native Ethiopians) and "dispersed" ones (refugees).[29] At any rate, verse 10 is unnecessary in its present context, and its inclusion is a bit puzzling—unless it comes from one who himself was of Ethiopian ancestry.

One cannot long expose himself to the prophecy of Zephaniah without becoming aware that theologically he bears the imprint of his immediate predecessor, Isaiah of Jerusalem (ca. 740–700 BCE). This is especially clear in the emphasis on the Day of the LORD, the remnant, and faith. But there is one passage in Zephaniah that is utterly unlike anything in Isaiah and indeed is unique in the Old Testament. Zephaniah lived after the long reign of Manasseh (687–642 BCE), during which Assyria was at the height of her power, and whether by necessity or choice, Manasseh actively promoted the paganizing of Judah (2 Kgs 21:3–9). Consequently, Zephaniah's prophecy has largely to do with judgment. But Zephaniah has the capacity to see beyond the judgment to the restoration of Judah and Jerusalem in

29. The text of 3:10 has created consternation for commentators and has led to the most diverse translations and interpretations. The major problem of interpretation centers in the words rendered, "my suppliants, the daughter of my dispersed." The meaning of "suppliants" for *'ătār* (perhaps to be vocalized as a participle) is now firmly established by its usage in Ugaritic (see Sabottka, *Zephanja*, 119). While *bat* is used in a rather exceptional way, "daughter of my dispersed" is still a legitimate rendering of *bat-pûsay*. The difficulty is not so much in the meaning of these two phrases as in their juxtaposition to each other. If the reference is not to native Ethiopians and refugee Israelites, as proposed in the text of this study, then "daughter of my dispersed" should perhaps be understood as an addition from the time of the Diaspora (after 587 BCE) to call attention to the Israelite presence in Ethiopia (see Isa 11:11) or to give the passage the meaning that the converted Ethiopians will bring the dispersed Israelites home. These words are absent from the Peshitta and among the witnesses to the Septuagint they are absent from Codex Alexandrinus, Codex Marchalianus, and nine of the manuscripts collated by Holmes and Parsons.

God's purpose (2:1–3; 3:11–13). In the concluding and climactic oracle of his prophecy, Zephaniah appropriates that future in a vision of great power and beauty (3:14–18a).[30]

So real is the future of Jerusalem and the covenant people for Zephaniah that he breaks forth into praise and celebration. So powerful is his hope that the somber, foreboding storm clouds that have overshadowed his ministry from the beginning give way to dazzling sunlight. Excitedly he summons Jerusalem to cry out for joy, to shout, to rejoice, to exult with all her heart (v. 14). The reason is that the LORD has removed her judgment, cleared away her enemies and Israel's king, the LORD, is in her midst; she need fear evil no more (v. 15). Jerusalem is not the only place where there is reason to rejoice; this is also an occasion of great joy for God himself. The portrait of God that follows is one of the most remarkable in the Bible. It is both earthy and sublime, both unabashedly anthropomorphic and delicately spiritual. God is King and as such the sublime ground of all existence. Yet his love for Israel and his involvement in his life is like that of a young man in the prime of his manly strength, who takes pride in defending his people and openly delights in them as a father in his son, as a bridegroom in his bride.

The divine joy is such that God cannot contain himself. The vocabulary of rejoicing is virtually exhausted in expressing his delight: "He will rejoice over thee with gladness, he composes a song expressive of his love,[31] he will joy over thee with spirited singing." Is not this marvelous picture of the rejoicing, loving, singing God indebted to the African heritage of Zephaniah?

The roots of the prophet Zephaniah is not the only subject of the Bible that does not permit the satisfaction of a definitive answer. A careful examination of this matter, however, points persuasively to the conclusion that he was of both royal and Ethiopian ancestry. There is nothing that stands in the way of the identification of the Hezekiah of Zephaniah's ancestry with King Hezekiah, nor with the identification of Kushi with one of Ethiopian descent. These identifications are so intrinsically natural, in fact, that the text requires qualifying notes to prevent them. Moreover, they

30. With the majority of scholars the writer views the first line of v. 18 as belonging to and completing the thought of v. 17. The remainder of ch. 3 I regard as a later addition, for it presupposes the exile. Those addressed have already suffered disaster and borne reproach (v. 18b–c), they have been oppressed and put to shame (v. 19), and they have been scattered abroad so that they must be brought home and their fortune restored (v. 20).

31. In this translation of a famous crux, I follow Sabottka, *Zephanja*, 132–34.

are powerfully enhanced by the fact of the alliance between Judah and the Ethiopian dynasty of Egypt in revolt against Assyria, and by Zephaniah's preaching. Zephaniah's significance depends, of course, not on his roots but on his message. But the fact that he is an Israelite prophet, probably also of Ethiopian origins, is in itself a message.

6

Africans and the Origin of the Worship of Yahweh[1]

It has always been puzzling to students of the Bible that Moses does not seem to know the name of God at the time of his call. After Moses turns aside to see the "great sight" of the burning bush and God commissions him to go to Pharaoh and bring the Israelites out of Egypt, Moses asks, "If I come to the Israelites and say to them, 'The God of your ancestors has sent me to you,' and they ask me, 'What is his name?' what shall I say to them?" (Exod 3:13 NRSV). God's response is to reveal the divine name as the LORD, that is, Yahweh.[2] The solemn affirmation with which Yahweh concludes the address to Moses, "This is my name forever, and this is my title for all generations," "seems to indicate that a new name was introduced into the circle of Moses."[3] What is implied by Exod 3:13–15 is confirmed by Exod 6:2–3. There God says to Moses, "I am Yahweh. I appeared to Abraham, Isaac, and Jacob as God Almighty, but by my name Yahweh I did not make myself known to them."

1. Dedicated to Dr. Charles B. Copher, Professor Emeritus of Old Testament at the Interdenominational Theological Center, Atlanta, GA, in celebration of his eightieth birthday and in appreciation for his contribution to biblical scholarship and to the spiritual health of America.

2. Lord of KJV, NRSV, and other modern translations represents the name of the covenant God of Israel, which sometime after the Babylonian Exile of 587–538 BCE, out of reverence, ceased to be generally spoken. To prevent the inadvertent utterance of the sacred name, the vowels of Adonai, Lord, were added to the consonants of the divine name, YHWH, directing one to say "Lord" or the equivalent. The original vocalization was therefore lost but in the judgment of most scholars was Yahweh.

3. Anderson, *Understanding the Old Testament*, 65.

I

Moses came to know God by the name Yahweh, not in Ur or Haran, the home of the patriarchs and matriarchs, or in Canaan, the promised land, but in a remote region far to the south of Canaan at a mountain that had long been home to Yahweh. The site of Moses's call was Mount Horeb (also called Mount Sinai), "the mountain of God" (Exod 3:1; 18:5; 1 Kgs 19:8) / "the mountain of Yahweh" (Num 10:33), traditionally identified with Jebel Musa ("Mountain of Moses") in the southern tip of the Sinai Peninsula. Yahweh was thought either to be enthroned upon or to descend from time to time to Horeb/Sinai from heaven (Exod 19:11, 18, 20; 24:10; 34:5; see Deut 33:16). As the special place of Yahweh's presence, the mountain was holy, so that Moses had to take off his sandals (Exod 3:5; see 19:12–13, 21–24).

Yahweh continues to be associated with Horeb/Sinai long after the departure of the Israelites. Moses asks Yahweh to accompany the Israelites to Canaan (Exod 34:9), but Yahweh declines Moses's request and instead sends an angel (Exod 32:34; 33:1–3; 23:20; see 33:12–17). More than a century after the covenant at Horeb/Sinai, when the newly settled tribes were suffering from Canaanite oppression, Yahweh came to their aid from "the region of Edom . . . yon Sinai" (Judg 5:4–5). When Elijah fled from Jezebel in search of spiritual renewal, he made a pilgrimage to "Horeb, the mount of God" (1 Kgs 19:8), and this was some four centuries after Moses.

With the building of the temple in Jerusalem, Yahweh's sacramental presence came to be located at the temple and Mount Zion (1 Kings 8). In the course of time an elaborate theology was developed affirming and celebrating Yahweh's presence in Zion (1 Sam 6; Pss 132; 46; 48; 76; 84; 122; Amos 1:2; Isa 8:18, etc.). Yet the new theology of Yahweh's presence in Zion never completely supplanted Yahweh's association with Horeb/Sinai. Yahweh continued to be identified as "the God of Sinai" (Ps 68:8 NRSV)[4] who "came from Sinai . . . from Mount Paran" (Deut 33:2; Hab 3:3; Ps 68:7–8; see Isa 63:1; Zech 9:14). The reason for this, according to Kyle McCarter,

4. NRSV retains and paraphrases *zeh sinay* (see NEB), which RSV and other modern translations omit as a gloss. Albright translates more literally, "The One of Sinai" ("A Catalogue of Early Hebrew Lyric Poems," 20). See also "Yahweh of Teman" in the inscriptions from Kuntillet 'Ajrud, which date from shortly before or after 800 BCE, in Emerton, "New Light on Israelite Religion," 2–3.

was "that the old Sinai tradition was so venerable and well known . . . so persistent and authentic that it couldn't be suppressed."[5]

If the Israelites were not the original worshipers of Yahweh, who was? Since at the time of his call Moses was a refugee in the "land of Midian" (Exod 2:15) tending the sheep of his father-in-law, Jethro (also called Reuel, Exod 2:18; Num 10:29), "the priest of Midian" (Exod 2:16; 3:1; 18:1), it would seem that the original worshipers of Yahweh were the Midianites. More particularly, Moses's in-laws are identified as Kenites (Num 10:29; Judg 1:16; 4:11), apparently a clan of the Midianites or possibly the priestly order of the Midianites. The homeland of the Midianites and Kenites was northwestern Arabia east of the Gulf of Aqabah, but they lived a nomadic existence and made their home at times in Moab (Gen 36:35), the Jordan Valley (Num 25:1, 6–7; 31:2–3; Josh 13:21), Canaan (Judg 6:1–6, 33; 7:1), and Sinai (Num 10:29), the site of the traditional location of the mount of revelation.

Some exciting archaeological finds support the biblical material connecting the Kenites with Yahweh. During excavations of the temple of Amon at Soleb in Nubia, two topographical lists were found that date from the time of Amenhotep III (1402–1363 BCE).[6] They include, among others, six references to lands of the Shasu, a partially nomadic and partially sedentary social class somewhat like the Hapiru.[7] One of these place names is called "the land of Shasu-*yhw*." Other names in this series, as Seir (Edom) and Laban (Deut 1:1), place "the land of Shasu-*yhw*" in southern Palestine.[8] W. F. Albright identified *yhw* as an abbreviated form of Yahweh and affirmed that "there is not the slightest doubt that we have here the same name as Hebrew Yahweh attached to a place or district of Eastern

5. McCarter, "The Origin of Israelite Religion," 128.

6. Giveon, "Toponymes Ouest-Asiatiques à Soleb," 244, col. 4A2; Giveon, *Les bédouins Shosou des documents égyptiens*, nos. 6a, 16a; Herrmann, "Der Name Jhw in den Inschriften von Soleb," 213–16.

7. See Ward, "Shasu," 1165–67. For depictions of some Shasu in the temple of Amon at Karnak, see Pritchard, ed., *The Ancient Near East in Pictures*, nos. 323, 326–29 and 287–88.

8. Place names adjacent to "the land of the Shasu-*yhw*" in the Soleb text were illegible but were restored on the basis of a copy of the Soleb inscription made at Amara West (near Soleb) during the reign of Rameses II (1290–1224 BCE). The place name *yhw*, apparently located in southern Palestine, is also found in two inscriptions from the time of Rameses III (1198–1166 BCE) at Medinat Habu. Gardiner published a text in 1917 that appears to contain the name *yhw* ("The Tomb of a Much-Travelled Theban Official," 36). The reading is uncertain, but if correct attests Yahweh as a place name as early as the Eleventh Dynasty (see Görg, "Jahwe—ein Toponym?" 7–9).

Palestine or the Negeb (including perhaps Midian) in the early thirteenth century BCE."[9] "The land of Shasu-*yhw*" comprehends both a place and its inhabitants,[10] designating the land of the Yahweh-Shasu in distinction from other Shasu lands. Is this name based on the presence of a temple of Yahweh somewhere in the land of the Shasu?[11] Or does the name relate specifically to the holy mountain where Yahweh was thought to dwell?[12]

At Timna, some eighteen miles north of the Gulf of Aqabah, large pieces of heavy red and yellow flax and wool fabric with beads woven into it and a copper snake image were discovered in a former temple of Hathor, Egyptian goddess of mining. Regularly placed postholes in the floor identified the fabric as the remnants of a tent shrine. "Much beautifully decorated Midianite pottery" and the location of Timna within Midianite territory confirmed that the tent shrine and copper snake image were Midianite. The date of the site where these objects were found (site 200, stratum 2) was determined to be ca. 1150 BCE.[13] Since a tent shrine (Exod 26; 36) and a copper serpent (Num 21:6–9; 2 Kgs 18:4) are associated with the worship of Yahweh among the Israelites, their presence at Timna implies worship of Yahweh by the Midianites and Kenites.

Moses's presence in Midian at the time of his call, the location of Horeb/Sinai in or near the land of Midian, the place "land of the Shasu-*yhw*" in Midianite territory attested in the Egyptian topographical texts

9. Albright, Review of *L'épithète divine Jahvé Seba' ôt* by B. Wambacq, Cross calls the Soleb inscriptions "the earliest appearance of what appears to be the independent form of the name [Yahweh]. . . . No other suggested occurrences seem to withstand close linguistic scrutiny" (*Canaanite Myth and Hebrew Epic*, 61–62). This judgment is also affirmed by Redford, *Egypt, Canaan, and Israel in Ancient Times*, 272–73, 418.

The determination of the original pronunciation of foreign words in Egyptian is difficult so that scholars differ slightly on the correct vocalization of *yhw*. Albright vocalizes Ya-h-we(a) (ibid.) or Y(a)hw(e?) (*Yahweh and the Gods of Canaan*, 171), while F. M. Cross thinks *yhw* should probably be read Ya-h-wi (ibid.).

10. Görg, "Jahwe—ein Toponym?" 11, 14.

11. So Giveon, "The Cities of Our God (2 Sam 10:12)," 415–16.

12. So Herrmann, "Der alttestamentliche Gottesname," 289; Knauf, *Midian*, 46–48. Johnson translates *zeh sinay* of Ps 68:8 as "Him of Sinai" or more literally "Who is Sinai" (*Sacral Kingship in Ancient Israel*, 71 n. 1).

13. Rothenberg, *Timna, Valley of the Biblical Copper Mines*, 112–89. For the location of Timna, see the map on 15; for examples of Midianite pottery, see plates 48–54; for a description of the remnants of the tent shrine and an artist's reconstruction of it, see 151–52; for the copper serpent with the gilded head, see 159, plates xix and xx; for a photograph of the temple area, see 189–190. See also Rothenberg and Glass, "Midianite Pottery," 65–24.

before the time of Moses, and the discovery of the tent shrine and copper serpent at Timna seem to confirm that the original worshipers of Yahweh were the Midianites and Kenites.

II

If the Midianites and Kenites were the original worshipers of Yahweh, and if Moses first came to know Yahweh at the time of his call, then the Israelites must have adopted the worship of Yahweh from the Midianites and Kenites. Strong support for this inference comes from Exod 18:5–12. After the liberation of the Israelites, Jethro meets Moses, rejoices in what Yahweh has done, and *presides* at a sacrificial meal. What is most remarkable about this is that Aaron, the archetypal high priest, and the elders of Israel are Jethro's guests. Declares H. P. Smith, "The fact of a foreigner officiating at a sacrifice at which Aaron and the elders of Israel are only guests is so extraordinary and so much out of harmony with later Hebrew thought that we are compelled to see in this account a very ancient tradition . . . [according to which] Yahweh was formally introduced to Israel by a Midianite priest."[14] Significantly, Moses is not mentioned, presumably because he had already been introduced to the proper rites for the worship of Yahweh.

Not only does Jethro preside at the sacrificial meal at which Aaron and the elders of Israel are guests, he gives advice and instructions to Moses concerning the administration of justice (Exod 18:13–27), "which was regarded as a religious rather than a civil function."[15] Concluding his instructions to Moses, Jethro says, "If you do this, *and God so commands you*, then you will be able to endure, and all these people will go to their home in peace" (Exod 18:23, emphasis added). This manner of speaking means that Jethro acts not merely as a concerned father-in-law but authoritatively as the priest of Midian.

In the light of the discovery of the tent shrine and copper snake at Timna "it seems at least plausible to consider the tented-shrine, the *Ohel Mo'ed*, of Israel's nomadic desert faith to be somehow connected with the relationship between Moses and Jethro."[16] The Midianite copper snake found at Timna could also account for Moses's introduction of the copper serpent, Nehushtan (Num 21:6–9; 2 Kgs 18:4), into Israelite worship. It is

14. Smith, *The Religion of Israel*, 50–51.

15. Rowley, *From Joseph to Joshua*, 151.

16. Rothenberg, *Timna*, 184.

difficult to conceive of the Israelites adopting the worship of Yahweh from the Kenites without including certain cult objects.

The union of different ethnic and political groups in the biblical world was conditional on the worship of a common deity. The Israelites were closely related ethnically to the Moabites, Ammonites, and Edomites but remained distinct from them because the Moabites, Ammonites, and Edomites worshiped deities other than Yahweh. The Kenites, however, did become one with the Israelites, and this very fact presupposes that both peoples worshiped Yahweh. Moses urged the Kenite Hobab to go with Israel to Canaan and in effect "offered Hobab a share in the promised land" (Num 10:29–32, note specially v. 32).[17] Hobab accepted, and the Kenites "went up with the people of Judah . . . into the wilderness of Judah which lies in the Negeb near Arad; and they went and settled with the people" (Judg 1:16 RSV; see 1 Sam 27:10).[18] The Kenites were treated with special favor by Saul (1 Sam 15:6) and David (1 Sam 30:29) and are reckoned with the tribe of Judah in 1 Chr 2:3–55.

Significantly, the occurrences of personal names compounded with an abbreviated form of Yahweh (*yeho* or *yo* at the beginning and *yahu* or *yah* at the end), with one exception, are found only from the time of Moses. Abraham means "the [divine] ancestor is exalted"; Sarah, "princess"; Isaac, "he laughs"; Ishmael, "God hears"; Jacob, "he supplants"; Israel, "God rules." Moses and Aaron have Egyptian names, but Joshua (Hebrew *Jeho*shua), Moses's successor, means "Yahweh is salvation." Names compounded with

17. Levine, *Numbers 1–20*, 316, 335.

18. Hobab's acceptance and guidance are omitted in order to give precedence to the divine guidance of the ark in Num 10:33–34 (Seebas, "Zu Num X 33f," 111–13). See also Weinfeld, "The Tribal League at Sinai," 306–7. Weinfeld emends *ʾaph hōbēb ʿammîm*, "surely loving peoples" in Deut 33:3 to *hōbāb ʿimmām*, "also Hobab was with them" (ibid., 307–8 and n. 30).

Mazar suggests that the passage on the Kenites in Judg 1:16 was included in Judges 1 "to accentuate the special importance of this noble clan, which most likely derived from a religious-cultic tradition from its nomadic days" ("The Sanctuary of Arad and the Family of Hobab the Kenite," in *Biblical Israel*, 73). Mazar thinks that the Kenites, one of whose ancestors was Irad (Gen 4:18), may have given the name Arad to the region where they settled and through their role as priests established the most important "sanctified spot" in the Negeb of Arad, which became the site of a sanctuary dating from the tenth to the seventh century BCE. (ibid., 75–77). Freedman considers it likely that "the inscriptions and drawings at such an out-of-the-way place as Kuntillet ʿAjrud may reflect the ancient form of Yahwism practiced by Midianites and other desert people" ("Who Is Like Thee Among the Gods?," 329).

Yahweh, as *Jo*nathan, *Jo*tham,[19] Athaliah (Hebrew, Athal*yah*), and Isaiah (Hebrew, yesha*yahu*), become especially frequent from the time of David. The absence of names formed with Yahweh prior to the time of Moses and their increasing frequency after Moses is hard to account for if Yahweh was known to the Israelites before Moses.

The leadership in the worship of Yahweh passed to the Israelites, but Kenites stand out from time to time as zealous champions of Yahweh. The Kenite woman Jael (Judg 5:24; 4:17) struck a critical blow to free the people of Yahweh from Canaanite oppression by killing the Canaanite general Sisera (Judg 5:24–27; 4:17–21).[20] When the northern kingdom had seriously compromised its loyalty to Yahweh during the reign of Ahab and Jezebel and their son Joram, the Kenite Jehonadab (1 Chr 2:55) supported Jehu's revolution and a return to the pure worship of Yahweh (2 Kgs 10:15–16, 23).[21] When Jerusalem was about to be invaded by Nebuchadnezzar, Jeremiah invited the Rechabites, an order founded by Jehonadab who lived in tents and refused to drink wine, to find refuge in the temple and commended them as the one group in Judah who had been obedient and kept the faith (Jeremiah 35). In the judgment of Karl Budde, the zeal of these Kenites, attested in texts over a period of four and one-half centuries, "goes far beyond a mere *participation* in the Yahweh religion. On the contrary, everything indicates that they did not adopt the worship of Yahweh from others, but were conscious of being the proper, the genuine, the original worshippers of Yahweh."[22]

Interestingly, there are striking similarities between the Kenites and the Levites.[23] The Kenites eschewed settled life and lived in tents (see Hab

19. Influenced by the tradition of spelling names established by the Latin Vulgate, English translations represent the Hebrew letter *y* by *j* in these names.

20. Apparently Jael and her husband Heber separated from fellow Kenites in order to establish a cult center at the sacred "oak of za-anan-nim" (Judg 4:11). That Jael was a prominent person is attested by the dating of the Canaanite oppression in the days of Shamgar and "in the days of Jael" (Judg 5:6). Mazar thinks Jael may have rallied the people to support Shamgar in the same way that Deborah rallied support for Barak, and that it was in her role as charismatic leader that she killed Sisera ("The Sanctuary of Arad," 73–75).

21. Morgenstern thinks Jehonadab "must have been an influential and active participant in [the Elisha-Jehu] revolution" and that he or his forebears also influenced and participated in Asa's reformation ("The Oldest Document of the Hexateuch," 115–16).

22. Budde, *The Religion of Israel to the Exile*, 21.

23. See Schmökel, "Jahwe und die Keniter," 217–19; Heyde, *Kain, der erste Jahwe-Verehrer*, 29–32.

3:7; Judg 5:24; Jer 35:5–10). The Levites had no tribal land, but they did have pasturelands scattered among the other tribes (Josh 21), a remarkable circumstance in Israel, where the promise and gift of the land played such a central role. The Kenites were zealous champions of the pure worship of Yahweh; so were the Levites. So zealous were the Levites that they disowned brothers and sisters and ignored their children in support of the true worship of Yahweh (Deut 33:8–9; Exod 32:25–29). The Kenites were scribes and presumably also teachers (1 Chr 2:55); the Levites were entrusted with the responsibility of teaching Israel Yahweh's ordinances and law (Deut 33:10). Since the early home of the Levites was near that of the Kenites (Num 26:57–58; Judg 17:7, 9), the two groups would have had occasion to get to know one another. Were the Kenites a priestly order (note the designation of Jethro as the priest of the people or country of Midian) whose role was adopted by the Levites? Did, in fact, the Levites absorb and take over the function of the Kenites as a priestly order?[24]

It was noted at the beginning of this essay that both Exod 3:13–15 and 6:2–3 affirm that Israel first came to know God by the name Yahweh in the time of Moses. On the other hand, there is the statement in Gen 4:26 that humankind began to worship Yahweh in the time of Enosh, the grandson of Adam. And there are a number of passages where Yahweh is identified as active in the life of the patriarchs and matriarchs, even addressing them as, "I am Yahweh" (Gen 15:7; 28:13). How does one account for this apparent contradiction?

The statement that the worship of Yahweh began in the time of Enosh (Gen 4:26) and the designations of God by the name Yahweh before the time of Moses belong to the J version of Israel's early history.[25] Originating in Judah, the J version was heir to the traditions of the Kenites, who after leaving their homeland and guiding Israel to Canaan, became a component of the tribe of Judah. As the original worshipers of Yahweh, the Kenites could say that the worship of Yahweh went back to time immemorial (Gen

24. Binns calls attention to three fragmentary inscriptions from a Minaean colony at *el-'Ola* in northwest Arabia that contain the Arabic words *lavi'u, lavi'at* (fem.), obviously the equivalent of Levite, Levitess, to designate a priest. The normal Arabic term for priest, however, is *rišw* or *šauwâ*. Since these Minaeans, apparently a trading colony, were a thousand miles from their homeland and living among the Midianites, they must have borrowed the terms *lavi'u, lavi'at* from the Midianites. This means that *Levite* was a Midianite word, and therefore that the Israelites must also have borrowed the term ("Midianite Elements in Hebrew Religion," 348–50).

25. See, e.g., Schmidt, *Old Testament Introduction*, for the identification, characterization, and dates of the J, E, and P versions of Israel's early history.

4:26)—and those who shared their traditions could also say this. The usage of Yahweh by J is also an acknowledgment that although Israel had not always known God by the name Yahweh, it was Yahweh who had been active in their history and in the history of humankind from the beginning. The E (Exod 3:13–15) and P (Exod 6:2–3) versions of Israel's beginnings preserve the more accurate memory that for Israel the worship of God by the name Yahweh began in the time of Moses. (Note the affirmation in Hos 12:9 and 13:4, "I am Yahweh your God from the land of Egypt.")

One of the most unpleasant features of the Bible is numerous references to rivalry and dissension within Israel. The root of this according to Murray Newman was the "unstable fusion" of two different experiences of Yahweh resulting from the Israelite adoption of the worship of Yahweh from the Kenites.[26] Scholars have observed that a close bond existed among Judah, Simeon, some Levites, Othniel, Caleb, and the Kenites. These allied tribes entered Canaan from the south independently of the other tribes (Num 21:1–3; 13–14; Judg 1:1–21; Josh 15:14–19). Because of the unity of this southern group, a number of scholars have concluded that they were members of a league that had existed from before the time of Moses. Because of the association with the Kenites, it is possible that Judah, Simeon, some Levites, Othniel, and Caleb may have been worshipers of Yahweh before the Exodus. If so, they would have shared with the Kenites a traditional, priestly, hierarchical form of Yahwism. Moses and the tribes with him in Egypt, on the other hand, had a personal, charismatic, democratizing experience of Yahweh. Thus when Moses rejoined fellow Levites, Judah, Simeon, Othniel, Caleb, and the Kenites after the Exodus, two fundamentally different experiences of Yahweh were brought together with resulting rivalry and dissension over who were the rightful and authoritative custodians of the worship of Yahweh (see Exod 15:22–17:1–7; 32:25–29; Numbers 11–20).

The one exception to names formed with Yahweh before the time of Moses is Jochebed, the mother of Moses (Exod 6:20; Num 26:59). While scholars are divided over whether the initial component of *Jo*chebed is an abbreviated form of Yahweh, for the purposes of this study Jochebed is assumed to be a genuine Yahweh name. That Israelites before Moses could have known Yahweh is further supported by Yahweh's self-identification to Moses in Exod 3:6 as "the God of your father." If, as suggested previously, some Israelite tribes were associated with the Kenites before the Exodus,

26. Newman Jr., *The People of the Covenant*, 25–26, 72–101.

individual Israelites, as Moses's mother, through intermarriage could have been given Yahweh names.[27] And the God of an ancestor of Moses through his mother's lineage could have been Yahweh.[28] This supposition would also explain why Moses fled to Midian after killing the Egyptian supervisor of forced labor (Exod 2:11–15). "If he had some Kenite blood on his mother's side, it would not be surprising for him to flee to his mother's kindred when he could not remain in Egypt."[29]

III

The first to suggest that Israel adopted the worship of Yahweh from the Kenites was F. Wq. Ghillany, writing under the pseudonym of R. von der Alm, in 1862.[30] Since that time the "Midianite" or "Kenite hypothesis" has been widely accepted.[31] But so far as I know, no one who affirms the Kenite hypothesis has gone on to point out that the Kenites most likely were Africans. To be sure, the home of the Midianites and Kenites was centered around the Gulf of Aqabah, but Africans were not confined to the boundaries modern geographers have assigned to Africa. There is ample

27. See Rowley, *From Joseph to Joshua*, 159–60.

28. Hyatt, "Yahweh as 'The God of My Father,'" 135–36.

29. Rowley, "Moses and Monotheism," 56–57.

30. Ghillany, *Theologische Briefe an den Gebilden der deutschen Nation*, vol. 1, 216, 480 (cited by Meek, *Hebrew Origins*, 93 n. 18).

31. One of the first to popularize the Kenite hypothesis was Budde in *The Religion of Israel to the Exile*, ch 1. The best presentation and defense with full bibliography is by Rowley, *From Joseph to Joshua*, 149–61 and "Moses and Monotheism," 48–59. The arguments against the Kenite hypothesis by Buber (*Moses*, 94–98), Meek (*Hebrew Origins*, 92–99), and Brekelmans ("Exodus XVIII and the Origin of Yahwism in Israel," 215–24) are effectively refuted by Rowley.

De Vaux's attempt to disprove the Kenite hypothesis by maintaining that the Kenites and Midianites had no relationship to each other has not commended itself to other scholars (de Vaux, "Sur l'origine kénite ou madianite du yahvisme," 28–32 and *The Early History of Israel*, 330–38).

Following Brekelmans, Fensham ("Did a Treaty between the Israelites and the Kenites Exist?" 51–54), Cody ("Exodus 18:12: Jethro Accepts a Covenant With the Israelites," 153–66), and Avishur ("Treaty Terminology in the Moses-Jethro Story [Ex 18:1–12]," 139–47) argue that Exod 18:1–12 is simply the account of the making of a covenant between Jethro and Moses and has nothing to do with the adoption of the worship of Yahweh from the Kenites. But the covenant relationship between the Kenites and Israel goes back to Moses's initial relationship to Jethro, as Weinfeld emphasizes ("The Tribal League at Sinai," 308).

evidence of an African presence before and during biblical times in Arabia, Transjordan, southern Palestine, and the Sinai Peninsula.

All except one of the sons of Kush, the eponymous ancestor of the Kushites or Ethiopians, are located in Arabia (Gen 10:7). Seba, Kush's oldest son, is associated with Kush and Egypt in Isa 43:3 and 45:14, placing him on the African mainland, more precisely according to Strabo (*Geographie* 16:4, 8, 10), on the African coast. The association of the Seba with Sheba (approximately identical with modern Yemen) in Ps 72:10 suggests that these two peoples belonged to a single kingdom, part of which was on the African mainland and part in Arabia. The other sons and grandsons of Kush are distributed along the northwestern coast of Arabia to the border of Edom (Gen 10:7–14).[32]

The Bible preserves the memory of Africans in the land of Midian in Hab 3:7, where Kushan stands parallel to Midian and evidently preserves the name of the ancient population of this region.[33] Extrabiblical evidence confirms the presence of Kushites in this part of the world before the time of Moses. In the Tale of Sinuhe (ca. 1950 BCE), the story of a high Egyptian official who fled Egypt and found refuge in Syria, Sinuhe names a certain Kenti-iaush from southern Kush who will vouch for his good character to his new Egyptian overlord.[34] The context in which this reference occurs points to Transjordan as the home of Kenti-iaush. Also, Egyptian Execration Texts from the nineteenth and eighteenth centuries BCE mention chieftains "of the tribes of Cush,"[35] which W. F. Albright locates in "the

32. See the identifications in Simons, *The Geographical and Topographical Texts of the Old Testament*; McCray, *The Black Presence in the Bible and the Table of Nations*, 82–85; Westermann, *Genesis 1–11*, 511–12, and the literature on Genesis 10, 495–96. Copher points out that the word *Kedar*, the name of a tribe in northwest Arabia (Isa 21:13–17; 60:6–7; Ezek 27:21) "and its derivatives range from 'to be dark' and 'swarthy' to 'very black,' 'dark skinned,' and 'dusky'" ("The Black Presence in the Old Testament," 152).

33. Kushan is a variant form of Kush in the same way that Kenan is of Kain and Lotan of Lot. The *-an* ending may be an Arabic element denoting ethnic origin. Four of the offspring of Abraham and Keturah, including Midian, have names that end in *-an*. From the parallelism with Midian in Hab 3:7, Kushan would seem to be an archaic, poetic synonym for Midian expressive of the dominant ethnic group of the Midianites. See Aharoni, *The Land of the Bible*, 146.

34. Pritchard, ed., *ANET*, 21, line 220. For the identification of the country of the ruler of line 220, see Posener, *Princes et pays d'Asie et de Nubie*, 88 and Aharoni, *The Land of the Bible*, 143–44.

35. Posener, *Princes et pays d'Asie et de Nubie*, 88–89. The Execration Texts are curses directed against certain rulers and groups who are identified by name and geographical location. The curses are written on pottery bowls, or the one to be cursed is represented

region from the Arnon southward into Midian, corresponding to the archaic Kushan of Hab 3:7, which appears as a synonym of Midian."[36]

A number of biblical passages refer to a legendary people variously called Anakim, Emim, Rephaim, and Zuzim or Zamzummim (Deut 2:10–11, 20) who were among the original inhabitants of Canaan (Num 13:28–29). They lived in Bashan (Deut 3:13), Philistia (Josh 11:22; see 2 Sam 21:16–22; 1 Chr 20:4–8), the hill country of Judah and Israel (Josh 11:21–22), and especially southern Judah (Num 13:22; Josh 14:12, 15; Judg 1:20). The most distinctive feature about these people was their great height (Num 13:32–33; Deut 1:28; 2:10, 21; 9:2; see Amos 2:9). King Og of Bashan, "one of the last of the Rephaim" (Deut 3:11; Josh 12:4; 13:12), had a bed nine cubits long and four cubits wide (Deut 3:11).[37]

Since the home of the Zuzim was Ham in northern Gilead (Gen 14:5),[38] a place name implying an African presence and located in the area called Kush in the extrabiblical material, and the Rephaim are mentioned in a list of people that includes the Kenites in Gen 15:19–20, were not these people Africans? Unusually tall persons may be found in every race, but this is characteristic only of Africans, especially those Africans nearest

---

by a stone, wood, or terra-cotta figurine that may or may not be inscribed. Groups of texts referring to rulers in Palestine-Syria were found at Thebes (now in Berlin), Mirgissa in Nubia, and Sakkara (now in Cairo and Brussels). Presumably these bowls and figurines were broken in order to subdue by sympathetic magic those beyond Egypt's direct control who were considered inimical to Egypt's political and commercial interests. Both the texts found at Thebes and Sakkara refer to two Kushite chieftains in a location that seems to coincide with that of Midian. The text cited by Posener is from the Cairo-Brussels group (E 50–51). For the publication, dating, and interpretation of the Execration Texts, see Thompson, *The Historicity of the Patriarchal Narratives*, 98–113.

[In his earlier writing Dr. Rice spelled Kush, Kushi, and Kushan with a C. In his later writing he spelled these words with a K, the favored spelling among Nubiologists. For consistency's sake, unless these words are in a quotation, they will be spelled with a K.]

36. Albright, "The Land of Damascus between 1850 and 1750 B.C.," n.8. Similarly, Helck, *Die Beziehungen Ägyptens zu Vorderasien im 3. und 2. Jahrtausend* v. *Chr*, 8.

There was also a district of Qusana-ruma, that is, "high Kushan" in North Syria in the thirteenth and twelfth centuries BCE mentioned in a list of Rameses III (Albright, *Archaeology and the Religion of Israel*, 205 n.49). For the text, see Edgerton and Wilson, *Historical Records of Ramses III*, 110. Is this Kush contiguous to the southern Kush of the Tale of Sinuhe (see n.33 of this study)?

37. Wilson, *Historical Records of Ramses III*, relates "the ruler of Iy'aneq" of the Egyptian Execration Texts to the Anakim (*ANET*, 328).

38. See Pritchard, ed., *The Harper Atlas of the Bible*, 33. Ham is included among the cities Thutmose III (ca. 1490–1436 BCE) claims to have subdued in his first Asiatic campaign (*ANET*, 242; Breasted, *Ancient Records of Egypt*, vol. 2, no. 402).

Palestine (see Isa 18:2; 45:4). In 1824 J. B. Buckingham wrote: "It is certainly a very marked peculiarity of the Arabs that inhabit this valley of the Jordan that they have flatter features, darker skins, and coarser hair than any other tribes."[39] Were these black Arabs described by Buckingham descended from an original African and Arab presence in Canaan?

Shur, the general area east of the Suez Canal and extending to the southern border of Canaan (Gen 16:7, 14; 20:1; 25:18; 1 Sam 15:7; 27:8), may have been the home of Hagar, the Egyptian maid of Sarah. When Hagar fled from Sarah, the angel of Yahweh came to her aid "in the wilderness . . . on the way to Shur" (Gen 16:7, 14). And it was in this general area—the wilderness of Paran—which lies directly south of Judah (Num 13:3, 26; Gen 14:6, 7), that Hagar raised Ishmael after she left Abraham's household (Gen 21:20, 21). (Note that Midian is adjacent to Paran according to 1 Kings 11:18.)

There is evidence also of an African presence at Ziklag, Gerar, and Gaza on the southwestern border of Canaan during and probably before biblical times. While pursuing the Amalakites who had raided his camp at Ziklag, David came upon an Egyptian nearby (1 Sam 30:11, 13). This incidental reference implies a larger African presence in the area. In fact, was it not from this area that David, who lived at Ziklag for a year and four months (1 Sam 27:7), recruited the Kushite soldier who later bore the news of Absalom's death (2 Sam 18:19–23)? (Or was the Kushite soldier of 2 Sam 18:19–23 the same person David found near Ziklag?)

Biblical references establish an African presence at Gerar on the southern border of Canaan (Gen 10:19) from the time of King Asa (913–873 BCE) to Hezekiah (715–687 BCE), a period of approximately two centuries. It was from Gerar that Zerah, the Ethiopian, invaded Judah (2 Chr 14:9–14) with an army of Ethiopians and Libyans (2 Chr 16:8) and almost defeated Asa.[40] Ethiopians were still at Gerar during the reign of King Jehoram of Judah (849–842 BCE). During his reign God stirred up against him "the anger of the Philistines and of the Arabs who are *near* [emphasis added] the Ethiopians" (2 Chr 21:16). The Philistines and Arabs did not live near the country of Ethiopia, which in biblical times lay to the south of Egypt (Ezek 29:10), but they were near Gerar. Ethiopians continued to reside at Gerar

39. Cited in Seale, "The Black Arabs of the Jordan Valley," 28.

40. Zerah is also the name of two Edomites (Gen 36:13, 17, 33; 1 Chr 1:37, 44) and a Simeonite (Num 26:13; 1 Chr 4:24), proof of the affinities of Zerah the Ethiopian with local peoples of Palestine.

until the time of Hezekiah (715–687 BCE) when they were displaced by the Simeonites (1 Chr 4:39–41).[41]

Famous for its great fertility (Gen 26:12) and "rich, good pasture" (1 Chr 4:39–41) and only six miles southeast of Gaza, the chief Egyptian administrative center in Canaan, Gerar seems to have been a military base and supply center. It was during the period following the expulsion of the Hyksos ca. 1550 BCE that Egypt was most concerned to maintain control of Canaan, and it may be that it was during this time that Gerar was established as a military base.[42] In the course of time, as Egyptian influence in Canaan declined, the Africans at Gerar settled down and became farmers. When the Simeonites invaded Gerar "they found rich, good pasture, and the land was very broad, quiet, and peaceful; for the former inhabitants there belonged to Ham" (1 Chr 4:41).

An African presence can also be assumed at Gaza, the southernmost coastal city in Canaan. Located on the road linking Europe, Asia, and Africa, the famous Via Maris, and the Egyptian capital in Canaan following the expulsion of the Hyksos, Gaza would have been the center of African administrators and military personnel.

More directly relevant to the African identity of the Midianites and Kenites is the reference to Moses's wife as a Kushite in Num 12:1.[43] A few have followed Josephus in understanding her as Tharbis, daughter of the

41. Reading Gerar with the Septuagint (Greek version) for the Masoretic (Hebrew) text Gedor in 1 Chr 4:39. See JB and TEV.

42. It is less likely that this Ethiopian colony was first established at Gerar by Shishaq in connection with his foray into Palestine in the fifth year of Rehoboam (ca. 918 BCE.) as Albright maintains in "Egypt and the Early History of the Negeb," 146–47. Hommel fails to see that Zerah's base of operation was Gerar, but does recognize the presence of Kushites in central Arabia that ultimately could have been Zerah's home ("Zerah the Kushite," 378–79).

An African presence in the general area of Gerar is attested by anthropoid clay coffins found at Tell el-Far'ah, Tell ed-Duweir, and Deir el-Balah (all south and west of Gerar), and at Beth-Shan. "These coffins represent without doubt an Egyptian burial tradition" (Ahlström, *The History of Ancient Palestine*, 320–24; see illustrations 7.29 and 7.30 in *Archaeology of the Land of the Bible*, by Mazar, 284).

From the Tell el-Amarna letters we know that Kushite troops were stationed in Byblos (EA 127:22, 36; 133:16–17; 131:13), Megiddo (246:Rev. 8), and Jerusalem (287:33, 72, 74). Letter 49 contains a request to Pharaoh for a Kushite physician. Many of these Kushites in Palestine and Syria no doubt became a part of the local population. See Klengel, "Das Land Kush in den Keilschrifttexten von Amarna," 227–32.

43. For the literary analysis of Num 12, see Burns, *Has the Lord Indeed Spoken Only Through Moses?*, 68–71, 77–79.

king of Ethiopia, who was smitten with love for Moses while he was in command of an Egyptian army that was besieging Saba (Meroë), the capital city of Ethiopia (*Ant.* 2:10).[44] But Josephus's elaboration of the biblical account seems to be based on a contemporary source of popular lore now lost, and its credibility is questionable.[45] The only wife of Moses the Bible knows is Zipporah, the daughter of the priest of Midian (Exod 2:16–21; 18:5–6).

Three objections have been raised to the identification of Moses' Kushite wife in Num 12:1 as Zipporah. First, "Kushite" normally designates one from the country that lies to the south of Egypt. Second, why would Miriam find fault with Zipporah when at the time of the controversy in Numbers 12 Moses had been married for some time and Zipporah was the mother of two sons (Exod 18:2–4)? Third, the statement "for he had married a Kushite woman" is interpreted by some to mean that Moses had recently married. But as pointed out previously, Kushites were not restricted to the region of modern Sudan but were to be found in Arabia, Transjordan, southern Palestine, and the Sinai Peninsula. The answer to the second and third objections is that Moses had left Zipporah behind when he returned to Egypt, and she became known to Miriam only after the liberation.[46]

Was Miriam's fault finding with Moses' Kushite wife racist?[47] The leprosy inflicted on Miriam would be a fitting penalty for a racist offense. But do we know Miriam's color? The real reason, as the rest of Numbers 12 makes clear, is resentment and jealousy over Moses's special role as the mediator of God's will. In fact, is not Miriam's complaint against Moses's Kushite wife in effect an accusation that Moses's role is based on his connection to the Kushite family of the priest of Midian, the original custodians of the worship of Yahweh?[48] God's reprimand to Aaron and Miriam sounds like a

44. So, e.g., Adamo, "The African Wife of Moses," 230–37.

45. See Shinan, "Moses and the Ethiopian Woman" 66–78; Feldman, *Josephus and Modern*, 151–52.

46. See Milgrom, *Numbers*, 93.

47. See Felder, "Race, Racism, and the Biblical Narratives," 42. The rabbis understood "Kushite" to connote beauty as well as ethnic origin. According to the rules of gematria, the numerical value of Kushite (*kûšîṯ*) in Hebrew equals "beautiful of appearance" (*yep̱aṯ mar'eh*). Rashi states that "Because of her beauty she was called 'the Aethiopian' just as a man calls his handsome son 'Moor'" (*Pentateuch With Rashi's Commentary: Numbers*, 59). In the Jewish tradition of interpretation *'l 'dwt* is taken to mean "on behalf of" rather than "because of" (NRSV) and Miriam and Aaron are understood to have spoken in Zipporah's interest "because they regarded her to have been wronged by Moses" (ibid., 192).

48. See with a different emphasis, Bailey, "Africans in Old Testament Poetry and Narratives," 179–80.

refutation of this charge. Moses's special role, God asserts, is not based on any connection to his Kushite wife and in-laws, but on a uniquely personal and intimate relationship between God and Moses (Num 12:7–8; see Exod 33:11; Num 11:24–30; Deut 34:1–12). Was there also professional rivalry between Miriam the prophet (Exod 15:20, see Mic 6:4) and Zipporah, "apparently a priestess in her own right" (see Exod 4:24–26)?[49]

IV

The Kenite hypothesis does not mean that Moses and the Israelites only learned a new name for God from the Kenites.[50] The new name entailed a new conception of God, proper forms of worship, and a new lifestyle in conformity with the worship of the bearer of the new name. That Jethro/Reuel was the priest of Midian and Moses's instructor in the administration of justice presupposes that the Kenites had old and well-established rites for the worship of Yahweh and legal traditions. (Note that Zipporah was well informed about how to approach Yahweh when Moses was threatened because he was not circumcised.) Julian Morgenstern[51] and H. H. Rowley[52] maintain that the so-called Ritual Decalogue of Exod 34:14–26 is Kenite in origin. Hartmut Schmökel goes so far as to say that the if-then laws of the Covenant Code (Exod 20:22–23:33) were adopted from the Kenites.[53]

49. Cross, *Canaanite Myth and Hebrew Epic*, 200. See Robinson, "The Jealousy of Miriam," 428–32 and Weems, *Just a Sister Away*, 74–81. There may also be overtones of the rivalry between the Mushite and Aaronide branches of the priesthood in Numbers 12. See Coats, *Rebellion in the Wilderness*, 261–64; Cross, *Canaanite Myth and Hebrew Epic*, 204.

50. This point is forcefully made by Heyde, *Kain, der erste Jahwe-Verehrer*, 34.

51. Morgenstern, "The Oldest Document of the Hexateuch," 1–138; Morgenstern, "The Kenite Code," 88–91. Morgenstern argues that the Decalogue of Exod 34:14–26 together with certain narrative portions of Exod 33, 34; Num 10:29–32, and the original of Exodus 18 were once part of an independent Kenite document.

Vischer thinks Kenite traditions have been preserved in Genesis 4; Exodus 18; Numbers 22; 24; and in the narratives of the Wilderness Wandering centering at Kadesh (Exod 15:22–17:16; Num 10:11–20:13). Also, Vischer finds traces of matriarchal thinking in the portrayal of Eve in Gen 4:1–16 and in the role of Deborah in Judges 5, which he attributes to Kenite influence (*Jahwe der Gott Kains*, 36–40, 64, 74–75).

52. Rowley, "Moses and the Decalogue," 88–91. Rowley dates the Decalogue of Exod 34:14–26 earlier than Morgenstern, relates it to those tribes that entered Canaan from the south, and allows for some modifications to adapt to life in Canaan.

53. Schmökel, "Jahwe und die Keniter," 224–26.

George Buchanan Gray conjectures that in the original form of Exodus 18 Jethro teaches Moses the oracular method for discerning Yahweh's will for difficult cases and also instructs him in the sacrificial system, "and thus the Hebrew priesthood is affiliated to the Midianite." Gray thinks that modifications were later made to Exodus 18 to obscure Israel's dependence on Midian.[54] L. Elliott Elliott-Binns, admitting that he may be overstating things, suggests that the tabernacle, incense altar, technical terms for sacrifice, and the ceremonies of the Day of Atonement were borrowed from or influenced by the Midianites.[55]

Most important of all, Israel came to know that Yahweh, the God of the Kenites, was a God who acts on behalf of the oppressed. There is a significant difference between the God of the patriarchs and matriarchs and the God of the Exodus.

"Yahweh the redeemer of a new people from bondage in Egypt is clearly new."[56] As descendants of Cain, the Kenites of old had worshiped One whose nature it was to act with compassion and to defend the vulnerable (Gen 4:1–16). Israel's experience of liberation verified these qualities of Yahweh in a dramatic way (Exod 18:1–11). And Israel's response to Yahweh in gratitude and commitment added a new dimension that deepened and enriched the original understanding of Yahweh.[57]

In addition to their contributions in religion, the Kenites, whose forebears were the progenitors of civilization according to Gen 4:17–22, enriched the cultural and material life of the Israelites. As scribes (1 Chr 2:55), the Kenites may have taught the art of writing to the Israelites.[58] According to Nelson Glueck, the Kenites, "whose very name reveals that they were smiths, . . . were the ones in all probability who introduced the Israelites to the arts of mining and metallurgy."[59] And in the judgment of

54. Gray, *Sacrifice in the Old Testament* (New York: KTAV, 1971), 206–8. See also Stade, "Das Kainzeichen," 307; Vischer, *Jahwe der Gott Kains*, 8–10, 37.

55. Binns, "Midianite Elements in Hebrew Religion," 337–54. Stade argues that the sign of Exod 13:9, 16; Deut 6:8; 11:18 (which later led to the practice of wearing phylacteries) was identical with or related to the mark of Cain ("Das Kainzeichen," 308–17).

56. Freedman, "Who Is Like Thee?," 329.

57. See Rowley, *From Joseph to Joshua*, 156 and "Moses and Monotheism," 57–58.

58. Schmökel cites with approval this suggestion by Sellin, "Jahwe und die Keniter," 224–26.

59. Glueck, "Kenites and Kenizzites," 22.

W. F. Albright, "it is quite possible" that the twelve-tribe organization of the Israelites "was suggested to Moses by his Midianite father-in-law."[60]

Not least of the legacies of the Kenites is their willingness to share their faith with others and their zeal for their faith when it was threatened. Jethro/Reuel cordially welcomed Moses into his family, rejoiced in what Yahweh had done in the liberation from Egyptian bondage, initiated Aaron and others into the worship of Yahweh, and instructed Moses in the role of priest and the administration of justice. Moreover, the Kenites joined Moses and the newly liberated tribes, guided them to Canaan, shared leadership and their ancient traditions with them, and mentored them in the rudiments of civilization. As a result, a bonding of the most diverse groups based on faith in Yahweh took place and a new people, Israel, was created with a sense of mission to "all the families of the earth" (Gen 12:3). This new people included not only the Kenites and those tribes who called Jacob father, but also the mixed multitude that went up with Moses from Egypt and many from the motley welter of peoples in Canaan deposited there by the ebb and flow of migrations from Africa, Asia, and Europe, including among others Amorites, Arameans, Arabs, Canaanites, Kushites, Egyptians, Hittites, and Philistines. Conversely, when Israel was in danger or about to compromise its commitment to Yahweh, a Jael, a Jehonadab, or the Rechabites were there to rally Israel and call it back to its true identity and destiny as Yahweh's covenant people.

V

While the Bible nowhere states explicitly that the Kenites were the original worshipers of Yahweh or that the Israelites adopted the worship of Yahweh from them, the Kenite hypothesis does shed light on a number of biblical passages and problems of interpretation. It accounts for the ancient and persistent association of Yahweh with a holy mountain in or near the land of Midian. That Yahweh was known in the region of Midian long before the Exodus is confirmed by the place name, "the land of shasu-*yhw*," attested in Egyptian topographical texts from the time of Amenhotep III. The Midianite tent shrine and copper serpent found at Timna provide tangible evidence for the worship of Yahweh among the Midianites and Kenites.

The assumption that the Israelites adopted the worship of Yahweh from the Kenites explains why Moses did not know the name of Yahweh

60. Albright, "Moses in Historical and Theological Perspective," 126–27.

at the time of his call, why Jethro officiated at a sacrifice where Aaron and the elders of Israel were present, and why Jethro gave instructions to Moses about the administration of justice. The Kenite hypothesis also provides an explanation for the union of the Kenites and Israelites, the giving of names compounded with Yahweh from the time of Moses, the zeal of the Kenites for the pure worship of Yahweh, the similarities of the Levites to the Kenites, the different traditions of the beginning of the worship of Yahweh, the persistent rivalry and dissension within Israel, and the reason Moses fled to Midian rather than some other place when it was no longer safe for him to stay in Egypt. No one of these considerations is decisive, but taken together they have a cumulative weight that is impressive.[61]

The location of the descendants of Kush in Arabia in Gen 10:7, the identification of Kushan with Midian in Hab 3:7, the reference to a Palestinian Kush in the Tale of Sinuhe, the mention of the tribes of Kush in Transjordan and Midian in the Egyptian Execration Texts, the place Ham in northern Galilee, the unusually tall inhabitants of Canaan prior to the Israelite settlement, and the evidence of Africans at Shur, Ziklag, Gerar, and Gaza document an African presence in Canaan long before Moses. This does not prove that the Kenites were Africans but does make it a credible inference. If Moses's Kushite wife in Num 12:1 is Zipporah, as I have argued, it is clear that Miriam and the biblical author regarded her and her kindred as Africans.[62]

61. After carefully considering the arguments for and against the Kenite hypothesis, Ringgren concludes: "Of the many theories explaining the origin of the religion of Yahweh, the Kenite hypothesis is the only one to which a certain probability attaches" (*Hannemann*, 34). For Staubli the discovery of the tent shrine at Timna gives "great probability" to the thesis of the Midianite-Kenite origin of the worship of Yahweh (*Das Image der Nomaden im Alten Israel*, 231). While not concerned with the Kenite hypothesis as such, Ahlström gives powerful support to it when he says: "It is likely that some clans of Edomite origin migrated to the central hill country of Palestine, taking with them the deity Yahweh" (*The History of Ancient Palestine*, 417). And Sadler Jr. pertinently asks: "Why would a group intentionally create the problem of an ethnically unrelated and distinct group, present in a significant manner at Sinai, at the defining event of the Israelite nation?" ("The Kenite Hypothesis Revisited," 18).

62. Calvin cites Bochart, who "endeavors to prove that the Kushites and Midianites were the same people"; and Shuckford (vol. 1, 166; edit. 1743) states his opinion that 'by the land of Kush is always meant some part of Arabia.' Habakkuk 3:7 . . . seems to corroborate this view." (*Commentaries on the Last Four Books of Moses*, 43 n.1).

7

The Alleged Curse on Ham

Genesis 9:18–29 has been popularly understood to mean that Ham was cursed, and this understanding has often been used to justify oppression of African people, the descendants of Ham. The text gives the impression that Ham offended his father Noah and because of this was cursed, but a careful reading of the passage reveals that this is not so, but rather that Canaan was the offender and was the one cursed. Confusion has arisen because Genesis is not a book in the modern sense, but an editorial synthesis of different traditions of Noah's family. Genesis 9:18–29 is concerned with giving an account of the political relationships between the Israelites, the Philistines, and the Canaanites in biblical times and has nothing to do with race. In fact, the Bible knows nothing of a curse on Ham and nowhere does it have anything negative to say about Africans because of their race. The theological heartbeat of the Bible is that we are all sons and daughters of God, that we are all related to one another as members of a family, that each one of us, whatever our race, ethnicity, and nationality, is special and precious to God, and that we were created for companionship with God—and fellowship with one another.

One of the most damaging misconceptions of the Bible is that it sanctions a curse on African people because Ham was cursed. Since Ham is regarded as the father of African people, this belief implies that Ham's descendants are also cursed. Incalculable harm has resulted from this supposition. It has provided a theological justification to Caucasian Americans and others for feelings of superiority, prejudice, and actions that are oppressive to African Americans. Conversely, this assumption has created resentment and anger among African Americans and caused many to reject the Bible.

The tragedy is that the belief that Ham was cursed rests on an erroneous interpretation of the Bible. The authority claimed for the curse on Ham is Gen 9:18–29, but this passage is complex and subject to misunderstanding.

A Careful Reading of Genesis 9:18–29

This passage is made up of three distinct parts. The centerpiece is a story in vv. 20–27 about Noah's discovery of wine and how this affected relationships between him and his sons. This story is framed by a summary statement in vv. 18–19 that the sons of Noah were the ancestors of all the peoples of the biblical world (*CEV*), and by the conclusion to the genealogy of Noah from Genesis 5:28–29.

According to Gen 9:18–19, Shem, Ham, and Japheth went forth from the ark, and in obedience to God's command (9:1, 7), peopled the whole earth. These verses condense a long history but no details are given. The concern is to make clear the identity of the ancestors of the various peoples of the biblical world and to establish that it was only from "these three" that all the peoples of the world are descended. The results of the procreative activity of Shem, Ham, and Japheth are given in Genesis 10. There, some seventy different peoples are listed and all are identified as descendants of Shem, Ham, and Japheth. Thus Gen 9:18–19 anticipate and prepare the reader for the extraordinary expansion of humankind from the three sons of Noah recorded in chapter 10.

Genesis 9:28–29 connect back to Genesis 5, take up, and bring to a close the genealogy and the life of Noah. In keeping with the interest of Genesis 5, Gen 9:28–29 informs us that Noah lived three hundred fifty years after the flood, "and died at the age of 950." A regular feature of the genealogy of Noah's ancestors is that after their first-born, they all had "more children" (Gen 5:4, 7, 10, 13, 16, 19, 22, 26, 30). Noticeable by its absence is any reference in 9:28–29 to Noah having other sons and daughters after the birth of Shem, Ham, and Japheth. This relates 9:28–29 to the emphasis in 9:18–19 that it was only from "these three" sons of Noah that all humankind is descended.

The story of Noah's discovery of wine in Gen 9:20–27 stands apart from its framing passages. Vv. 18–19 of chapter 9 lead one to expect an account of the increase and dispersal of Noah's descendants following the flood. Instead, vv. 20–27 deal with the relationships of Noah's sons and their descendants in the land of Canaan or Palestine, and connect these relationships to Noah's discovery of wine. According to this story, Noah was the first to plant a vineyard and to discover wine. This new development has significant connections with the previous history of humankind.

Because of Adam's sin, the ground was cursed and Adam had to earn his livelihood by the sweat of his brow (Gen 3:18–19). But with the birth of Noah, his father saw an omen in Noah's name and expressed the hope that "he will give us comfort, as we struggle hard to make a living on this land that the Lord has put under a curse." (Gen 5:29). Lamech's wish was inspired by the similarity of sound between the name Noah in Hebrew, *noach*, and the Hebrew word for relief or comfort, *nicham*. Thus Noah's discovery of wine, God's gift "to cheer us up" (Ps 104:15; Judg 9:13; Prov 31:6–7; Jer 16:7), is regarded as the fulfillment of his father's wish and a blessing. But wine can be a mixed blessing (Prov 23:29–35; Hos 4:11, 18).

Ignorant of the properties of wine, Noah drank some, became drunk, uncovered himself because of the heat from the wine, and lay naked in his tent. Noah betrays no consciousness of wrongdoing in becoming drunk nor does the text condemn him, but his nakedness created problems for his sons.

From the references to nakedness in the Old Testament, it appears that the Israelites observed a modesty about their physical being comparable to that of Muslims today. Exposure of one's nakedness was a source of shame, humiliation, and degradation. To be clothed was the first need of the man and the woman after eating the forbidden fruit (Gen 3:7). One was not to go up by steps to the altar because "you might expose yourself when you climb up" (Exod 20:26). Prisoners were led away naked and barefoot, with buttocks uncovered (Isaiah 20). The degradation and humiliation of defeat and exile is likened to the exposure of a woman's nakedness (e. g., Hos 2:10; Isa 47:3; Jer 13:26; Ezek 16:37, 39; Nah 3:5).

Thus Noah's nakedness posed a delicate problem for his sons, whose responsibility to respect and care for their parents is presupposed here and spelled out in Israelite tradition (Exod 20:12; 21:15, 17; Deut 27:16; Prov 30:17; Isa 51:17–19).

Ham, according to Gen 9:22, behaved very badly. He discovered his father in his tent in his drunken condition, paused to look upon him, then went outside and told his brothers. Shem and Japheth, however, took an outer garment (*the garment* in Hebrew probably Noah's discarded garment) which also served as a blanket (Exod 22:26–27; Deut 24:12–13), put it "over their shoulders and walked backward [gingerly, and awkwardly, no doubt] into the tent. Without looking at their father, they placed it over his body" (Gen 9:23). The detail and vividness of this scene emphasize the modesty, respect, and sense of duty of Shem and Japheth for their father and highlight, by contrast, the offense of Ham. Ham looked at Noah in his naked condition, made no effort to cover his father, and talked about his father's nakedness.

Some time later Noah awoke "and knew what his youngest son had done to him." Noah's son is not named in the Hebrew text of Gen 9:24, but a few translations, as the King James Version, identify Noah's son in verse 24 as Ham by referring to him as the "younger son." The grammar permits either the comparative or the superlative degree, but the more natural construction because of the three sons, and the one adopted by most modern translators, is the superlative, "the youngest."

The text does not tell us how Noah came to know what had been done to him. Did Shem and Japheth tell Noah about their brother viewing and talking about their father's nakedness? Or was more involved than seeing and talking about it? In any case, Noah was highly offended and cursed his son.

In Hebrew mentality a curse has a self-fulfilling energy and power to bring about the malady prescribed in the curse. The king of Moab hired Balaam to curse Israel to prevent the Israelites from entering his land, confident that Balaam's curse was as effective as a military force (Numbers 22–24). After conquering and burning Jericho, Joshua pronounced a curse on anyone who would rebuild the city (Josh 6:26). Centuries later in the days of Ahab, Hiel rebuilt Jericho and, because of Joshua's curse, lost his first-born and his youngest son (1 Kgs 16:34). The text leads us to expect Ham to be cursed but takes us by surprise by naming Canaan as the one cursed and by identifying him as Noah's youngest son! Ham, however, is consistently referred to as Noah's middle son (Gen 5:32; 6:10; 7:13; 9:18; 10:6). The curse is that Canaan is to be the lowest of slaves to his brothers. Canaan's brothers, whom he is to be subject to, are then named. Again the text takes us by surprise and mystifies us. The brothers Canaan is to be a slave to are Shem and Japheth! Shem and Japheth, however, are blessed and after each is blessed it is reiterated that Canaan is to be their slave, making the curse all the more binding, for repetition strengthens and intensifies (Gen 41:32).

As a curse has a self-fulfilling energy and power, so does a blessing when rightly spoken. And the blessing, like the curse, has the power to determine destiny and to shape the future. Jacob's ascendancy over Esau (Genesis 27), Ephraim's pre-eminence over Manasseh, the first-born (Gen 48:8–20), and the destinies of all Jacob's sons (Gen 49:1–27) are attributed to blessing. So also the relationships of Noah's descendants in Canaan are understood in terms of curse and blessing. The motive for the blessing of Shem and Japheth is not stated, but from the context it is clearly because of their respect and care for their father.

Noah blesses Shem by way of blessing the Lord, the God of Shem. The thought here is that of Ps 144:15 (NKJV): "Happy are the people whose God is the Lord!" To bless the Lord is to express thanksgiving and praise in acknowledgment of the Lord as God. Since among the descendants of Shem the Lord became the covenant God of Israel, Shem at this point in time represents the future Israelites. The blessing of Japheth takes the form of a wish that God may extend, *yaph* a play on Japheth, his territory and that he may dwell in the tents of Shem.

With the blessing of Japheth it becomes clear that we are not dealing with individuals alone but with groups of people and their political relationships to one another. Canaan obviously represents the Canaanites, Shem the Israelites, and Japheth, the ancestor of Greek peoples (Gen 10:2), the Philistines, who were immigrants from the Aegean basin (Amos 9:7; Jer 47:34). This way of referring to peoples in their relationships to one another is confirmed by Genesis 10. There, a combination of geographical, political, ethnic, racial, and linguistic relations among people is expressed in terms of genealogical relationships. When Canaan is said to be the son of Ham (Gen 10:6), for example, this expressed the fact that Canaan is geographically adjacent to Egypt and was, from earliest times, either under the hegemony or directly ruled by Egypt. As the list of Canaan's descendants in Gen 10:15–19 shows, the Canaanites were not properly an African people, but Semites and Indo-Europeans who all lived in Palestine.

Problems of Interpretation

One comes to the end of Gen 9:18–29 perplexed and with a host of questions. Verse 22 implies that Ham was liable to be cursed for acting disrespectfully to his father, but it is Canaan who is cursed. One might infer that Canaan was cursed for the infraction of his father, but if this were so one would expect a reason to be given for it; but none is. In fact, Canaan is explicitly identified as the offender in verses 24–25. "When Noah woke up and learned what his youngest son had done, he said, 'I now put a curse on Canaan!'" (CEV). Since Canaan is called Noah's son, and the brothers he is to be subjected to are identified as Shem and Japheth, how does this accord with the statement in Gen 9:18 that the sons of Noah were Shem, Ham, and Japheth? Moreover, the descendants of Shem, Ham, and Japheth are said to populate the whole earth in 9:19, but Shem and Japheth rule over and jointly occupy only the land of Canaan in 9:26, 27. In the flood story, Shem, Ham, and Japheth have wives (Gen 7:7, 13; 8:15, 18), but Noah's sons in 9:20–27 seem to be living at home with their father and there is no mention of their wives. Why is it said in 9:18 and 9:22 that Ham was the father of Canaan, but there is no reference to Ham's other sons, Kush, Egypt, and Put? And why is there no mention of Shem and Japheth being the father of anyone? How can Ham be the father of Canaan when according to 9:24–25, Noah was the father of Canaan? When did Shem (Israel) and Japheth (the Philistines) jointly rule Canaan and did these old enemies live in peace? Finally, what is the point of the passage?

The Literary Character of Genesis

One of the established results of biblical criticism is the recognition that Genesis speaks with not one, but four voices. By paying attention to the terms used for the deity, God (Hebrew, *Elohim*) and the Lord (Hebrew, YHWH, traditionally pronounced Yahweh) together with literary style and theological point of view, scholars have distinguished two creation stories, two lists of patriarchs before the flood, two versions of the flood, two versions of the family of nations in chapter 10, etc. These different voices continue throughout Genesis and into Exodus, Leviticus, and Numbers. Scholars call the voice that consistently refers to God as the Lord, J (from the German spelling, Jahweh), and a widely accepted date is ca. 950 BCE. Another voice begins with God (*Elohim*), changes to God All-Powerful (*El Shaddai*) at Genesis 17, and to the Lord in Exodus 6. This voice has a pronounced interest in priestly matters and for this reason is called P; it is generally dated to ca. 550–450 BCE. A third voice calls the deity God (*Elohim*) until the time of Moses, then the Lord (but not consistently), but it is fragmentary and difficult to date. Because of its preference for Elohim and its place of origin in the Northern Kingdom, also called Ephraim, this voice is named E. Proposed dates range from ca. 900–750 BCE. The fourth voice of Genesis is that of the one(s) who carefully and purposefully placed J, E, and P in the order in which we now find them.

While there is a profound theological harmony between these versions of the early history of humankind, they often differ in detail. The universe in Gen 1:1—2:4a is brought into being by eight creative acts of God's Word over a period of six days. In Gen 2:4b–25 creation is accomplished by four creative acts by the Lord's hands and there is no reference to the time involved. In the parallel genealogies of humankind before the flood in Gen 4:17–26 and Genesis 5, the names are sometimes spelled differently and they do not consistently follow the same order of birth. (Note also the differences in the genealogy of Jesus in Matthew and Luke.) According to one version of the flood, Noah took two of every kind of animal into the ark (Gen 6:19–20; 7:9, 15). In the other version, Noah took seven pairs of clean and one pair of unclean animals and seven pairs of birds into the ark (Gen 7:2–3). Nor is this phenomenon confined to the Old Testament. We have not one, but four versions of the life and ministry of Jesus, and the differences between Mark and John are as striking as anything in Genesis. But whereas the New Testament Gospels have been preserved separately, the different literary sources in Genesis have been "braided" together.

These differences in detail are the inevitable results of the oral transmission of information and traditions for generations in different geographical locales and under different historical circumstances. The Bible leaves these differences uncensored and thereby indicates that it accepts and embraces them. The combined witness of the different voices in Genesis (and elsewhere in the Bible) gives us a fuller and better understanding than any one voice alone.

Two Versions of Noah's Family

The recognition of the composite nature of Genesis provides the key to the proper understanding of 9:18–29. As there are two versions of creation, two genealogies of humankind before the flood, and two versions of the flood, so there are two versions of Noah's family. Verses 18–19 represent one tradition; verses 20–27 embody another. Verses 18–19 and also 28–29 belong with Genesis 1, 5, and 10 (the P voice) and reflect the view that the (married) sons of Noah were Shem, Ham, and Japheth and that they were the ancestors of all the peoples of the biblical world. In 9:20–27, on the other hand, the (apparently unmarried) sons of Noah are Shem, Japheth, and Canaan. In this version of Noah's sons the one cursed is Canaan and the purpose of these verses is to account for relations between Israelites, Canaanites, and Philistines in the land of Canaan. These verses speak with the voice of J, also found in Genesis 2–4; 11:1–9, and chapter 12. This tradition of Noah's sons seems also to be reflected in Gen 10:21 where Shem is referred to as the elder brother of Japheth.

The understanding of Gen 9:18–29 is so confused because the Hebrew text at an early stage of its transmission has been edited to harmonize the two traditions of Noah's sons. This was done by adding the note in 9:18b, "and Ham, he was the father of Canaan" (to give a literal translation of the Hebrew text), and by inserting the phrase, "Ham the father of," before Canaan in 9:22a. These editorial additions interrupt the flow of the narrative and stand out like a bandaged thumb. The concern of 9:18–19 is to establish that Shem Ham, and Japheth, and only "these three," were the forebears of all the peoples of the biblical world. The note that explains Ham's relationship to Canaan in 9:18b introduces a new and unrelated subject. And this note is made conspicuous as an addition by the absence of similar information about Shem and Japheth.

The insertion of "Ham the father of" in 9:22 is equally intrusive and stands in conflict with 9:24. This editorial note makes Ham, the middle son of Noah, the offender, but Noah explicitly identifies the guilty party as his youngest son (9:23–24).

The editorial nature of "and Ham, he was the father of Canaan" in 9:18b is acknowledged in the translations of The New International Version, The New American Bible, and Today's English Version by placing these words in brackets or parentheses. The same should be done for "Ham the father of" in 9:22, as in the Moffatt Translation and the Confraternity Version. Notes added to the Hebrew text by a later editor to explain changes in place names, etc. are found throughout the Bible. The New Revised Standard Version, the New International Version, and the New King James Version use parentheses to designate part of the following passages in Genesis as editorial additions: 14:8; 23:2, 19; 35:6, 19, 27; 48:7. Other translations, including the *CEV*, integrate these editorial additions into the text.

It is understandable that someone confronted by the two traditions of Noah's family in Gen 9:18–29 would attempt to harmonize them, especially since Noah's sons are identified by name as Shem, Ham, and Japheth in the P version of the flood (Gen 6:10; 7:13), and the P version of Noah's sons (9:18–19) stands immediately before Noah's curse and blessing (9:20–27).

In the J version of the flood the sons of Noah are not named. When they are referred to, it is as Noah's "whole family" (Gen 7:1) and "the others in the boat" (7:23). The authority for the editorial additions in 9:18 and 9:22 is Gen 10:6, where it is stated that Ham indeed was the father of Canaan. However, the author of these editorial notes overlooks the fact that in Gen 9:24, 25 Noah is the father of Canaan.

The recognition that there are two traditions of Noah's sons in Gen 9:18–29 opens the way to the correct interpretation of the passage. The only basis for identifying Ham as the offender is the note in 9:18, "and Ham, he was the father of Canaan," and the insertion in 9:22, "Ham the father of." When it is understood that these notes were not a part of the original narrative but later, editorial additions to the Hebrew text, the offender as well as the one cursed is Canaan. Ham was not the one cursed because in Gen 9:1 God blessed Ham and his brothers. As Baalam could not curse Israel whom God had blessed (Num 22:12; 23:8), so Noah could not have cursed Ham whom God had blessed.

If the editorial notes about Ham being the father of Canaan are accepted as original, no satisfactory explanation of Gen 9:18–29 is possible. These notes make Ham the offender but give no reason why Canaan is cursed. There is the additional awkwardness that Ham is consistently referred to as Noah's middle son, but the one cursed is identified as Noah's youngest son. Those who interpret the passage on the assumption that the notes in 9:18 and 9:22 are an integral part of the narrative are forced to resort to speculation or to declare other portions of the passage secondary. This approach has achieved no consensus of interpretation and has led to widely diverging and sometimes bizarre expositions.

The Purpose of 9:18–29

In Gen 12:7 God promises Abraham that the land of Canaan will be given to his descendants. Preceding and following this promise (12:6; 13:7) is the notation that the Canaanites were then living in the land and therefore were the native inhabitants of Canaan. This raises an important question: What right did the Israelites have to Canaan when its native population were Canaanites? In the course of time the Israelites did occupy Canaan and subjected the native population to forced labor (Josh 16:10; 17:12–13; Judg 1:27–35; 1 Kgs 9:20–21), but they shared possession of the land with the Philistines. If God promised the land to the Israelites, why did they share it with the Philistines?

Gen 9:20–27 provides answers to these questions. According to this passage, the Canaanites lost their right to their land because of an inherent perversity in their ancestor Canaan which was perpetuated by his descendants. The Canaanites, especially those of Sodom, were "wicked, great sinners against the Lord" (Gen 13:13; 15:16; 18:20–21; 19; Amorites in 15:16 is a synonymous term for Canaanites). According to Leviticus 18:24–25, it was because of the abominable sexual practices of the native population of Canaan that the land "vomited" them out (see also Deut 9:4–5; 12:29–31; 1 Kgs 14:24; 2 Kgs 17:7, 11). Because of the notoriety of the Canaanites for sexual misconduct, it is tempting to infer that what was "done" to Noah (Gen 9:24) was homosexual rape and that a fuller account of what happened has been curtailed to avoid offending readers. To see the nakedness of another leads naturally to sexual relations (Lev 20:17). And to look upon a forbidden object opens the way to succumbing to temptation, as in the case of Eve with the forbidden fruit (Gen 3:6) and David with Bathsheba (2 Sam 11:2–5). In whatever way we understand what was done to Noah, Canaan did not honor his father. And as the fifth commandment makes clear, honoring one's parents is the basis for maintaining the tenure of one's land.

Noah's curse and blessing are in effect a theological mandate for Israel's supremacy over Canaan. A remarkable feature of this mandate is that it also includes the Philistines. The Israelites and Philistines entered Canaan about the same time and at first were rivals for control of the land. Under David, the Israelites conquered the Philistines (2 Sam 5:17–25; 8:1, 12; 2:15–22; 23:9–17), but the Philistines were allowed to retain their holding along the coastal plain of Canaan and to maintain their separate identity. This is all the more remarkable in that the Israelites claimed the territory occupied by the Philistines. In the boundary lists of the promised land (Exod 23:31; Num 34:3; Josh 15:11; Ezek 47:20) the western boundary does not stop at Philistine territory but is placed at the Mediterranean Sea.

The wish that God may enlarge Japheth probably refers to an extension of Philistine territory in the direction of Egypt. This would not only be a blessing to Japheth but also a source of security to Israel from the threat of Egyptian incursion into Palestine.

David may have contributed to the Israelite acceptance of the Philistine presence "in the tents of Shem," for he had enduring relationships with the Philistines, especially Achish, king of Gath. David lived as a refugee with

Achish for one year and four months (1 Sam 27:7). Achish later gave David the city of Ziklag as a feudal holding (1 Samuel 27). After David became king of all Israel and conquered the Philistines, Achish continued to be king of Gath into the reign of Solomon (1 Kgs 2:39). Also, there was in David's army a contingent of troops from Gath willing to follow him into exile (2 Sam 15:18–22). And the royal bodyguard of David and Solomon was composed of Cherethites and Pelethites (2 Sam 8:18; 23:23; 1 Kgs 1:44), who were either components or relatives of the Philistines (Ezek 25:16; Zeph 2:5). In any case, it is true that personal relationships with the "enemy" and those who are different can lead to blessing and dwelling together in peace.

No Evidence of a Curse on Ham Anywhere in the Bible

Not only is there no shred of evidence in Gen 9:18–29 of a curse on Ham; nowhere in the Bible is there any reference or even an allusion to such a curse. Genesis 10 contains a list of the descendants of Shem, Ham, and Japheth (from the P source; portions of the chapter also belong to J). If there were any negative thoughts and feelings toward Ham and his descendants, this passage, following immediately on Noah's curse and blessing, would have been the place to express them. But no disparaging remark is made about anyone. (In Deut 23:7, 8 Israelites are expressly forbidden to be unkind to Egyptians because "you lived as foreigners in the country of Egypt.") Rather, all the descendants of Noah are listed as related to one another as brothers and sisters. The one person given special attention is Nimrod, the son of Kush, and he is credited with being the first to exercise imperial political power in Mesopotamia (Gen 10:8–12). The point of Genesis 10 is that humankind is conceived as a unity, and the diversity of peoples with "their own languages, tribes, and land" (vv. 5, 20, 31) is understood as the fulfillment of God's command to Noah and his sons to be fruitful and to multiply, and to fill the earth (Gen 9:1, 7). As God inspected the creation in Genesis 1 and declared it to correspond exactly to the divine intention, that it is good, so Genesis 10 implies that humankind in all its ethnic and racial manifestations corresponds to God's intention and is good. Abraham had no reservation about going to Egypt, the land of Ham (Pss 78:51; 105:23, 27; 106:22), when there was a famine in Canaan (Gen 12:10–20). Nor did Abraham and Sarah have any qualms about using Hagar, an Egyptian, as a surrogate mother so they could have an heir (Genesis 16). In fact, Abraham would gladly have accepted Ishmael, Hagar's son, as the father of the covenant people (Gen 17:18). The mother of the tribes of Ephraim and Manasseh was Asenath, an Egyptian (Gen 41:45, 50–52; 46:20), and Jacob was at pains to adopt her sons so that they could be recognized as fully Israelite (Gen 48:5, 6).

Moses was married to a Kushite (the Hebrew word for the peoples living south of Egypt whom the Greeks called Ethiopians, a word meaning literally, "burnt faces") and while Miriam and Aaron spoke out against her, the context shows that what they were really protesting was Moses's exclusive authority to speak for God (Numbers 12). If Moses's Kushite wife was Zipporah from the land of Midian where Moses found refuge (Exod 2:11–22), then Moses accepted instruction in the administration of justice from his Kushite father-in-law, Jethro (Exod 18:13–27). It is worthy of note that Aaron's grandson and successor as high priest (Exod 6:25), and also one of the sons of Eli the priest (1 Sam 1:3), given the Egyptian name, Phinehas, which means literally, "The Southerner" (in relation to Egypt), that is, the Ethiopian or the Nubian.

David had Ethiopian troops in his army (2 Sam 18:19–32). Solomon made an alliance with Egypt and took an Egyptian wife (1 Kgs 3:1). Solomon graciously received, and treated as an equal, the queen of Sheba whose kingdom embraced both Arabian and African territory (1 Kgs 10:1–13).

Amos likens Israel to the Ethiopians to make the point that the distant and different Ethiopians were just as near and dear to God as the covenant people (Amos 9.7, 8a). The Targum on this passage quotes God as saying: "Are you [the Ethiopians] not greatly beloved unto me."

Hezekiah made an alliance with Egypt, then ruled by the Twenty fifth (Ethiopian) Dynasty, and with the support of his ally revolted against Assyria. Isaiah, who called for repentance and faith, objected to this alliance and makes some disparaging remarks about Egypt's help (e.g., Isa 30:5, 7) because the Egyptians were men and not God (31:3), but nowhere does he appeal to an ancient curse on Egypt (nor do other prophets who criticize Israel for turning to Egypt or who announce judgment on Egypt, e.g., Hos 7:11; Jer 2:18; Ezekiel 30). Hezekiah's revolt was not successful, but the Ethiopian general and later pharaoh, Tirhakah, stood by Hezekiah and fought for him (2 Kgs 19:9; Isa 37:9).

As a result of Hezekiah's alliances with the Twenty-fifth Dynasty of Egypt, close contacts were established between the two peoples. Soon afterwards we find Ethiopians as members of Israelite society and Israelite settlers in Ethiopia. The father of the prophet Zephaniah was an Ethiopian as his name, Kushi, indicates, and Zephaniah's great-great grandfather was (King) Hezekiah of Judah (Zeph 1:1). Jehudi, son of Nethaniah, son of Shelemiah, son of Kushi, was a trusted member of King Jehoiakim's cabinet (Jer 36:14, 21, 23). And Jeremiah's life was saved by the royal servant, Ebed-melech, "the Ethiopian" (Jer 38:7–13; 39:15–18). Throughout Israel's history, Egypt and Ethiopia were places of refuge (e.g., Isa 11:11; Jeremiah 42–44; Matt 2:13–15). But for Israelite refugees and converts to the religion of Israel, Zion was their spiritual home and those in foreign lands looked forward to worshipping in Zion. Isa 18:7 anticipates the time when gifts will be brought to the Lord by the Ethiopians. So does Zephaniah in 3:10 of his prophecy, and the Psalmist in Ps 68:31. Psalm 87 pictures such a gathering of pilgrims in Zion, not only from Egypt and Ethiopia, but also from Babylon, Philistia, and Tyre, who all say, "I was born in Zion" (v. 4). And Isa 19:23b–25 (CEV) anticipates the time when "The Egyptians and the Assyrians will travel back and forth from Egypt to Assyria, and they will worship together. Israel will join with these two countries . . . then the Lord All-Powerful will bless them by saying, 'The Egyptians are my people. I created the Assyrians and chose the Israelites.'" Note also the diverse peoples gathered in Jerusalem at the time of Pentecost (Acts 2:5–11), and the "large crowd . . . from every race, tribe, nation, and language" gathered before the throne and the Lamb in Rev 7:9–10.

Simon, from the North African city of Cyrene (Matt 27:32; Mark 15:21; Luke 23:26), was not regarded as unworthy to carry Jesus's cross. Nor did Philip feel obligated to discuss Gen 9:18–29 with the Ethiopian minister of Queen Candace before baptizing him (Acts 8:26–40).

Origin of the Idea of a Curse on Ham

If there is no basis in the Bible for a curse on Ham, how did this idea originate? It was not until the last quarter of the nineteenth century that biblical scholars convincingly clarified the composite literary character of Genesis. To one unaware of the two traditions of Noah's family and the editorial nature of the references to Ham as the father of Canaan in Gen 9:18, 22, the offender is obviously Ham. And if Ham is the offender, the inference naturally suggests itself that Ham was also the one cursed. A few manuscripts of the early Greek translation, the Septuagint (ca. 250–100 BCE), name Ham as the one cursed. Ham is also named as the one cursed in the Arabic version (thirteenth century CE). In early rabbinic literature and the writings of the Church Fathers, one occasionally finds references to Ham as affected by Noah's curse. But it was not until the Middle Ages that Jewish, Christian, and Islamic authorities alike began generally to identify Ham as cursed. Luther and Calvin also name Ham as cursed, as well as Canaan. Still, the interpretation of Gen 9:18–29 during the Middle Ages for the most part was homiletical and moralistic, not intentionally racist. Ham was criticized for his immodesty or for speaking disrespectfully about his father, or for failing to care for his father, or for causing dissension in the family. Nevertheless, the focus on Ham during the Middle Ages helped establish the popular notion that Ham was cursed and made it possible for racists to seize upon this passage and to use it as theological justification for the oppression of African people.

The misunderstanding and abuse of Gen 9:18–29 illustrate what a responsibility it is to rightly interpret Scripture. The erroneous idea that there is a curse on Ham is not the fault of the Bible. At the least, it is poor exegesis and reflects lack of knowledge of biblical scholarship. Used in a racist sense, this erroneous idea is a reminder of the ingenuity and perversity with which humans find ways to justify their sin to themselves and to others. However one reads Gen 9:18–29, it is absolutely clear that there is no basis for a curse on Ham in this passage. The curse is on Canaan and it is because of behavior, not race. And the passage is concerned with political relationships between Israelites, Canaanites, and Philistines in Canaan in the tenth century BCE, not with Africans or African Americans. Even if the passage is accepted as an organic literary unit speaking with a single, coherent voice, it has nothing to do with race. Read this way, its point is that the behavior of parents may bring a curse on their children. The erroneous idea of a curse on Ham stands in violent conflict with the theological heartbeat of the Bible that we are all sons and daughters of God, that we are all related to one another as members of a family, that each one of us, whatever our race, ethnicity, and nationality, is special and precious to God, and that we were created for companionship with God—and fellowship with one another.

8

Book Review

The Rescue of Jerusalem: The Alliance between Hebrews and Africans in 701 B.C. Henry T. Aubin. Toronto: Doubleday Canada; New York: Soho, 2002. HB. $16.95.

One of the most dramatic and perplexing mysteries in biblical studies is how Jerusalem was rescued from the Assyrian siege of the city in 701 BCE.

In a David-and-Goliath-like struggle, Judah was invaded and Jerusalem was besieged by the militaristic and cruel superpower of the time, Assyria. The very life of Judah and the future of God's covenant people were at stake.

As the Assyrians toyed with Jerusalem, the siege was broken and Jerusalem was rescued in some mysterious way. That much is clear. But what actually happened has defied scholars. The problem is not one of lack of sources, however; the rescue of Jerusalem is one of the best-documented events in the Bible.

Sources that Refer to the Rescue of Jerusalem

The primary biblical account is found in 2 Kings 18–20. Although Isaiah 36–39 is virtually identical to 2 Kings 18–20, most scholars regard 2 Kings as the original of the two accounts. A highly selective version of the Kings account, 2 Chr 32:1–23, dates from several centuries later, serves concerns different from those of 2 Kings, and is not generally taken into account. Second Kings 20 is set in the time of the siege of Jerusalem, but it does not deal directly with the deliverance of the city. A number of passages from Isaiah and Micah contribute to the larger picture of the Assyrian invasion but do not shed light on the mystery of the rescue of Jerusalem. The introduction in 2 Kgs 18:1–12 to the reign of Hezekiah mentions Hezekiah's revolt but does not go into the outcome. The mystery of Jerusalem's deliverance is concealed within 2 Kgs 18:13—19:37, and it is here that scholarship has focused.

Since the publication of Bernhard Stade's article in 1886,[1] most scholars have distinguished three sources in 2 Kgs 18:13—19:37: an archival source of Sennacherib's siege of Jerusalem (18:13–16, designated A), and two parallel accounts of the Assyrian demand that Hezekiah surrender unconditionally (18:17—19:9a, 36, designated B1, and 19:9b–35, designated B2). B1 is thought to have been composed within a generation or two after 701 and to offer a reliable account of what happened. B2 is judged to date from the Babylonian exile (587–538 BCE) and to be more legendary and theological than B1 and, therefore, less reliable.

Fortunately, the biblical account is complemented by an inscription of 700 words by the Assyrian king, Sennacherib, who besieged Jerusalem. That text is translated in *Ancient Near Eastern Texts Relating to the Old Testament*, edited by James B. Pritchard, hereafter referred to as *ANET*.[2] A passage from Herodotus's *History* is usually also taken into account in the discussion of the deliverance of Jerusalem.

Apparent Scenario of the Rescue of Jerusalem

The combined biblical and Assyrian sources yield the following scenario of what happened in 701 BCE. King Hezekiah of Judah, a vassal of Assyria, the most powerful empire in the biblical world at that time, had joined other subject states in a wide-scale revolt against Assyria when its ruler, Sargon II, died in 705 BCE. After subduing Babylonia, the most powerful of the subject states, Sennacherib, the successor of Sargon II, turned to the small states on the western perimeter of his kingdom, most of which had been subject to Assyria since 734. The leader of the rebellion in Phoenicia, Luli, the king of Sidon, fled without a fight to Cyprus. King Luli's flight prompted rulers of adjacent kingdoms, such as Ashdod, Byblos, Edom, and Moab, to

1. Stade, "Anmerkungen zu 2 Ko. 15–21," 122–92.

2. Pritchard, ed., *Ancient Eastern Texts Relating to the Old Testament*, 3rd ed., 287–88.

come to Sennacherib at Sidon and to reaffirm their allegiance. Absent from that gathering were Ashkelon, Ekron, and Judah, who, counting on Egypt's help, defied Sennacherib.

Proceeding down the Mediterranean coast to "the plain of Eltekeh" about twelve miles south of modern Tel Aviv, Sennacherib was confronted by an army from "the kings of Egypt (and) the bowmen, the chariot (corps), and the cavalry of the king of Ethiopia, an army beyond counting."[3] Sennacherib was victorious, but no details are given of prisoners or booty taken. After subduing Ashkelon and Ekron, Sennacherib turned inland and began systematically to conquer Judah. He boasts of besieging and capturing forty-six walled cities, chief of which was Lachish, about thirty miles southwest of Jerusalem, and Judah's second most important city. Then Sennacherib turned to Jerusalem, claiming that he had shut up Hezekiah "like a bird in a cage."

From Lachish, Sennacherib sent three high officials with "a great army" to Jerusalem and demanded that Hezekiah surrender unconditionally. Hezekiah went to the temple, sent for the prophet Isaiah, and reported to him the Assyrian demand to surrender. Isaiah assured the king that God would cause Sennacherib to hear a rumor that would make him return to his own land where he would be killed.

In the meantime, Sennacherib moved from Lachish to Libnah, a few miles to the north, apparently because he had learned that an army led by the Kushite, Tirhakah, was advancing against him. But nothing is said of the outcome of Tirhakah's challenge, in either the biblical or the Assyrian account. Instead, the biblical narrator informs us that Sennacherib sent another delegation to Jerusalem and again demanded in insulting and blasphemous language that Hezekiah surrender. Hezekiah again went to the temple and prayed, and Isaiah again assured him even more emphatically that the Assyrians would not succeed. That night the angel of the Lord smote 185,000 in the camp of the Assyrian army; Sennacherib broke the siege and departed for Nineveh, where he was slain by his sons.

Mystery of the Rescue

Of all the kings who rebelled against Sennacherib, only Hezekiah did not have to flee his kingdom or give up his throne. Of all the cities threatened by Sennacherib, only Jerusalem was rescued—but how? We know that

3. *ANET*, 287b.

Tirhakah survived the siege of Jerusalem and had a long and impressive reign afterward (from 690 to 664). But what happened militarily? And what actually happened to the Assyrian army? Is the angel of the Lord to be understood literally, or is the angel a metaphor for some human cause? Despite all the sources available to us, and even though there are numerous studies in commentaries on 2 Kings and Isaiah, in special articles, in monographs, and even in entire books, the mystery remains. Scholars tend to feel that a solution is beyond us in our present state of knowledge.

Yale's Brevard Childs stated in 1967 that "it seems unlikely that a satisfactory historical solution will be forthcoming without fresh extra-biblical evidence."[4] A generation later, the European Seminar on Methodology in Israel's History devoted its 2000 meeting to the invasion of Sennacherib in 701.[5] The scholars of the European Seminar had no breakthroughs to report, and the issues they debated are still those from the nineteenth century. They carefully explain and defend their methodologies, but the only historical sources they are certain of are Sennacherib's annals and 2 Kgs 18:13–16. The chronology of Hezekiah's reign remains uncertain, Jerusalem's rescue is still "considerably debated," and the role of Tirhakah in the events of 701, if any, remains questionable.

Henry T. Aubin's Attempt to Solve the Mystery of Jerusalem's Rescue

A refreshingly new attempt to solve the mystery of Jerusalem's rescue in 701 BCE has been undertaken by Henry T. Aubin in a thoroughly researched and brilliantly written study, *The Rescue of Jerusalem: The Alliance between Hebrews and Africans in 701 BCE.* Aubin is a European American now living in Montreal, where he writes for the *Montreal Gazette.* In his search for edifying reading material for his adopted son of African descent, Aubin learned of the Ethiopian Tirhakah's involvement in the rescue of Jerusalem, and he became convinced that Tirhakah played a significant role in that event. Aubin asserts that there is no need for new sources because the known sources are "chock full of telling but overlooked clues." In fact, "like Edgar Allan Poe's purloined letter that lies in so obvious a place that the searchers do not find it, the Bible's evidence lies in full view" (96). The

4. Childs, *Isaiah and the Assyrian Crisis*, 120.

5. Their findings are published in Grabbe, ed., *The Invasion of Sennacherib in 701 BCE.*

trick to finding those obvious clues is "to be free of preconceptions that the Kushites were incapable" (83). Aubin is a man with a mission: to correct mistaken ideas about Africa and to bring to light the role of Tirhakah in one of the most dramatic and critical events in Hebrew history.

Although a newspaper man by profession, Aubin has produced a solid work of scholarship, which was researched over several years and documented by 112 pages of fine print endnotes (almost 400 authorities are listed in the author index). The endnotes constitute an excellent survey of scholarship and are one of the most valuable contributions of the book. Aubin is fully aware of the spectrum of scholarly opinion, and he gives a helpful summary of the traditional, conventional or standard, and minimalist critical stances in biblical scholarship on pages xviii–xxii. Drawing primarily on works in the standard spectrum, Aubin argues his case with passion but fairness. He considers and evaluates every option and—like a skilled lawyer—builds an impressive case to support his position concerning Tirhakah's role in the rescue of Jerusalem. The book is clearly written and has the sustaining interest of a mystery novel.

Importance of Jerusalem's Rescue in Israelite and World History

To correct "the unrecognized impact on our world" of the role of Tirhakah and the Kushites in the rescue of Jerusalem in 701 BCE, Aubin calls this event the high point in the history of the Israelite monarchy and stresses its importance in Jewish and world history (xvi). The northern Israelite kingdom called Israel or Samaria (separated from Judah after the death of Solomon) had been defeated by the Assyrians in 722. The leading members of society had been exiled throughout the Assyrian Empire, the homeland had been resettled by foreigners, and the identity of the ten northern tribes had been damaged beyond repair. In 701, only Judah remained as the bearer of God's purposes in the world. The Jewish identity and destiny hung in the balance. Had Jerusalem and Judah fallen and gone the way of the northern Israelite kingdom, the religion of Israel would have died out and there would have been no Judaism, without which "both Christianity and Islam become inconceivable. And without these faiths, the world as we know it becomes unrecognizable: profoundly, utterly different" (21).[6]

6. Quoted from McNeill, professor of history at the University of Chicago, "Infectious Alternatives," 80.

In short, the rescue of Jerusalem in 701 BCE is one of world history's "most audacious," "pivotal," and "most influential events" (xxiii). In 1998, thirty-seven historians named the rescue of Jerusalem in 701 as the most important victory in the military history of the West (21). In terms of theological significance, the deliverance of Jerusalem is second only to the Exodus. Aubin maintains that this event gave rise to the full understanding of the nature of God, to Israel's identity as the covenant people, and to the sanctity of Jerusalem.

Kush's Capability of Rescuing Jerusalem

A second major concern of Aubin is to establish that Kush, the Egyptian and biblical term for the land lying directly south of Egypt (called Ethiopia or "land of burnt faces" by the Greeks and roughly equivalent to modern Sudan), was capable of playing a significant role in the rescue of Jerusalem. Kush had been conquered by Egypt in the sixteenth century BCE, but Egyptian control had ceased by the eleventh century. By the eighth century BCE, Kush was stronger militarily than Egypt. By the middle of the eighth century, the Kushite, Kashta, exercised control over Upper Egypt, while the Delta was the scene of the rivalry of petty, warring states. Around 728 BCE, a coalition of Delta rulers invaded Upper Egypt to curb the growing power of Kush, only to be soundly repulsed by the Kushite, Piye (also called Piankhi), "the valorous equivalent of David, Arthur, or Charlemagne" (xvi). But Piye did not follow up his victory by occupying Lower Egypt, and local "pharaohs" continued to rule there.

In the meantime, Assyria began its imperialistic expansion in the region of Khor, an Egyptian term adopted by Aubin to designate the collective Palestinian states, including Ammon, Edom, Moab, Philistia, Phoenicia, and Syria, as well as the Israelite states of Samaria and Judah (16). Assyrian rulers penetrated to the border of Egypt and occasionally beyond in 734, 732, 720, 716, and 712 BCE. This alarming development would have been noted and appropriate action would have been taken by Kushite authorities to equip themselves to defend all Egypt against Assyrian aggression. Around 712, Shabako, the successor of Piye, conquered Lower Egypt and established the Twenty-fifth Dynasty, which ruled Egypt and Ethiopia until 663 BCE. "Under the Kushite pharaohs, Egypt underwent a veritable renaissance" (71). Kushite Egypt had a large reservoir of experienced soldiers, many of whom had served as mercenaries throughout the biblical world

(324–25, note 97), and it was fully capable of providing significant help to Judah at the time of Sennacherib's siege in 701 BCE. While not noted for imperialistic ambition, it was in Kushite Egypt's self-interest for security and trade to have free access and influence with the neighboring Palestinian states, including Samaria and Judah.

Although the Kushite rulers of Egypt were clearly capable of supplying help to Hezekiah in 701 BCE, virtually all contemporary scholars have ignored them and have offered unconvincing alternative explanations. Because Isaiah assures Hezekiah that Sennacherib will hear a rumor that will cause him to break off the siege and return home (2 Kgs 19:6–7), some scholars propose a "troubles elsewhere" theory. On the basis of a story in Herodotus, other scholars have inferred that the work of the angel of the Lord was actually a plague.

In his *History*, Herodotus says that Sennacherib invaded Egypt and that at Pelusium during the night mice "ate their quivers, their bowstrings, and the leather handles of their shields, so that on the following day, having no arms to fight with, they abandoned their positions and suffered severe losses during their retreat."[7] Because mice are known to transmit plague, a large number of scholars hold that the work of the angel represents a plague. Still others hold that the rescue was simply a surrender. The explanation of the parallel accounts in 2 Kings by the theory that Sennacherib invaded Judah twice, first in 701 and again about 688, Aubin dismisses as having been refuted by recent scholarship (335–36 n. 1).

Aubin refutes all of the alternative explanations and advances the Kushite rescue theory as the most plausible. If troubles elsewhere had caused Sennacherib to break off the siege of Jerusalem, why did he not return once he had taken care of the situation? But Sennacherib left Khor "*permanently*" (117). Moreover, both Herodotus and the Bible represent the withdrawal as being the result of duress and compulsion coming from close at hand, not from far away.

As for the epidemic theory, "Divinely appointed epidemics enjoy a perfectly honorable place in biblical tradition," as in the plagues of Egypt at the time of the liberation. Would not the epidemic be plainly mentioned in the rescue of Jerusalem if it were the cause? Also, Sennacherib's forces were scattered throughout Judah; 185,000 of them would not likely have been concentrated in one place. If Hezekiah surrendered, why did not

7. Herodotus, *History* II.141, which was cited by Aubin, 94–95.

Sennacherib say so and incorporate Judah into the Assyrian Empire? How could the Bible represent surrender as a miraculous deliverance?

Six Reasons in Support of the Kushite Rescue of Jerusalem

Aubin offers six reasons the Kushite rescue theory best accounts for the deliverance of Jerusalem:

First Reason

If 2 Kgs 19:9b–35 (B2), which is generally regarded as secondary and late, is removed from 18:17—19:9a, 36–37 (B1), the connection between the approach of Tirhakah and the withdrawal of Sennacherib is clear. The rumor that Isaiah announces in 2 Kgs 19:7 is fulfilled in 19:9a in the report of the approach of Tirhakah. The conclusion of B1 in 19:36–37—interrupted by B2 (19:9b–35)—establishes that Sennacherib's departure was because of the approach of Tirhakah. The answer to the mystery of the rescue of Jerusalem is as obvious as Poe's purloined letter!

Second Reason

Not one but two Kushite-Egyptian armies fought against the Assyrians. The army that fought at Eltekeh, while containing Kushite contingents, was mustered by "the kings of Egypt" and led by "princes of Egypt."[8] It was after Sennacherib had not only defeated the Egyptian-Kushite army at Eltekeh but also conquered Ashdod and Lachish that Tirhakah appeared on the scene. The statement by Herodotus that Sennacherib's army suffered "severe losses during their retreat" and passages in Isaiah (22:1–14; compare 14:24–25; 17:12–14; 29:5–7; 31:8–9) attest to Assyria's military defeat. The only force capable of defeating the Assyrians at Jerusalem was the second Kushite army led by Tirhakah, who was about twenty years old at the time and later became pharaoh.

8. *ANET*, 287–88.

Third Reason

Egypt had free access to Khor and enjoyed thriving commercial relations with Khor after 701, exercising control over the strategic city of Gaza. But Sennacherib, although he reigned for another twenty years, never returned to Khor.

Fourth Reason

After 701, Egypt became famous for its military prowess. It defeated an Assyrian army in Egypt in 674, provided help to Tyre and Ashkelon in 671, and struck fear in the heart of Esarhaddon, Sennacherib's successor, at the prospect of fighting the Kushites (160–61). Strabo, a Greek geographer and historian of the first century CE, includes Tirhakah, as a great military leader, along with leaders such as Cyrus and Xerxes of Persia. And the Hebrew prophet Nahum credits Ethiopia with being the real strength of Egypt (Nah 3:9).

Fifth Reason

The positive attitude of Judahites to Kushites after 701 is expressive of their appreciation for having been saved by Kushites. Aubin notes that "several passages in the Bible that deal with Kushites are, in the opinion of the overwhelming majority of biblical experts, decidedly hostile toward that African people" (164). On the contrary, Aubin maintains that the Hebrew Bible depicts Africans "in exceptionally generous terms" (165), and he devotes all of chapter 13 to setting the record straight. Of the fifty-six references to Kushites in twenty-nine different passages (excluding duplicate passages in Isaiah 36–39), "not once does the Hebrew Bible cast aspersions on the Kushites' national character, way of life, or religion" (168).

Sixth Reason

There are no valid reasons against the Kushite theory. The scholars who belittle the ability of the Kushites to aid Hezekiah base their reasoning on the Assyrian official's characterization of Egypt as "that broken reed of a staff, which will pierce the hand of anyone who leans on it" (2 Kgs 18:21).

According to Aubin, the larger context of the passage affirms that just as Judah was right to trust in God, so it was right to lean on Egypt.

Aubin's Imaginative Reconstruction of the Kushite Rescue of Jerusalem

Aubin believes that his "thesis—that Kushite Egypt turned back Sennacherib—is unshakable" (188) and shares his "musings" of how it might have happened. Aubin conjectures that the Assyrian forces were widely dispersed—some stationed at Lachish and Libnah, others besieging the forty-six walled cities Sennacherib claims to have conquered—so that a relatively small force may have been at Jerusalem. Aubin thinks that a month or more after the battle of Eltekeh and the conquest of Lachish, Tirhakah, at the head of a second army largely comprising Kushites, avoided the coastal highway ("the Way of the Sea") and came to Jerusalem by "the back door." Using the highway from Beersheba by way of Debir and Hebron, a journey of about forty-four miles, Tirhakah may have taken the Assyrians at Jerusalem by surprise. Contributing to Tirhakah's success was the fact that the Assyrian soldiers and their horses did not have access to water. Not only had Hezekiah provided a secure water supply for himself by cutting a tunnel from the Gihon spring that brought water inside Jerusalem (2 Kgs 20:20), but also he had stopped up the springs and other sources of water in the countryside outside the city (2 Chr 32:2–4).

Following the Kushite victory, Aubin thinks that a deal was worked out with Sennacherib whereby Hezekiah retained his independence but paid tribute. Both the biblical author (2 Kgs 18:13–16) and Sennacherib acknowledge that Hezekiah paid tribute. However, Sennacherib did not victoriously "carry away" the spoils of Jerusalem but received them "later," suggesting a negotiated settlement.[9] And a negotiated settlement presupposes a Judahite victory and the support of Tirhakah, giving Judah bargaining power.

Why the Role of the Kushites Has not Been Recognized

If such a strong case exists for Tirhakah and Kushite Egypt being the source of Jerusalem's rescue, why has that role not been widely recognized? Aubin

9. *ANET*, 288a.

deals with this question in the third part of his book, "Why History Has Distorted the Kushites' Achievement." The first to obscure the role of Tirhakah was the B2 source, 2 Kgs 19:9b–35. During the Babylonian exile (587–538 BCE) when B2 was written, the historical situation was profoundly different from the time of B1 (about fifty years after 701), and the needs of the people were different. Egypt had become an ally of Assyria and the enemy of Judah. The Twenty-sixth Dynasty had been established by the Assyrian monarch Ashurbanipal; when Assyria was threatened by Babylonia, Egypt came to the aid of Assyria. Under King Josiah, Judah made a bid for independence and tried to stop Pharaoh Necho II, who was on the way to help Assyria. But Josiah lost his life, and Judah became the vassal of Egypt (2 Kgs 23:29–30). Later, with the assurance of Egyptian aid, Judah revolted against Babylonia, but sufficient aid was not forthcoming. Thus, those who produced the B2 account had reason not to give credit to Egypt for rescuing Jerusalem in 701. Their concern was not to honor Egypt for a past deed, but to give hope to a defeated and exiled people.

Aubin maintains that B2 is to be understood in the light of Deuteronomy 7 and the role of the angel of the Lord in the Exodus and the conquest. According to Deuteronomy 7, God requires strict obedience to the laws given by Moses. One who fulfills this requirement can expect a miraculous intervention on his or her behalf. To explain why Jerusalem was delivered, the author of B2 idealizes Hezekiah as one who trusted in God and kept the commandments that the Lord gave to Moses. According to Deuteronomy 7, those who blatantly oppose God are liable to suffer swift retaliation. Therefore, B2 attributes the deliverance of Jerusalem to the angel of the Lord. "Despite the fact that, historically speaking, it is a total fabrication, B2 does not spring from a calculated effort to 'cover up' as such the Kushite accomplishment" (218). The angel of the Lord is made the agent of deliverance for didactic purposes. "The angel gives majesty to the Deliverance story and helps to elevate it to a high level of significance" (218). "The ancients saw the revision of texts (or the writing of entirely new ones) as essential precisely in order to be truthful" (210).

A second reason that the achievement of Kushite Egypt in the rescue of Jerusalem is not well known is traceable to modern scholars. Almost to a person, modern scholars charge Kushite Egypt with maliciously and ineptly instigating revolt among the small states of Khor and, therefore, with being "to blame for the devastation of Judah and much of Khor" (233). The only source cited in support of this view is the visit of the Kushite ambassadors to Jerusalem in Isaiah 18. Aubin argues that those ambassadors could just as well have urged Hezekiah not to revolt or could have cautioned Hezekiah to prepare for invasion. Moreover, a number of passages in Isaiah, such as 20:1–6; 31:1; and 30:1–2, 6–7, make it clear that it was Judah who sought an alliance with Egypt. Also, inscriptions from Sargon and Sennacherib identify Judah and neighboring states as imploring Egypt to send military aid. Furthermore, there is no evidence of the Kushite leadership of Egypt being imperialistic. The hard life under Assyrian domination was the real reason for Hezekiah's revolt. Four of the five Philistine city-states were subject to Assyria, and Hezekiah's expansion into Philistine territory (2 Kgs 18:8) was ample reason for Sennacherib's retaliation. Aubin also points out that scholars are indulgent of Assyria for its imperialistic ventures, but they are reproachful and disdainful of Kushite Egypt's involvement in Judah's affairs.

Just when Aubin thought he had completed his research, he chanced upon a book written by A. H. L. Heeren, a famous professor at the University of Göttingen, and published in 1838.[10] Heeren expressed admiration for Kushites and gave Tirhakah credit for rescuing Jerusalem! This discovery spurred Aubin on to read further in eighteenth- and nineteenth-century scholarship. To his surprise, he found a consistently positive attitude toward Kushites. He also found that the story of Jerusalem's deliverance was well known. When Lord Byron wrote "The Destruction of Sennacherib" in 1815, he did not have to explain who Sennacherib was or even to identify the city Sennacherib threatened. Major popular works of the nineteenth century and earlier gave credit to Kushites for the rescue of Jerusalem in either a supporting or a leading role.

Aubin regards John Calvin's (1509–64) discussion of the Isaiah version of the rescue of Jerusalem as showing "an understanding of the politics behind the conflict of 701 that is . . . far more penetrating than that of any modern scholar" (238). Aubin also found a respectful attitude toward Africans in the arts, as evidenced by Verdi's Aida (1871); by an 1872 bronze statue of an African woman holding up the globe along with Caucasian, Amerindian, and Oriental women; and by an 1881 painting by Edward Burne-Jones of a black African king wooing a white maiden.

Then suddenly, beginning about 1880, "respect for Africa makes way for disdain . . . a societal sea change took place in both the arts and in scholarship . . . and alternatives to the Kushite-rescue theory gain an unprecedented degree of acceptance" (243). A factor in this turnaround

10. Heeren, *Historical Researches*, 2nd ed., vol. 1, 209–91, 471.

was the influence of Darwin's *On the Origin of Species* of 1859. But the real cause was the European subjugation of all Africa between 1880 and 1900. To subjugate Africa, Europeans found it necessary to regard Africans as intellectually and morally inferior.

The European states were able to carve up Africa with a clear conscience at the end of the nineteenth century because of an alliance between the state, the university, and the church. Imperialists in the national government needed experts from the university to "establish" the inferiority of Africans, and they needed the church to bless the work of the state as a mission of civilizing and Christianizing the "benighted." This mutual reinforcement worked especially well in Britain, the foremost of the European imperialist countries, and the prime exemplar of the arrangement was Archibald Henry Sayce (1845–1933).

Sayce was an ordained deacon of the Anglican Church, professor of Assyriology at Oxford University, and active archaeologist who spent seventeen winters in the Nile Valley—and he was widely published. His achievements are impressive: he wrote the first English grammar of Assyriology, he knew twenty or more ancient and modern languages, he deciphered the ancient Armenian cuneiform, he was the first to copy and publish the Hebrew inscription commemorating the completion of Hezekiah's tunnel, he was the first to detect the existence of the ancient Hittite Empire in Asia Minor, and he was the first to identify the ruins of Meroe. He was also the friend and confidant of British Prime Minister William Ewart Gladstone, as well as the military commanders and governors of Egypt and Sudan. Through those friendships and associations, Sayce "lost all critical distance between himself—as a scholar and cleric who was originally probably quite devoted to ideals like truth and justice—and empire" (260). That loss may explain Sayce's behavior and thoughts about race.

While Sayce was on an archaeological expedition through central Egypt in 1884–85, the provincial governor asked Sayce what to do about one hundred thirty brigands who had been arrested on suspicion of robbing and killing peasants. British authorities in Cairo had insisted on trials, but the governor feared that a jury would not convict them. Sayce's advice: execute them immediately and tell Cairo that their telegram had arrived too late. Sayce had an ambivalent attitude toward the Kushite rulers of Egypt, at one time placing them with the white race and characterizing them as the most handsome of people and at another time calling them

Negroes, whom he regarded as inept and the ugliest of humans. Aubin cites the following quote from Sayce's *The Races of the Old Testament*[11] "The Negro, in fact, stands about as much below the European as he stands above the orang-outang."

A Critical Evaluation of Aubin's Position

Critical to Aubin's position is his contention that there were two Kushite Egyptian armies involved in the events of 701. Although it is not explicitly stated in Assyrian or biblical sources, it is a valid deduction in my judgment. Sennacherib refers to the army that fought against him at Eltekeh as an army of the "kings of Egypt," that is, rulers from Lower Egypt, and he refers to them as led, not by Tirhakah, but by "Egyptian princes." This army had been defeated and posed no threat to Sennacherib, nor did it offer any hope to Jerusalem. The biblical material places Tirhakah's appearance to fight against Sennacherib after Lachish had been captured and Sennacherib had left Lachish to fight against Libnah (2 Kgs 19:8–9a). This event would have been some time after the battle at Eltekeh, which was fought in Philistine territory, before Sennacherib invaded Judah. If the B2 material (2 Kgs 19:9b–35) is regarded as a later addition, the connection between Tirhakah's advance and Sennacherib's departure is obvious. While neither biblical nor Assyrian sources refer to a military engagement between Tirhakah and Sennacherib, Herodotus says Sennacherib's army "suffered severe losses during their retreat,"[12] and Isa 22:1–14 is a witness to a military engagement (see also Isa 14:24–27; 17:12–14; and 31:8–9).

In Aubin's concern to call attention to the importance of the rescue of Jerusalem in Israelite and Western history, he takes critical positions and expresses views about the religion of Israel that not everyone will agree with. A number of scholars regard the deliverance of Jerusalem in 701 as second in importance to the Exodus. Aubin (220) agrees with this and goes a step further:

> So if, as much belief-neutral research now holds, the exodus is largely myth (and at best an inflation of a minor migration from Egypt), and if the date of the exodus narrative's composition was long after 701 BCE (as is now widely acknowledged), then it would follow that the rescue of Jerusalem was far more important *as an*

11. Sayce, *The Races of the Old Testament*, 253.

12. Herodotus, *History*, 141.

> *historical event* than a journey from Egypt in shaping the Hebrew identity as a chosen people. As a factual event that shaped the Hebrew identity as the chosen people, the city's rescue would be in a class by itself.

While this view of the exodus is not without (minimalist) scholarly support, it would undoubtedly be news to the authors of the Song of Moses (Exodus 15:1–18), the Yahwist and Elohist epics, and the books of Amos and Hosea and to the many scholars who regard the Exodus as the primal, birthing, formative event of Israel's existence.

Aubin conjectures that "if pious Yahwists from Jerusalem several centuries after Sennacherib's invasion could have traveled back in time and visited their city in the months leading up to the crisis, they would have found the local religion almost unrecognizable" (25). They would have found that most of the people were polytheists, that religion consisted primarily of sacrificial rites, that the Mosaic laws and the Ten Commandments were unknown, that there was no canonical scripture, and that circumcision was not practiced. Furthermore, Aubin surmises, there was no covenant between God and Israel; the Hebrews did not think of themselves as the chosen people; the citizens of Judah were not Jews, for Judaism had not yet evolved; Zion was only one of many sacred mounts, not an inviolable, holy city; and Yahweh was a local deity whose sovereignty was pretty much confined to Judah. How one evaluates this characterization will depend on one's critical stance. Aubin finds support for those views among some established scholars, but one suspects that the major factor leading Aubin to espouse such positions is his concern to highlight the importance of Jerusalem's deliverance as a creative power in shaping the religion of Israel—and the importance of Tirhakah's role in that deliverance.

Aubin also holds that the biblical portrait of Hezekiah should be regarded as a later, idealized version. Hezekiah was *a* leader, not *the* leader of the opposition to Assyria, as is generally maintained. Hezekiah was a weak monarch; he did not have a commanding personality, and important military leaders deserted him when Jerusalem was threatened. While Isaiah does not mention Hezekiah by name, the prophet is very critical of the king's policies and regards Hezekiah's revolt as a "serious miscalculation." The workers who cut the tunnel for the Gihon spring to provide water for Jerusalem did not think enough of Hezekiah to mention him in their inscription. Hezekiah centralized worship in Jerusalem so that he could control the cult and benefit from it financially. He is credited with no social reform. He is never pictured on the battlefield with his troops. And during his sickness, Hezekiah "appears . . . to have provided his people with something less than exemplary helmsmanship" (38).

In my judgment, Aubin has overdrawn the negative aspects of Hezekiah's character. Sennacherib refers to Hezekiah as "overbearing and proud."[13] While Luli, the king of Sidon, fled at the approach of Sennacherib, Hezekiah stood his ground.[14] It took a bold and daring person to defy Assyria, the strongest power in the biblical world at that time. Hezekiah "attacked the Philistines as far as Gaza" (2 Kgs 18:8); removed Padi, the pro-Assyrian king of Ekron; and kept him a prisoner in Jerusalem.[15] Those acts demonstrated vigorous and courageous leadership. Hezekiah's destruction of the high places and his centralization of worship in Jerusalem were so radical that they made news in Assyria (2 Kgs 18:22). A weak person would not have undertaken such a fundamental change. Is not Aubin critical of Hezekiah because he wants to shift the credit for the rescue of Jerusalem from Hezekiah to Tirhakah? Why not give credit to both?

Whatever one's critical stance regarding the history and religion of ancient Israel, and however one regards Hezekiah, Aubin has made a significant contribution to biblical studies by placing Kushite Egypt prominently and justifiably on the stage of Israelite and world history. Aubin's answer to the mystery of how Jerusalem was rescued from the Assyrian siege of 701 BCE is attractive and convincing. He has made us aware of what a tragic loss it would have been if Jerusalem had not been rescued—and of how great was the contribution of Tirhakah to the rescue of the city. And Aubin's demonstration of the correlation between the negative attitude toward Kushites and European imperialistic expansion in Africa during the latter part of the nineteenth century is powerful confirmation of the influence of social location on interpretation.

13. *ANET*, 288b.

14. *ANET*, 287b.

15. *ANET*, 287b.

Bibliography

Adamo, David T. "The African Wife of Moses: An Examination of Numbers 12:1–9." *ATJ* 18 (1989) 230–37.

Addis. William E. *The Documents of the Hexateuch*. London: Nutt, 1892.

Aharoni, Yohanan. *The Land of the Bible*. Rev. ed. Translated by Anson F. Rainey. Philadelphia: Fortress, 1979.

Ahlström, Gösta W. *The History of Ancient Palestine*. Edited by Diana Edelman. Minneapolis: Fortress, 1993.

Albright, W. F. *Archaeology and the Religion of Israel*. Baltimore: Johns Hopkins University Press, 1953.

———. "A Catalogue of Early Hebrew Lyric Poems." *HUCA* 23 (1950–51) 1–39.

———. "Egypt and the Early History of the Negeb." *JPOS* 4 (1924) 146–47.

———. "The Land of Damascus between 1850 and 1750 B.C." *BASOR* 84 (1941) 30–36.

———. "Moses in Historical and Theological Perspective." In *Magnalia Dei: The Mighty Acts of God: Essays on the Bible and Archaeology in Memory of G. Ernest Wright*, edited by Frank Moore Cross, et al., 120–31. Garden City, NY: Doubleday, 1976.

———. Review of *L'épithète divine Jahvé Seba'ôt: Étude philologique, historique et exégétique* by B. N. Wambacq, O. Praem. In *JBL* 67 (1948) 377–81.

———. *Yahweh and the Gods of Canaan*. Garden City, NY: Doubleday, 1969.

Allen, Don Cameron. *The Legend of Noah: Renaissance Rationalism in Art, Science, and Letters*. Urbana: University of Illinois Press, 1949.

Allier, Raoul. *Une énigme troublante: La race nègre et la malédiction de Cham*. Les cahiers missionnaires 16. Paris: Société des Missions, 1930.

Alt, Albrecht. "The Formation of the Israelite State." In *Essays on Old Testament History and Religion*, 171–238. Translated by R. A. Wilson. 1966. Reprint, Biblical Seminar 9. Sheffield: JSOT Press, 1989.

Amsler, Samuel. *Osée, Joël, Abdias, Jonas, Amos*. Commentaire de l'ancien Testament 11a. Paris: Neuchâtel, Delachauz & Niestlé, 1965.

Anderson, Bernhard W. *Understanding the Old Testament*. 4th ed. Englewood Cliffs, NJ: Prentice Hall, 1986.

Armstrong, Gregory T. *Die Genesis in der Alten Kirche*. Beiträge zur Geschichte der biblischen Hermeneutik 4. Tübingen: Mohr/Siebeck, 1962.

Aubin, Henry. *The Rescue of Jerusalem: The Alliance between Hebrews and Africans in 701 BC*. Toronto: Doubleday Canada/New York: Soho, 2002.

Avishur, Yitzhak. "Treaty Terminology in the Moses-Jethro Story Ex 18:1–12." *AuOr* 6 (1968) 139–47.

Bibliography

Bacon, Benjamin W. *The Genesis of Genesis*. Hartford: Student, 1893.

———. "Notes on the Analysis of Genesis XV." *Hebraica* 7 (1890/91) 75–76.

Bailey, Randall C. "Africans in Old Testament Poetry and Narratives." In *Stony the Road We Trod: African American Biblical Interpretation*, edited by Cain Hope Felder, 165–84. Minneapolis: Fortress, 1991.

Ball, C. J. *The Book of Genesis*. Sacred Books of the Old Testament 1. Leipzig: Hinrichs, 1896.

Bassett, F. W. "Noah's Nakedness and the Curse on Canaan: A Case of Incest?" *VT* 21 (1971) 232–37.

Bastide, Roger. "Color, Racism, and Christianity." *Daedalus* 96 (1967) 312–27.

Beardsley, Grace Hadley. *The Negro in Greek and Roman Civilization*. New York: Arno, 1979.

Beck, Eleonore. *Gottes Traum: Eine menschliche Welt Hosea–Amos–Micha*. Stuttgarter Kleiner Kommentar 14. Stuttgart: Katholisches Bibelwerk, 1972.

Bede. Edited by D.H. Farmer. Translated by Leo Sherley-Price. *Ecclesiastical History of the English People*. London: Penguin Classic, 1991.

Bennett, Robert A., Jr. "Africa and the Biblical Period." *Harvard Theological Review* 64 (1971) 483–500.

Bennett, W. H. *Genesis*. Century Bible. Edinburgh: Jack, 1904.

Bentzen, Aage, *Introduction to the Old Testament*. 2 vols. in 1. Copenhagen: Gads, 1948.

Bewer, J. A. *The Book of the Twelve Prophets 1*. Harper's Annotated Bible Series. New York: Harper, 1949.

Böhl, Franz. *Kanaanäer und Hebräer: Untersuchungen zur Vorgeschichte des Volkstums und der Religion aufdem Boden Kanaans*. Beiträge zur Wissenschaft vom Alten Testament 9. Leipzig: Hinrichs, 1911.

Bosse, Käthe. *Die menschliche Figur in der Rundplastik der ägyptischen Spätzeit von der XXII. bis zur XXX. Dynastie*. Aegyptologische Forschungen 1. Glückstadt: Augustin, 1936.

Bič, Miloš. *Das Buch Amos*. Berlin: Evangelische Verlagsanstalt, 1969.

Binns, L. Elliott. "Midianite Elements in Hebrew Religion." *JTS* 31 (1930) 337–54.

Blank, Sheldon, H. *Jeremiah: Man and Prophet*. Cincinnati: Hebrew Union College Press, 1961.

Bochart, Samuel, *Hierozoicon Sive biparti Operis De Animalibus Scripturae*. London: Roycroft, 1663.

Breasted, James Henry. *Ancient Records of Egypt*. Vol. 2. Chicago: University of Chicago Press, 1906.

———. *A History of the Ancient Egyptians*. New York: Scribner, 1908.

———. *A History of Egypt*. 2nd ed. New York: Scribner, 1909.

Brekelmans, Chr. H. W. "Exodus XVIII and the Origin of Yahwism in Israel." *OtSt* 10 (1954) 215–24.

Bright, John. *A History of Israel*. Philadelphia: Westminster, 1981.

Browne, Thomas. *Pseudodoxia epidemica* (1646). In *The Works of Sir Thomas Browne, III*. Edited by G. Keynes. London: J.C. for G. Beedle and T. Collins, 1928.

Brueggeman, Walter. "David and His Theologian." *CBQ* 30 (1968) 156–81. Reprinted in *David and His Theology: Literary, Social, and Theological Investigations of the Early Monarchy*, 1–28. Eugene, OR: Cascade Books, 2011.

Briggs, Charles A. *Messianic Prophecy*. New York: Scribner, 1886.

Brightman, Edgar Sheffield. *The Sources of the Hexateuch.* 1918. Reprint, Eugene, OR: Wipf & Stock, 2017.

Buber, Martin. *Moses: The Revelation and the Covenant.* Harper Torchbooks. New York: Harper, 1958.

Budde, Karl. *Die biblische Urgeschichte (Gen. 1—12, 5).* Giessen: Ricker, 1883.

———. *The Religion of Israel to the Exile.* American Lectures on the History of Religions. New York: Putnam, 1899.

———. "Zu Text und Auslegung des Buches Amos." *JBL* 44 (1925) 63–122.

Budge, E. A. Wallis. *The Egyptian Sudan: Its History and Monuments.* Vol. 2. London: Kegan Paul, Trench, Trübner, 1907.

Burns, Rita J. *Has the Lord Indeed Spoken Only through Moses? A Study of the Biblical Portrait of Miriam.* SBL Dissertation Series 84. Atlanta: Scholars, 1987.

Buswell, James O., III. *Slavery, Segregation and Scripture.* Grand Rapids: Eerdmans, 1964.

Calkins, Raymond. *The Modern Message of the Minor Prophets.* New York: Harper, 1947.

Calvin, John. *Commentaries on the Last Four Books of Moses,* Vol. 4. Translated by C. W. Bingham. Grand Rapids: Baker, 1979, Vol. 1, 1743 edition.

Calvoer, Caspar. *Gloria Mosis.* Goslar, 1696.

Carpenter, J. Estlin, and C. Hartford-Battersby. *The Hexateuch according to the Revised Version,* II. New York: Longmans, Green, 1900.

Cassuto, Umberto. *A Commentary on the Book of Genesis.* Vol. 2, *From Noah to Abraham.* Translated by Israel Abrahams. Jerusalem: Magnes, 1964.

Chaine, Joseph. *Le Livre de la Genèsis.* Lectio divina 3. Paris: Cerf, 1951.

Charles, P. "Les noirs, fils de Cham le maudit." *Nouvelle Revue Théologique* 55 (1928) 721–39.

Cheyne, T. K. *Traditions and Beliefs of Ancient Israel.* London: Black, 1907.

Childs, Brevard S. *Isaiah and the Assyrian Crisis.* Studies in Biblical Theology 2/3. London: SCM, 1967.

Clamer, Albert. *La Genèsis.* La Sainte Bible. Paris: Letouzey & Ané, 1953.

Clark, W. Malcolm. "The Flood and the Structure of the Pre-patriarchal History." *ZAW* 83 (1971) 184–211.

Clop, P. E. "La prose 'dies irae' et l'ordre des Frères Mineurs." *Review de Chant Gregorien* 16 (1907) 43–53.

Coats, George W. *Rebellion in the Wilderness: The Murmuring Motif in the Wilderness Traditions of the Old Testament.* New York: Abingdon, 1968.

Cody, Aelred. "Exodus 18:12: Jethro Accepts a Covenant with the Israelites." *Biblica* 49 (1968) 153–66.

Condamin, Albert. *Le Livre de Jérémie.* Paris: Gabalda, 1920.

Copher, Charles B. "The Black Presence in the Old Testament." In *Stony the Road We Trod: African American Biblical Interpretation.* Edited by Cain Hope Felder. Minneapolis: Fortress, 1991.

Cornill. Carl H. *Introduction to the Canonical Books of the Old Testament.* Translated by G. H. Box. Theological Translation Library 23. 1907. Reprint, Eugene, OR: Wipf & Stock, 2006.

Cowles, Henry. *The Minor Prophets.* New York: Appleton, 1868.

Cripps, Richard S. *A Critical and Exegetical Commentary on the Book of Amos.* Edited, with introduction, notes and excursuses by Richard S. Cripps. New York: Macmillan, 1929.

Cross, Frank M. *Canaanite Myth and Hebrew Epic: Essays in the History of the Religion of Israel.* Cambridge: Harvard University Press, 1973.

Crowfoot, J. W., and Grace M. Crowfoot. *Early Ivories from Samaria.* Samaria-Sebaste. London: Palestine Exploration Fund, 1938.

Cunliffe-Jones, Hubert. *Jeremiah: Introduction and Commentary.* Torch Bible Commentaries. London: SCM, 1960.

Davidson, A. B. "The Prophet Amos." *The Expositor,* 3rd series, 5 (1887) 161–79.

Davis, David Brion. *The Problem of Slavery in Western Culture.* Ithaca, NY: Cornell University Press, 1966.

de Fraine, Jean. *Genesis.* De Boeken van het Oude Testament. Roermond: Romen & Zonen, 1963.

Delitzsch, Franz. *A New Commentary on Genesis.* Vol. 1. Translated by Sophia Taylor. New York: Funk & Wagnalls, 1889.

Desnoyers, L. "Le Prophète Amos." *Revue Biblique* 14 (1917) 218–46.

Dillmann, August. *Genesis Critically and Exegetically Expounded,* I. Translated by William Barron Stevenson. Edinburgh: T. & T. Clark, 1897.

Dods, Marcus. *The Book of Genesis.* Expositor's Bible. Edinburgh: T. & T. Clark, 1907.

Donner, Herbert, "The Separate States of Israel and Judah." In *Israelite and Judaean History,* edited by John H. Hayes and J. Maxwell Miller, 381–434. Philadelphia: Westminster, 1977.

Driver, S. R. *The Book of Genesis.* Westminster Commentaries. 15th ed. London: Methuen, 1948; 1st ed., 1904.

———. *The Books of Joel and Amos.* Cambridge Bible. Cambridge: University Press, 1897.

DuBois, W. E. B. *The World and Africa.* 2nd ed. New York: International, 1965.

Duhm, Bernhard. "Anmerkungen zu den Zwölf Propheten." *ZAW* 31 (1911) 161–204.

Dummelow, John R. "Genesis." In *A Commentary on the Holy Bible,* edited by J. R. Dummelow, 1–46. New York: Macmillan, 1916.

Dussaud, René. "Cham et Canaan." *Revue de l'Histoire des Religious* 59 (1909) 221–30.

Eaton, J. H. *Obadiah, Nahum, Habakkuk, Zephaniah.* Torch Bible Commentaries. London: SCM, 1961.

Edens, A. "A Study of the Book of Zephaniah as to the Date, Extent and Significance of the Genuine Writings." PhD diss. Vanderbilt University, 1954.

Edghill, Ernest Arthur. *The Book of Amos.* Westminster Commentaries. London: Methuen, 1914.

Edgerton, William F., and John A. Wilson. *Historical Records of Ramses III: The Texts in Medinat Habu.* Studies in Ancient Oriental Civilization 12. Chicago: University of Chicago Press, 1936.

Eerdmans, B.D. *Die Composition der Genesis.* Reprint. Pranava Books, 2019; Original, 1908.

Ehrlich, Arnold B. *Randglossen zur Hebräischen Bible.* Vol. 5, *Ezechiel und die kleinen Propheten.* Leipzig: Hinrichs, 1912.

———. *Randglossen zur Hebräischen Bible: Textkritisches, Sprachliches und Sachliches.* Vol. 1: *Genesis und Exodus.* Leipzig: Hinrichs, 1908.

Eichrodt, Walther. *Die Quellen der Genesis von neuem untersucht.* BZAW 31. Giessen: Töpelmann, 1916.

Eissfeldt, Otto. "Genesis." In *Interpreter's Dictionary of the Bible,* edited by George Arthur Buttrick, 2:366–80. New York: Abingdon, 1962.

———. *Hexateuch-Synopse.* Leipzig: Hinrich, 1922.

Elliott, Ralph H. *The Message of Genesis.* St. Louis: Broadman, 1961.
Emerton, J. A. "New Light on Israelite Religion: The Implications of the Inscriptions from Kuntillet 'Ajrud." *ZAW* 94 (1982) 2–20.
Encyclopedia of World Art. Vol. 4. New York: McGraw-Hill, 1961.
Erbt, Wilhelm. *Jeremia und seine Zeit: die Geschichte der letzten fünfzig Jahre des vorexilischen Juda.* Göttingen: Vandenhoeck & Ruprecht, 1902.
Erdmans, B. D. *Alttestamentliche Studiën I: Die Komposition der Genesis.* Giessen: Töpelmann, 1908.
Ewald, Heinrich. *Die Composition der Genesis.* 1823. Reprint, Kessinger, 2010.
Farrar, Frederic William. *The Minor Prophets.* Men of the Bible. New York: Randolph, 1910.
Felder, Cain Hope. "Race, Racism and the Biblical Narratives." In *Stony the Road We Trod: African American Biblical Interpretation*, edited by Cain Hope Felder, 127–45. Minneapolis: Fortress, 1991.
———, ed. *Stony the Road We Trod: African American Biblical Interpretation.* Minneapolis: Fortress, 1991.
Feldman, Louis H. *Josephus and Modern Scholarship 1937–1980.* Berlin: de Gruyter, 1984.
Fensham, F. C. "Did a Treaty between the Israelites and the Kenites Exist?" *BASOR* 175 (1964) 51–54.
Fohrer, Georg. *Introduction to the Old Testament.* Translated by David E. Green. New York: Abingdon, 1968.
Freedman, David Noel. "Who Is Like Thee among the Gods? The Religion of Early Israel." In *Ancient Israelite Religion: Essays in Honor of Frank Moore Cross*, edited by Patrick D. Miller et al., 315–35. Philadelphia: Fortress, 1987.
Fretheim, Terence E. *Creation, Fall, and Flood: Studies in Genesis 1–11.* Minneapolis: Augsburg, 1969.
Frey, Hellmuth. *Das Buch der Anfänge: Kapitel 1–11 des ersten Buches Mose, für Freunde und Verächter der Bibel.* Die Botschaft des Alten Testaments. Stuttgart: Calwer, 1950.
Friedel, Lawrence M. "Is the Curse of Cham on the Negro Race?" *Ecclesiastical Review* 106 (1942) 447–53.
Fritsch, Charles T. *The Book of Genesis.* Layman's Bible Commentary. Richmond: John Knox, 1959.
Gardiner, Alan H. "Piankhi's Instructions to His Army." *JEA* 21 (1935) 219.
———. "The Tomb of a Much-Travelled Theban Official." *JEA* 4 (1917) 28–38.
Genebrard, Gilbert. *Chronographiae libri quatuor.* Paris: Martinum Iuuenis, 1580.
Gerleman, Gillis. *Zephanja: Textkritisch und Literarisch Untersucht.* Lund: CWK Gleerup, 1942
Ghillany, F. W. (pseudonym: R. von der Alm). *Theologische Briefe an den Gebilden der deutschen Nation.* Vol. 1. Leipzig: Wigand, 1863.
Giesebrecht, Friedrich. *Das Buch Jeremia: Ubersetzt und Erklart.* Handkommentar zum Alten Testament. Göttingen: Vandenhoeck & Ruprecht, 1907.
Ginzberg, Louis. *Die Haggada bei den Kirchenvätern und in der apokryphen Literatur.* Berlin: Calvary, 1900.
———. *The Legends of the Jews.* Vol. 1. Philadelphia: Jewish Publication Society of America, 1925.
Giveon, Raphael. *Les bédouins Shosou des documents égyptiens.* Documenta et Monumenta Orientis Antiqui 18. Leiden: Brill, 1971.
———. "The Cities of Our God (2 Sam 10:12)." *JBL* 83 (1964) 415–16.

———. "Toponymes Ouest-Asiatiques à Soleb." *VT* 14 (1964) 239–55.

Glass, Jonathan, and Beno Rothenberg, "The Midian Pottery." In *Midian, Moab and Edom: the History and Archaelogy of the Late Bronze and Iron Age Jordan and North-West Arabia*, edited by John F. A. Sawyer and David J.A. Clines, 65–124. Sheffield: JSOT Press, 1983.

Glueck, Nelson. "Kenites and Kenizzites." *PEQ* 72 (1940) 22–24.

Goldman, Solomon. *In the Beginning*. Philadelphia: Jewish Publication Society, 1949.

Gordon, Alexander Reid. *The Early Traditions of Genesis*. Edinburgh: T. & T. Clark, 1907.

Görg, Manfred. "Jahwe—ein Toponym?" *BN* 1 (1976) 7–14.

Gottwald, Norman K. *All the Kingdoms of the Earth: Israelite Prophecy and International Relations in the Ancient Near East*. 1964. Reprint, Minneapolis: Fortress, 2008.

Grabbe, Lester L., ed. *Like a Bird in a Cage: The Invasion of Sennacherib in 701 BCE*. JSOTSup 363. New York: Sheffield Academic, 2003.

Graf, Karl Heinrich. *Der Prophet Jeremia erklärt*. Leipzig: Weigel, 1862.

Graves, Robert, and Raphael Patai. *Hebrew Myths: The Book of Genesis*. Garden City, NY: Doubleday, 1964.

Gray, George Buchanan. *Sacrifice in the Old Testament*. New York: Ktav, 1971.

Green, W. Henry. "The Pentateuchal Question." *Hebraica* 5 (1888/89) 137–89.

———. *The Unity of the Book of Genesis*. New York: Scribner, 1895.

Gressmann, Hugo. *Die älteste Geschichtsschreibung und Prophetie Israels*. 2nd ed. Schriften des Alten Testaments 2. Göttingen: Vandenhoeck & Ruprecht, 1921.

Grispino, J. A. "Note." In *The Old Testament of the Holy Bible*, Confraternity Version, 23. New York, 1964.

Gunkel, Hermann. *Die Genesis übersetzt und erklärt*. Handkommentar zum Alten Testament. 3rd ed. Göttingen: Vandenhoeck & Ruprecht, 1910.

———. *Die Urgeschichte und die Patriarchen*. Die Schriften des Alten Testaments. Göttingen: Vandenhoeck & Ruprecht, 1911.

Guthe, Herman. *Der Prophet Amos*. 4th ed. Die Heilige Schrift des Alten Testament 2. Tübingen: Mohr/Siebeck, 1923.

Halder, Alfred. "Canaan." *Interpreter's Dictionary of the Bible*, edited by George Arthur Buttrick, 1:494. New York: Abingdon, 1962.

———. "Canaanites." *Interpreter's Dictionary of the Bible*, edited by George Arthur Buttrick, 1:494–98. New York: Abingdon, 1962.

Halévy, J. *Recherches Biblique*. Vol. 1. Paris: Leroux, 1895.

Hall, H. R. *Cambridge Ancient History* 3: *The Assyrian Empire*. Cambridge: Cambridge: University Press, 1929.

Hallo, William W. "From Qarqar to Carchemish: Assyria and Israel in the Light of New Discoveries." *Biblical Archaeologist* 23/2 (1960) 34–61.

Hammershaimb, E. *The Book of Amos: A Commentary*. Oxford: Blackwell, 1970.

Hannemann, J. L. *Curiosum scrutinum nigridinis filiorum Cham*. Kiel: n.p., 1677.

Hansberry, William Leo. *Pillars in Ethiopian History*. Edited by Joseph E. Harris. Washington, DC: Howard University Press, 1974.

Hardt, H. von der. *Ephemerides philologicae*. Helmstadt: Hammius, 1696.

Harper, W. R. *A Critical and Exegetical Commentary on Amos and Hosea*. International Critical Commentary. New York: Scribner, 1905.

———. "The Pentateuchal Question. I. Gen. 1:1–12:5." *Hebraica* 5 (1888/89) 18–73.

Harrison, R. K. *Introduction to the Old Testament*. Peabody, MA: Hendrickson, 2004.

Hauret, Charles. *Amos et Osée*. Verbum Salutis Ancien Testament 5. Paris: Beauchesne, 1970.

Heemroodt, J. "Kanaän Vervloekt." *Het Heilig Land* 12 (1959) 129–31.

Heeren, A. H. L. *Historical Researches into the Political, Intercourse, and Trade of the Carthaginians, Ethiopians, and Egyptians*. 2nd ed. vol. 1. Translated by D. A. Talboys. London: Bohn, 1857.

Heinisch, Paul. *Das Buch Genesis*. Die Heilige Schrift des Alten Testamentes. Bonn: Hanstein, 1930.

Helck, Wolfgang. *Die Beziehungen Ägyptens zu Vorderasien im 3. und 2. Jahrtausend v. Chr*. 2nd ed. Ägyptologische Abhandlungen 5. Wiesbaden: Harrassowitz, 1971.

Heller, Jan. "Zephanjas Ahnenreihe: eine redaktionsgeschichtliche Bemerkung zu Zeph 1." *VT* 21 (1971) 102–4.

Henderson, E. *The Book of the Twelve Minor Prophets*. Andover, MA: Draper, 1868.

Heras, Henry. "The Curse of Noe." *Catholic Biblical Quarterly* 12 (1950) 64–67.

Hermann, J. "Zu Gen. 9:18–27." *ZAW* 30 (1910) 127–131.

Herrmann, Siegfried. "Der alttestamentliche Gottesname." *EvT* 26 (1966) 281–93.

———. "Der Name Jhw in den Inschriften von Soleb." In *Fourth World Congress of Jewish Studies*. Vol. 1, 213–16. Jerusalem: Magnes, 1967.

Herodotus. *The Histories*. Oxford World's Classics. Translated by Robin Waterfield. Oxford: Oxford University Press, 2008.

Herner, S. "Athalja: Ein Beitrag zur Frage nach dem Alte des Jahwisten und des Elohisten.' in *Vom alten Testament: Festschrift Karl Marti*. BZAW 41. Berlin: de Gruyter, 1925, 137–41.

Heschel, Abraham Joshua. *The Prophets*. New York: Harper & Row, 1962.

Heyde, Henning. *Kain, der erste Jahwe-Verehrer*. Stuttgart: Calwer, 1965.

Hicks, R. Lansing. "Ham." In *Interpreter's Dictionary of the Bible*, edited by George Arthur Buttrick, 2:15. New York: Abingdon, 1962.

Hitzig, Ferdinand. *Der Prophet Jeremia*. Brussels: Lang, 1866.

Hoftijzer, J. "Some Remarks on the Table of Noah's Drunkenness." In *Studies on the Book of Genesis*, 22–27. Oudtestamentische Studiën 12. Leiden: Brill, 1958.

Holzinger, H. *Einleitung in den Hexateuch*. Leipzig: Mohr/Siebeck, 1893.

———. *Genesis*. Kurzer Hand-Commentar zum Alten Testament 1. Leipzig: Mohr/Siebeck, 1889.

Hommel, Fritz. "Zerah the Cushite." *ExpTim* 8 (1896–97) 378–79.

Hoonacker, A. van. *Les douze petits Prophetes*. Etudes bibliques. Paris: Gabalda, 1908.

Horton, R. F. *The Minor Prophets*. Century Bible. Edinburgh: T. C. & E. C. Jack, n.d.

Huber, Friedrich. *Jahwe, Juda und die Anderen Völker Beim Propheten Jesaja*; BZAW. 1918. Reprint, Berlin: de Gruyter, 1976.

Hughes, R. L. "A Critical Study of the Meaning of *'RWR* in Genesis 9:18–27." PhD diss., New Orleans Baptist Theological Seminary, 1956.

Hyatt, J. Philip. "Yahweh as 'The God of My Father.'" *VT* 5 (1955) 135–36.

Jack, James William. *Samaria in Ahab's Time*. Edinburgh: T. & T. Clark, 1929.

Jacob, Benno. *Das erste Buch der Tora: Genesis*. Berlin: Schocken, 1934.

James, Fleming. "Amos." In *The Seventh-Day Adventist Bible Commentary*, 4:953–84. 7 vols. Washington, DC: Review & Herald, 1955.

———. *Personalities of the Old Testament*. New York: Scribner, 1951.

Jansma, Taeke. "Investigations into the Early Syrian Fathers on Genesis." In *Studies on the Book of Genesis*, 69–181. Oudtestamentische Studiën 12. Leiden: Brill, 1958.

Janssen, Jozef M. A. *Que sait-on actuellement du Pharaon Taharqa. Biblica* 34 (1953) 23–43.
Johnson, Aubrey R. *Sacral Kingship in Ancient Israel.* Cardiff: University of Wales Press, 1955.
Jordan, Winthrop D. *White Over Black.* Chapel Hill: University of NC Press, 1968.
Junker, Hubert. *Genesis.* Echter-Bible. 3rd ed. Würzburg: Echter, 1953; 1st ed., 1949.
Kapelrud, Arvid Schou. *The Message of the Prophet Zephaniah: Morphology and Ideas.* Oslo, Norway: Universitetsforlaget, 1975.
Kasher, Menahem. *Encyclopedia of Biblical Interpretation: A Millennial Anthology.* Vol. 2. Translated by Harry Freedman et al. New York: American Biblical Encyclopedia Society, 1955.
Kautzsch, E. *Die Heilige Schrift des Alten Testaments: Beilagen.* Leipzig: Mohr/Siebeck, 1894.
Kees, Hermann. *Aegyptische Kunst.* Breslau: Hirt, 1926.
Keil, C. F. *The Twelve Minor Prophets.* Biblical Commentary on the Old Testament. Edinburgh: T. & T. Clark, 1880.
Keller, Carl-Albert and René Vuilleumier. *Michee, Nahoum, Habacuc, Sophonie.* CAT 11b; Neuchâtel: Delachaux & Niestlé, 1971.
Kennett, R. H. "The Early Narratives of the Jahvistic Document of the Pentateuch." In *Old Testament Essays*, 1–41. Cambridge: Cambridge University Press, 1928.
Kent, C. F. *Narratives of the Beginning of Hebrew History.* New York: Bloch, 1908.
———. *The Heroes and Crises of Early Hebrew History.* New York: Scribner's, 1908.
Kenyon, Kathleen. *Royal Cities of the Old Testament.* New York: Schocken, 1971.
Kitchen, Kenneth A. *The Third Intermediate Period in Egypt* (1100–650 B. C.). Warminster, England: Aris & Phillips, 1973.
Klengel, Horst. "Das Land Kush in den Keilschrifttexten von Amarna." In *Ägypten und Kush*, edited by Erika Endesfelder et al., 227–32. Berlin: Akademie, 1977.
Knauf, Ernst A. *Midian.* Wiesbaden: Harrassowitz, 1988.
Koehler, Ludwig. *Amos.* Zürich: Beer, 1917.
Köhler, August. *Lehrbuch der Biblischen Geschichte: Alten Testament.* Vol. 1. Erlangen: Deichert, 1875.
König, Eduard. *Die Genesis.* Gütersloh: Bertelsmann, 1919.
Kraeling, Emil Gottlieb. "The Earliest Hebrew Flood Story." *JBL* 66 (1947) 279–293.
Kuenen, A. *An Historico-Critical Inquiry into the Origin and Composition of the Hexateuch.* Translated by Philip H. Wicksteed. 1886. Reprint, Eugene, OR: Wipk & Stock, 2005.
Kulp, K. "Der Hymnus *Dies irae, dies ilia.*" In *Monatsschrift für Gottesdienst und kirkliche Kunst* (1933), 256–63.
Laetsch, Theodore Ferdinand Karl. *The Minor Prophets.* Bible Commentary. St. Louis: Concordia, 1956.
Lamparter, Helmut. *Prophet wider Willen: der Prophet Jeremia.* Felixstowe, UK: Calwer, 1974.
Leclant, Jean. "Kushites and Meroites: Iconography of the African Rulers in the Ancient Upper Nile." In *From the Pharaohs to the Fall of the Roman Empire*, 89–132. The Image of the Black in Western Art 1. New York: Morrow, 1976.
Leclant, Jean, and Jean Yoyette. "Notes d'histoire et de civilisation éthiopiennes." *Bulletin de l'Institut Francais d'Archéologie Orientale* 51 (1952) 1–39.
Leslie, Elmer A. *Jeremiah.* Nashville: Abingdon, 1954.
Leupold, H. C. *Exposition of Genesis.* Columbus, OH: Wartburg, 1942.

Levene, Abraham. *The Early Syrian Fathers on Genesis*. London: Taylor's Foreign Press, 1951.

Levine, Baruch A. *Numbers 1–20*. Anchor Bible 4. New York: Doubleday, 1993.

Lewis, Jack P. *A Study of the Interpretation of Noah and the Flood in Jewish and Christian Literature*. Leiden: Brill, 1968.

Lipinski, Edward. Review of Arvid Schou Kapelrud, *The Message of the Prophet Zephaniah: Morphology andIdeas*. Oslo: Universitetsforlaget, 1975 in *VT* 25 (1975) 689.

Lippi, H. J. *Das Buch des Propheten Sophonias*. Biblische Studien XV/3. Freiburg: Herder, 1910.

Lods, Adolphe. *Historier de la Littérature Hébraïque et Juive: depuis les origines jusqu'à la ruine de l'état juif (135 après J.-C.)*. Bibliothèque historique. Paris: Pavot, 1950.

Logan, William M. *In the Beginning God*. Richmond: John Knox, 1957.

Löhr, Max. *Untersuchungen zum Buch Amos*. BZAW 4. Giessen: Töpelmann, 1901.

Luther, Martin. *Die Martin Luthers Werke: kritische Gesammtausgabe*. Vol. 44: *Genesis-vorlesung (cap. 31–50)*. Weimar: Böhlau, 1543/45.

Maag, Victor. *Text, Wortschatz und Begriffswelt des Buches Amos*. Leiden: Brill, 1951.

Maly, E. H. "Genesis." In *The Jerome Biblical Commentary*, edited by Raymond E. Brown et al., 7–46. Englewood Cliffs, NJ: Prentice-Hall, 1968.

Margoliouth, D. S. "Ham." In *A Dictionary of the Bible: Dealing with Its Language, Literature, and Contents, including the Biblical Theology*, edited by James Hastings, 2:288–89. 5 vols. New York: Scribner, 1899.

Marks, John H. "Noah." In *The Interpreter's Dictionary of the Bible*, edited by George Arthur Buttrick, 3:554–56. 4 vols. New York: Abingdon, 1962.

Marsh, John. *Amos and Micah*. Torch Bible. London: SCM, 1959.

Marti, Karl. *Dodekapropheten* 1. Kurzer Hand-Commentar zum Alten Testament. Tübingen: Mohr/Siebeck, 1904.

Maston, T. B. *The Bible and Race*. Nashville: Broadman, 1959.

Mays, James Luther. *Amos: A Commentary*. OTL. Philadelphia: Westminster, 1969.

Mazar, Amihai. *Archaeology of the Land of the Bible*. Anchor Bible Reference Library. New York: Doubleday, 1992.

Mazar, Benjamin. "The Sanctuary of Arad and the Family of Hobab the Kenite." In *Biblical Israel: State and People*, 67–77. Jerusalem: Magnes, 1992.

McCarter, P. Kyle, Jr. "The Origins of Israelite Religion." In *The Rise of Ancient Israel*, edited by Hershel Shanks, 118–41. Washington, DC: Biblical Archaeology Society, 1992.

McCown, Chester C. *The Ladder of Progress in Palestine: An Archaeological Adventure*. New York: Harper, 1943.

McCray, Walter Arthur. *The Black Presence in the Bible and the Table of Nations, Genesis 10:1–32: With Emphasis on the Hamitic Genealogical Line from a Black Perspective*. Chicago: Black Light Fellowship, 1990.

McNeile A. H., and T. W. Thacker. "Ham." In *Hasting's Dictionary of the Bible*, 361. Revised by F. C. Grant and H. H. Rowley. New York, 1963.

McNeill, H. "Collapse of the Cunard of Cham." *Interracial Review* (Sept. 1940) 135–37.

McNeill, W. H. "Infectious Alternatives." *Quarterly Journal of Military History* 10 (1998) 80.

Meek, Theophile J. *Hebrew Origins*. Rev. ed. New York: Harper, 1950.

Meyer, Eduard. *Die Israeliten und ihre Nachbarstämme: Alttestamentliche Untersuchungen*. Halle: Niemeyer, 1906.

Midrash Rabbah, I. Translated and edited by H. Freedman and Maurice Simon. London: Soncino, 1939.
Milgrom, Jacob. *Numbers*. JPS Torah Commentary. Philadelphia: Jewish Publication Society, 1990.
Mitchell, H. G. *Amos: An Essay in Exegesis*. Rev. ed. Boston: Houghton, Mifflin, 1900.
Möller, Wilhelm. *Wider den Bann der Quellenscheidung: Anleitung zu einer neuen Erfassung des Pentateuch-Problems*. Gütersloh: Bertelsmann, 1912.
Moore, George Foot. *Judaism in the First Centuries of the Christian Era: The Age of the Tannaim*. 3 vols. Cambridge: Harvard University Press, 1927.
Morgenstern, Julius. "The Kenite Code." *HUCA* 21 (1948) 88–91.
———. "The Oldest Document of the Hexateuch." *HUCA* 4 (1927) 115–16.
Mowinckel, Sigmund. *The Two Sources of the Predeuteronomic Primeval History (JE) in Gen. 1–11*. Oslo: Dybwad, 1937.
Murillo, Lino. *El Génesis*. Scripta Pontificii Instituti Biblici 10. Rome: Pontificio Instituto Biblico, 1914.
Myers, Jacob M. *Hosea, Joel, Amos, Obadiah, Jonah*. Layman's Bible Commentary. Richmond: John Knox, 1959.
Neher, André. *Amos: Contribution à l'étude du prophétisme*. Paris: Librairie Philosophique J. Vrin, 1950.
Neiman, David. "The Date and Circumstances of the Cursing of Canaan." In *Biblical Motifs*, edited by A. Altmann, 113–34. Cambridge: Harvard University Press, 1966.
Neumark, D. "The Beauty of Japheth in the Tents of Shem." *Journal of Jewish Lore and Philosophy* 1 (1919) 5–17.
Newman, Murray Lee, Jr. *The People of the Covenant*. New York: Abingdon, 1962.
Noth, Martin. *Das Buch Josua*. 2nd ed. Handbuch zum Alten Testament 7. Tübingen: Mohr/Siebeck, 1953.
Nötscher, Friedrich. *Zwölfprophetenbuch*. Echter-Bibel. Würzburg: Echter, 1948.
Nowack, W. *Die kleinen Propheten*. Göttinger Handkommentar zum Alten Testament. 3rd ed. Göttingen: Vandenhoeck & Ruprecht, 1922.
Orelli, C. von. *The Twelve Minor Prophets*. Translated by J. S. Banks. Edinburgh: T. & T. Clark, 1893.
Orlinsky, Harry M. *Notes on the New Translation of the Torah*. Philadelphia: Jewish Publication Society, 1969.
Orchard, W. E. *Oracles of God: Studies in the Minor Prophets*. London: James Clarke, 1922.
Paterson, John. *The Goodly Fellowship of the Prophets: Studies, Historical, Religious, and Expository in the Hebrew Prophets*. New York: Scribner, 1950
Patton, Walter M. *Israel's Account of the Beginnings*. New York: Pilgrim, 1916.
Peake, A. S. "Genesis." *Peake's Commentary on the Bible*. Edited by A. S. Peake. 2nd ed. New York: Nelson, 1937.
Perbal, Albert. "La race nègre et la malédiction de Cham." *Revue de l'Université d'Ottawa* 10 (1940) 156–77.
Pfeiffer, Robert H. *Introduction to the Old Testament*. 2nd ed. New York: Harper, 1948; 1st. ed., 1941.
Posener, G. *Princes et pays d'Asie et de Nubie*. Brussels: Fondation Egyptologique Reine Elisabeth, 1940.
Priese, Karl-Heinz. "Nicht-ägyptische Namen und Wörter in den ägyptischen Inschriften der Könige von Kush I." *Mitteilungen des Instituts für Orientforschung* 14 (1968) 166–75.

Pritchard, James B., ed. *The Ancient Near East in Pictures Relating to the Old Testament*. 2nd ed. Princeton: Princeton University Press, 1969.

———, ed. *The Harper Atlas of the Bible*. New York: Harper & Row, 1987.

Procksch, Otto. *Die Genesis*. KAT 1. 2nd and 3rd ed. Leipzig: Deichert, 1924.

———. *Theologie des Alten Testaments*. Gütersloh: Bertelmann, 1950.

Pusey, E. B. *The Minor Prophets*. Vol. 1. New York: Funk & Wagnalls, 1885.

Rad, Gerhard von. *Genesis: A Commentary*. Translated by John H. Marks. OTL. Philadelphia: Westminster, 1961.

Rashi. *Pentateuch with Rashi's Commentary: Numbers*. Translated by M. Rosenbaum and A. M. Silbermann. New York: Hebrew Publishing, 1929.

Redford, Donald B. *Egypt, Canaan, and Israel in Ancient Times*. Princeton: Princeton University Press, 1992.

Redlich, E. Basil. *The Early Traditions of Genesis*. Coler Library 4. London: Duckworth, 1950.

Rendtorff, Rolf. "Genesis 8:21 und die Urgeschichte des Yahwisten." *Kerygma und Dogma* 7 (1961) 69–78.

Rice, Gene. "Africans and the Origin of the Worship of Yahweh." *Journal of Religious Thought* 50 (1993–94) 27–44.

———. "The African Roots of the Prophet Zephaniah." *Journal of Religious Thought* 36 (1979) 21–31.

———. "The Alleged Curse on Ham." In *Holy Bible: African American Jubilee Edition*, 127–43. New York: American Bible Society, 1999.

———. "The Curse That Never Was (Genesis 9:18–27)." *Journal of Religious Thought* 29 (1972) 5–27.

———. "Joseph and Jim Crow." *Journal of Religious Thought* 21 (1964–1965) 3–14.

———. Review of *The Rescue of Jerusalem: The Alliance between Hebrews and Africans in 701 BC* by Henry T. Aubin. *Journal of Religious Thought* 57 (2005) 181–92.

———. "Two Black Contemporaries of Jeremiah." *Journal of Religious Thought* 32 (1975) 95–109.

———. "Was Amos a Racist?" *Journal of Religious Thought* 35 (1978) 35–44.

Richardson, Alan. *Genesis I—XI: The Creation Stories and the Modern World View*. Torch Bible Commentaries. London: SCM, 1953.

Ringgren, Helmer. *Israelite Religion*. Translated by David E. Green. Philadelphia: Westminster, 1966.

Robinson, B. P. "The Jealousy of Miriam: A Note on Num 12." *ZAW* 101 (1989) 428–32.

Robinson, H. Wheeler. "Amos." In *The Abingdon Bible Commentary*, edited by Frederick Carl Eiselen et al., 775–86. New York: Abingdon, 1929.

Robinson, T. H. *Die Zwölf Kleinen Propheten: Hosea bis Mica*. Handbuch zum Alten Testament. 3rd ed. Tübingen: Mohr/Siebeck, 1964.

Rost, Leonhard. "Noah der Weinbauer." In *Geschichte und Altes Testament: Aufsätze*, edited by W. F. Albright, 169–78. Beiträge zur historischen Theologie 16. Tübingen: Mohr/Siebeck, 1953.

Rothenberg, Benno. *Timna: Valley of the Biblical Copper Mines*. London: Thames & Hudson, 1972.

Rothenberg, Benno, and Jonathan Glass. "The Midianite Pottery." In *Midian, Moab, and Edom*, edited by J. F. A. Sawyer and David J. A. Clines, 65–125. JSOTSup 24. Sheffield: JSOT Press, 1983.

Rowley, H. H. "Moses and Monotheism." In *From Moses to Qumran*, 56–57. New York: Association Press, 1963.
———. "Moses and the Decalogue." *Bulletin of the John Rylands Library* 34 (1950–51) 88–91.
———. *From Joseph to Joshua*. London: Oxford University Press, 1950.
Rudolph, Wilhelm. *Joel–Amos–Obadja–Jona*. KAT 13/2. Gütersloh: Mohn, 1971.
Ryle, Herbert E. *The Book of Genesis*. Cambridge Bible. Cambridge: Cambridge University, 1914.
Sadler, Rodney S., Jr. "The Kenite Hypothesis Revisited." Unpublished paper. November, 1993.
Sagottka, L. *Zephanja. Versuch einer Neuübersetzung mit philologischem Kommentar*. Rome: Biblical Institute, 1972.
Sayce, A. H. *The Races of the Old Testament*. By-paths of Bible Knowledge 16. London: Religions Tract Society, 1891.
Scharff, Alexander and Anton Moortgat. *Ägypten und Vorderasien im Altertum*. Vol. 1 of *Weltgeschichte in Einzeldarstellung*. Hannover: Bruckmann, 1950.
Scharff, Alexander and Anton Moortgat. *Ägypten und Vorderasien Im Altertum*. Weltgeschichte in Einzeldarstellungen. Munich: Bruckmann, 1950.
Schmidt, Werner H. *Old Testament Introduction*. Translated by Matthew J. O'Connell. New York: Crossroad, 1984.
Schmökel, Hartmut. "Jahwe und die Keniter." *JBL* 52 (1933) 212–29.
Schrader, Eberhard. *Studien zur Kritik und Erklârung der biblischen Urgeschichte: Gen Cap. I–XI*. Zurich: Meyer & Zeller, 1863.
Schumann, G. A. *Genesis Hebr. et Graece*. Leipzig: Fleischer, 1829.
Schumpp, Meinrad. *Das Buch der zwölf Propheten*. Herders Bibelkommentar 10/2. Freiburg: Herder, 1950.
Schwally, Friedrich. "Das Buch Sefanjâ: eine historisch-kritische untersuchung." *ZAW* 10 (1890) 165–240.
Seale, M. S. "The Black Arabs of the Jordan Valley." *ExpTim* 68 (1956–57) 28.
Seebass, Horst. "Zu Num. X 33f." *VT* 14 (1964) 111–13.
Sellin, Ernst. *Das Zwölfprophetenbuch*. KAT. Leipzig: Deich-ert, 1922.
———. *Einleitung in das Alte Testament*. 5th ed. Heidelberg: Quelle & Meyer, 1929.
Selms, A. van. "The Canaanites in the Book of Genesis." In *Studies on the Book of Genesis*, 182–213. Oudtestamentische Studiën, 12. Leiden: Brill, 1958.
———. "Judge Shamgar." *VT* 14 (1964) 294–309.
Shanks, Herschel, et al. *The Rise of Ancient Israel*. Washington, DC: Biblical Archaeology Society, 1992.
Shinan, Avigdor. "Moses and the Ethiopian Woman." In *Studies in Hebrew Narrative Art*, edited by Joseph Heinemann and Schmuel Werses, 66–78. ScrHier 27. Jerusalem: Magnes, 1978.
Shuckford, Samuel. *Commentaries on the Last Four Books of Moses*. Vol. 4. Translated by C. W. Bingham. Grand Rapids: Baker, 1979.
Simons, Jan J. *The Geographical and Topographical Texts of the Old Testament*. Studia Francisci Scholten memoriae dicata 2. Leiden: Brill, 1959.
Simpson, Cuthbert A. "The Book of Genesis: Introduction and Exegesis." In *The Interpreter's Bible*, edited by George Arthur Buttrick , 1:437–829. New York: Abingdon, 1952.
———. *The Early Traditions of Israel: A Critical Analysis of the Pre-Deuteronomic Narrative of the Hexateuch*. Oxford: Blackwell, 1948.

Skinner, John. *A Critical and Exegetical Commentary on Genesis*. International Critical Commentary. 2nd ed. Edinburgh: T. & T. Clark, 1930.

Smart, James D. "Amos." In *Interpreter's Dictionary of the Bible*, edited by George Arthur Buttrick, 1:116–21 New York: Abingdon, 1962.

Smend, Rudolf. *Die Erzählung des Hexateuch*. Berlin: Reimer, 1912.

Smith, George Adam. *The Book of the Twelve Prophets, Commonly Called the Minor, in Two Volumes*. Vol II, *Zephaniah, Nahum, Habakkuk, Obadiah, Haggai, Zechariah, Malachi, Joel, Jonah*. New York: Doubleday, 1930.

———. *The Early Poetry of Israel in its Physical and Social Origins*. London: Oxford University Press, 1927.

Smith, Henry Preserved. *The Religion of Israel*. New York: Scribner, 1914.

Smith, William Stevenson. *Ancient Egypt as Represented in the Museum of Fine Arts, Boston*. 4th ed. Boston: Beacon, 1961.

Snaith, N. H. *Amos, Hosea and Micah*. Epworth Preacher's Commentaries London: Epworth, 1956.

———. *Notes on the Hebrew Text of Amos, Part II: Translation and Notes*. London: Epworth, 1946.

Snowden, Frank. *Blacks in Antiquity: Ethiopians in the Greco-Roman Experience*. Cambridge, MA: Belknap, 1970.

———. "Ethiopians and the Graeco-Roman World." In *The African Diaspora: Interpretive Essays*, edited by Martin L. Kilson and Robert I. Rotberg, 11–36. Cambridge: Harvard University Press, 1976.

Speiser, E. A. *Genesis*. Anchor Bible 1. Garden City, NY: Doubleday, 1964.

Stade, Bernhard. "Anmerkungen zu 2 Ko. 15–21." *ZAW* 6 (1886) 122–92.

———. "Das Kainszeichen." *ZAW* 14 (1894) 250–318.

———. *Geschichte des Volkes Israel*. Vol. 1. Berlin: Grote, 1889.

Staubli, Thomas. *Das Image der Nomaden im Alten Israel und in der Ikonographie seiner sesshaften Nachbarn*. Orbis biblicus et orientalis 107. Fribourg: Universitätsverlag, 1991.

Steindorff, George, and Keith C. Seele, *When Egypt Ruled the East*. Chicago: University of Chicago Press, 1963.

Steinmann, Jean. *Le Prophète Jérémie: Sa Vie, Son Oeuvre et Son Temps*. Paris: Cerf, 1952.

Steuernagel, Carl. *Lehrbuch der Einleitung in das Alte Testament*. Sammlung theologischer Lehrbücher. Tübingen: Mohr/Siebeck, 1912.

Strabo. *The Geography of Strabo: in Eight Volumes*. Edited and translated by Horace Leonard Jones. Loeb Classical Library: Cambridge: Harvard University Press, 1917–1932.

Strack, H. L. *Die Bücher Genesis, Exodus, Leviticus und Numeri*. Kurzgefasster Kommentar. Munich: Beck, 1894.

Streane, Annsley William. *The Book of the Prophet Jeremiah: Together with the Lamentations; With Map, Notes and Introduction*. Cambridge: Cambridge University Press, 1952.

Surfeit, J. Ernest. "Noah's Curse and Blessing." *Concordia Theological Monthly* 17 (1946) 779–800.

Sutcliffe, T. H. *The Book of Amos*. Biblical Handbooks. New York: Macmillan, 1939.

Tadmor, Hayim. "The Campaigns of Sargon II of Assur: A Chronological-historical Study." *Journal of Cuneiform Studies* 12:1, 3 (1958) 22–40, 77–100.

Taylor, C.L. "The Book of Zephaniah: Introduction and Exegesis," in. *Interpreter's Bible*, edited by George Arthur Buttrick, 6:1007–34. New York: Abingdon, 1956.
Thompson, E. T. "The Curse Was not on Ham." *Presbyterian Outlook* 137/10 (1955) 7.
Thompson, Thomas L. *The Historicity of the Patriarchal Narratives: The Quest for the Historical Abraham*. BZAW 133. Berlin: de Gruyter, 1974.
Tilson, Everett. *Segregation and the Bible*. Nashville: Abingdon, 1958.
Toynbee, A. J. *A Study of History*. Vol. 1. New York: Oxford UniversityPress, 1934.
Ullendorff, Edward. *Ethiopia and the Bible*. London: Oxford University Press, 1968.
Utley, Francis Lee. "Noah's Ham and Jensen Enikel." *Germanic Review* 16 (1941) 241–49.
Van Wyk, W. C. "The Cushites in Amos 9:7." *Hervormde Teologiese Studies* 22 (1967) 38–45.
Vaux, Roland de. *The Early History of Israel*. Translated by David Smith. Philadelphia: Westminster, 1978.
———."Sur l'origine kénite ou madianite du yahvisme." *ErIsr* 9 (1969) 28–32.
Vischer, Wilhelm. *Jahwe der Gott Kains*. Munich: Kaiser, 1929.
Volz, P. *Der Prophet Jeremia*. 2nd ed. KAT 10. Leipzig: Deichertsche Verlagsbuchhandlung Scholl, 1922.
Ward, William A. "Shasu." In *ABD* 5:1165–67.
Watts, John D. W. *The Books of Joel, Obadiah, Jonah. Nahum, Habakkuk and Zephaniah*. Cambridge Bible Commentaries on the Old Testament. Cambridge: Cambridge University Press, 1975.
Weems, Renita J. *Just a Sister Away: A Womanist Vision of Women's Relationships in the Bible*. San Diego: LuraMedia, 1988.
Weinfeld, Moshe. "The Tribal League at Sinai." In *Ancient Israelite Religion: Essays in Honor of Frank Moore Cross*, edited by Patrick D. Miller et al., 303–14. Philadelphia: Fortress, 1987.
Weiser, Artur. *Das Buch der zwölf kleinen Propheten*. 5th ed. Das Alte Testament Deutsch. Göttingen: Vandenhoeck & Ruprecht, 1967.
———. *Die Prophetie des Amos*. BZAW 53. Giessen: Töpelmann, 1929.
Welch, Adam C. *Jeremiah: His Time and His Work*. 1955. Reprint, Westport, CT: Greenwood, 1980.
Wellhausen, Julius. "Die Composition des Hexateuchs." *Jahrbuch für Deutsche Theologie* 21 (1876) 392–450, 531–602; 22 (1877) 408–79.
———. "Die geschichtlichen Bücher (Richter, Samuelis, Ruth, Könige)." In *Einleitung in das Alte Testament*, by Friedrich Bleek, 181–267. Einleitung in die Heilige Schrift 1. 4th ed. Berlin: Reimer, 1878.
———. *Die kleinen Propheten*. Skizzen und Vorarbeiten 5. 3rd ed. Berlin: Reimer, 1896
Westermann, Claus. *Genesis 1–11*. Translated by John J. Scullion. Continental Commentaries. Minneapolis: Augsburg, 1984.
Westphal, Alexandre. *Les sources du Pentateuque: étude historique sur la critique littéraire des livres mosaïques*. Vol. 1. Paris: Chauvin, 1888.
Williams, Arnold. *The Common Expositor: An Account of the Commentaries on Genesis 1527–1633*. Chapel Hill: University of North Carolina Press, 1948.
Williams, Ethel L., and Clifton F. Brown. *Afro-American Religious Studies: A Comprehensive Bibliography with Locations in American Libraries*. Metuchen, NJ: Scarecrow, 1972.
Wilson, John A. *The Culture of Ancient Egypt*. Phoenix Books. Chicago: University of Chicago Press, 1951.

Wiseman, D. J. *Chronicles of Chaldean Kings (626–556 B.C.): In the British Museum.* London: Trustees of the British Museum, 1956.

Wolf, Walther. *Kulturgeschichte des Alten Ägypten.* Stuttgart: Kroener Alfred, 1990.

Wolff, Hans Walter. *Dodekapropheton 2: Joel und Amos.* Biblischer Kommentar. Neukirchen-Vluyn: Neukirchener, 1969.

———. *Joel and Amos: A Commentary on the Books of the Prophets Joel and Amos.* Hermeneia. Minneapolis: Fortress, 1977.

———. "Das Kerygma des Jahwisten." *Evangelische Theologie* 24 (1964) 73–98.

———. "The Kerygma of the Yahwist." In *The Vitality of Old Testament Traditions*, Walter Brueggemann and Hans Walter Wolff, 41–66. Atlanta: John Knox, 1982.

Wolfendale, James. *A Homiletical Commentary on the Minor Prophets.* New York: Funk & Wagnalls, 1892.

Woodson, Carter G. *The African Background Outlined.* The Woodson Series edition. Baltimore: Black Classic Press, 2016.

Wreszinski, Walter. "Eine Statue des Monthemhêt." *Orientalische Literaturzeitung* 19 (1916) 10–18.

Wright, George Ernest. "Samaria." *Biblical Archaeologist* 22 (1959) 67–78.

Zeissl, Helene von. *Äthiopen und Assyrer in Ägypten.* Ägyptologische Forschungen 14. Hamburg: Augustin, 1955.

Zimmerli, Walther. *Mose 1–11.* 2nd ed. Zürich: Zwingli, 1957.

Scripture Index

OLD TESTAMENT

Genesis

Scripture Index

PSEUDEPIGRAPHA

ANCIENT NEAR EASTERN TEXTS

ANCIENT JEWISH WRITERS

RABBINIC WORKS

NEW TESTAMENT

EARLY CHRISTIAN WRITINGS

GRECO-ROMAN LITERATURE

Author Index

CPSIA information can be obtained
at www.ICGtesting.com
Printed in the USA
LVHW091934171220
674387LV00056B/657